The Hand Book

The Hand Book

Interpreting Handshakes,
Gestures, Power Signals, and
Sexual Signs

Linda Lee
and James Charlton

Prentice-Hall, Inc., Englewood Cliffs, New Jersey

The authors express appreciation for permission to reprint quotations from the following works:
Victory Within My Hands by Harold Russell and Victor Rosen. Copyright 1949, renewed © 1976 by Harold Russell and Victor Rosen. Reprinted by permission of Farrar, Straus and Giroux, Inc.
Sinister People by Jack Fincher © 1977, G. P. Putnam's Sons.
Facts and Theories of Psychoanalysis by Ives Hendrick, Alfred A. Knopf, Inc., 1941.
Selected Writings of Edward Sapir, University of California Press, 1949.
Quote by the Rev. John J. McLaughlin © 1974 by The New York Times Company. Reprinted by permission.
Nurse by Peggy Anderson, St. Martin's Press, Inc.
Manwatching by Desmond Morris, published by Harry N. Abrams, Inc. Text © 1977.

All photographs, unless otherwise noted, are by Nancy Crampton © 1980.
All drawings, unless otherwise noted, are by Mary Kornblum.

The Hand Book
by Linda Lee and James Charlton
Copyright © 1980 by Linda Lee and James Charlton

Address inquiries to Prentice-Hall, Inc., Englewood
Cliffs, N.J. 07632
Printed in the United States of America
Prentice-Hall International, Inc., London/Prentice-Hall of Australia, Pty. Ltd., Sydney/Prentice-Hall of Canada, Ltd., Toronto/Prentice-Hall of India Private Ltd., New Delhi/ Prentice-Hall of Japan, Inc., Tokyo/ Prentice-Hall of Southeast Asia Pte. Ltd., Singapore/ Whitehall Books Limited, Wellington, New Zealand
10 9 8 7 6 5 4 3 2 1

Library of Congress cataloging in Publication Data
Lee, Linda.
   The hand book.
   Bibliography: p.
   Includes index.
   1. Hand—Psychological aspects.   2.   Nonverbal
communication.   I.   Charlton, James, date   II.   Title.
BF908.L43   153   79-18000
ISBN 0-13-372425-5

Acknowledgments

We would like to thank Milt Machlin and the Lion's Head for their early help and encouragement in this project. The book would not have been possible without the extraordinary and inexhaustible collection of art and writing at the New York Public Library. We are also grateful for the research facilities in the London Museum Library and the Smithsonian Institution in Washington.

Beyond mere book research we are grateful to Amarjit Singh and Elizabeth Dane for their wisdom, help, and advice on the subject of hands. And we thank those who guided us to these two and to others in the field.

Of the hundreds of people who helped us in various ways we would like especially to thank Brendan Gill, Nancy Crampton, Barbara Binswanger, Genie Chipps, Maggie Askew, Peter Throckmorton, John Giroux, Pat McNees, Jill Smolowe, Christopher Evans, George Harpootlian, Bonnie Boston, Ethan Cliffton, Bob Abel, Bruce Petri, Jane and Andy Bradtke, Helene Schwartz, Annette Joseph,

Doug Smith, the Klinglers, Tim, Kevin, and Anne Charlton, Mrs. Robert E. Lee, our agents Elaine Markson and Sheryl Dare, and our patient editor Robert Stewart.

Further we thank all of those who listened to us expound on the subject in bars, restaurants, offices, and homes around New York. We thank those who resisted saying M.E.G.O. (my eyes glaze over) whenever the word "hands" was uttered. When we offered fascinating facts about hands ("Did you know that the fingernails on the right hand grow point zero eight six millimeters a day?") our friends were always polite, at times even enthusiastic. When our families and others wondered if the book and our obsession would ever be finished, they were kind enough not to inquire about it. And when the book *was* finished, not a single person said, "It's about time."

To all who took the Touch Test, who frantically clipped any mention of hands from newspapers and magazines, who answered endless questions about the ways people in other parts of the country and other parts of the world gestured, who steered us to sources and palmists, travelers and storytellers, we lift our hands in salute. Thank you.

Contents

The Hand Book

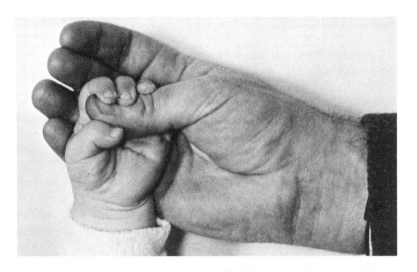

Introduction/The Hand in Western Civilization

I kept coming back to my hands. I couldn't get them out of my mind. What wonderful, efficient machines they were. So simple. Just some bones, muscles, nerves, blood vessels and skin. Nothing to them, really. And yet, how valuable, how perfect, how cunningly contrived to do so many marvelous things. Like pitching a ball or painting a picture or caressing someone you loved.

        Harold Russell and Victor Rosen, Victory Within My Hands

They seem to lead a life of their own, our hands: sometimes burrowing into our pockets for warmth, then flailing out at the inopportune moment to convey just the opposite meaning to that we had intended; then, wretched traitors, returning to the fold with disingenuous offers of solace and food, illicit cigarettes and drink. Hands are tempters:* intractable, wayward, deceitful, clumsy hydra-headed monsters leashed to us by the wrist.

Paul Tabori, in his *The Book of the Hand,* quotes Gaston Rageot as saying: "All the problems of the finite and infinite world— are they not contained within the small space between the wrist and the tip of the fingers? The hand represents destiny grappling with free will, the individual volition with the collective power; temperament fighting education and training."[1] Exactly.

Yet our hands are also eloquent, sensual, persuasive, healing, comforting, lovely to look at, delightful to hold, and heaven to kiss, an inspiration and obsession of writers and poets. In the Bible we read: "In his hands are the deep places of the earth; the strength of the hills is his also. The sea is his, and he made it; and his hands formed the dry land." (Psalms 95:4–5) And much later, in Willa Cather, we read of the less dramatic but equally astonishing work of the secular hand: "That irregular and intimate quality of things made entirely by the human hand." The hand is among the very first things, is perhaps *the* first thing, we see when we are born; the priest's, the doctor's, or the loved one's hand may well be the last thing we see on earth when we die.

Like other essentials in life—good health, freedom, love— hands may be most appreciated only when they are lacking. Harold Russell, whose quote opened this chapter, lost both hands in a training accident in World War II. "I couldn't get them out of my mind," he said. How unlike our own feelings about our hands. They are often the furthest things from our minds. Just as we do not recognize the recorded sound of our own voices, most of us would not recognize the recorded patterns of our own gestures. If anyone draws attention to our hands, we immediately become self-conscious.

Why are we so unaware of our hands and why are they so

Temptresses? In Latin the word for hand is masculine, but in French, Italian, and German (die Hand) the word is feminine. Spanish, peculiarly, gives the word a feminine article with a masculine-sounding ending on the noun: la mano.

difficult to control? Why do we take them for granted and why are we afraid of what they are really saying about us? (We *are* afraid; for this reason books on body language sell and sell.) If the hands are, as Jacob Bronowski said, "the cutting edge of the mind," why doesn't the following edge of the mind (the part involved in quotidian observations) have any idea what they are doing? And why, throughout history, and even before history, were hands regarded with awe and with reverence?

Before we can begin to consider these questions, we have to go back to the time when man first had hands—real, workable hands with opposable fingers. Frogs have "hands," squirrels have "hands," but only humans have the ability to join the end of their thumb with the end of their forefinger (as in the okay sign), an operation that allows hands to do fine precision work. Of course, in order to approach this fine precision work humans had first to get up off the ground to stand on two feet, to allow their once foot-like front appendages to evolve into the exquisite tools of their burgeoning brain power.

Let us consider premature babies. They have an instinctive urge to grip with their hands and, because of their light weight, they have the ability to support themselves solely by the hands. This gripping response fades soon after birth; within a few weeks the baby matures to the point where it can no longer support its weight.[2] What the baby has just done is to recapitulate, in a small way, what the prototypical *homo erectus* must have discovered—that there were better uses for those opposable thumbs and fingers than hanging onto a doctor's or nurse's finger, or hanging from the nearest tree. Once the hands are freed from this frozen grasp they are able to explore, to bring small bits of the world within view, smell, and taste. Even more crucial to early human beings was the fact that these new gadgets could enter small spaces and explore on their own. They could begin studying and shaping the world around them.

Man the Toolmaker, then, owed his career to the hands. He paid homage to them as if to an idol. He painted outlines of them in his caves, he developed rituals in which they dominated, and he began formulating hand habits, superstitions, and customs—all of which placed the hand in the realm of magic.

It was not only early man who felt this way. Isaac Newton said: "In the absence of any other proof, the thumb alone would convince me of God's existence." The thumb. In cosmologies of the hand the thumb is said to represent the ego. Of all the phalanges the thumb alone has a name devoid of the word "finger." We have a little finger, ring finger, middle finger, forefinger, and we have a thumb. It even looks like its name—something squat, avuncular, practical, outcast, comforting, softly rounded, Anglo-Saxon. "The thumb is a masterpiece of nature, an anatomical work of art," proclaimed Luigi Giacometti.[3]

So the hand was magic and the thumb a work of art. Humans' development and intelligence were directly related to the mastery of their hands. In *Man and His Ancestry,* Alan Houghton Brodrick proclaimed: "We think because we speak—and we are intelligent because we have hands." In 1620 Cresollius remarked that the hand is "the minister of reason and wisdom" and that "without it there is no eloquence." Immanuel Kant called hands "the outside brain of man."[4]

Because they symbolize so much, hands have been mistreated as well as revered. Hands have been chopped off as punishment, mutilated as a sign of homage, thumbs were taken in battle (the ancient mariners of Athens cut off the thumbs of their naval rivals, the Aeginetans, because without thumbs the men would be useless for sail).[5] Hands were studied to find the seat of ancient illnesses; priests' and conjurers' hands then healed those illnesses. Hands have been held high during religious moments as symbols of reverence and benediction and—contrarily and inevitably—they have been held high during moments of insult and obscenity. Hands seduce and, having seduced, make love. They are considered the maps of our past and future by palmists and the scribe of our present by graphologists. In rhetoric, "the hand is the onely speech that is naturall to man" (John Bulwer, *Chironomia,* 1644). In political campaigns the use of the hands can make the difference between success and defeat. There are regional and national "dialects" of gestures, yet there are—amazingly, when one considers the diversity of human culture—true universal gestures. While most of us have developed an ability to lie with our faces (if only to play poker), few of us have learned to lie with our hands, except in bed. In the Mediterranean and in South America and Southeast Asia there are over fifteen different amulets in the shape of the hand. And no wonder.

Consider the way words for the hand have crept into our language. "Handicap" is a corruption of "hand in cap," the original method for choosing lots at sporting events and in public affairs, by drawing lots from a hat. The word "hand" itself is from Anglo-Saxon, as befits most such everyday objects in the English language, not from Latin or French as were more exotic objects like the "garage." We have "at hand," "in hand," and "by hand"; "on hand," "off our hands," and "out of our hands." If we are skilled, we are "handy," and if we are goodlooking, we are "handsome," which originally meant something in "good measure," or a handful. Objects have useful appendages called "handles." Homes are filled with "hand-me-downs" and "handicrafts." If we are living "hand-to-mouth," we might ask for a "handout" and you might give us a "handsel," defined as "a gift as a token of good luck," or "first gift on any occasion." As children we would much rather play "handball" than do "handwork" for mother. A jockey can win a race "hands down" if he is ahead and doesn't have to use his whip. We "hand it to you" if we admire you; if we are ingrates we "bite the hand that feeds us." If we are involved in something, it is "hand and foot," as in the Latin *manibus pedibusque*. And we are "in safe hands with Allstate."

Then there are the hidden "hand" words, those that come to us through French and Latin, *main* and *manus*. We delight in "manual dexterity," but some people "manage" without it. Some writers have to be "manacled" to the typewriter so they will turn in their "manuscripts" on time. An officer might give a "mandate" to his troops during a crucial "maneuver." Someone who "manipulates" his betters might find it his "manifest" destiny to be "mangled" at the hands of fate. Abraham Lincoln's most controversial campaign issue was the "manumission" of the slaves. And when we make something by machinery, in a huge factory, we perversely call it "manufacture," to make by hand. On an earthier note, the word "manure" is a contraction of the Old French *manoeuvrer*, for manual work, i.e., the cultivation of the land with fertilizer. We have some slang words for hands—mitts and paws, for instance—that come from similar objects, mittens and a cat's paws. There are some slang words whose origins we can only guess: something we do with our hands, "glomming onto" an object, may have been a back formation from the noun "glomeration," which meant to gather into a ball. There is one slang word for hands, "dukes," whose origin may be totally obscure to Americans. The word comes from the Cockney slang for fingers, which was "forks," and Cockney rhyming slang, which produced "Duke of Yorks." So "Dukes" meant "forks," and "forks" meant "fingers," and the fingers stood for the hand.

We have immortalized the hand in endless proverbs and sayings in all languages ("cold hands—warm heart," "*Kalte Hände— warme Liebe,*" "*mains froides—coeur chaud*"). The authors' two favorites: the African proverb, "Were it not for the fingers, the hand would be a spoon," and the Russian proverb in reference to corporal punishment, "The hands sin but the back is guilty."[6]

We asked the question earlier, "Why are we unaware of our hands?" Perhaps the partial answer to that is that there are so many of them. They are everywhere, in our language, in our culture, religion, and superstition. They are evident in our work and in our play. They can be used consciously, yet often, below our level of awareness, they use us.

In *Travels in West Africa,* May Kingsley relates that for the Bubi tribe gesture is so important a part of communication Bubis say they cannot "talk" in the dark. We in Western culture seem almost to prefer the opposite situation. We *like* to "talk in the dark," as far as gestures are concerned. By using the telephone we can lie with our voices while our unseen hands go to our mouths to stifle a yawn or turn pages of the newspapers on our desks. In public we keep things in our hands—the ubiquitous newspaper, the handbag, cigarettes, whiskey glasses, pencils, gloves, lapels—anything so that our hands are "occupied" and will stay out of trouble. Our hands terrorize us. They are, when considered apart, like dangerous wild beasts, beautiful when asleep or playing, feasome when pushed to the limit.

We hope to show you that your hands need not terrorize you, need not misrepresent you, need not mystify you. You just have to get to know them a little better. "The hand created our entire civilization and culture," spoke Geza Revesz.[7] Surely such a creature deserves praise and examination. If through this book we can instruct and delight you on "hands and Western civilization"— perhaps the broadest subject possible—we will have succeeded. You will read about hands in the office and hands at home; about hand fetishes and hand phobias; about all the human character traits that show up in the way the hands are used. You will find palmistry lore, hand facts and fancies, information on masturbation and the use of the hands in sex with others. You will find tests for handedness, touching, a do-it-yourself palmistry guide, hand drawings and photographs, quotes from some famous people and some not so famous people on the subject of hands. And you will find out why a benign, or even friendly gesture in one country could land you in jail in another.

The hands are sometimes to be feared, true. But that is simply because they are so powerful. We hope in this book to teach you not only of the hands' power but also of the hands' gentle comfort, of their pleasures and delights.

A word on the origins of this book: it began when one of us, who was then an editor at a major publishing house, commented that a woman coming in for a job interview had "the worst handshake ever personally recorded." That bad handshake—cold, wet, timorous, *slimy* in fact—lingered through the entire interview. The prospect of meeting it again at the close loomed as a distasteful monument, seen first at a distance but coming closer and closer as the minutes ticked by. Finally, the evil deed was done and the woman walked out the door. The crawling ectoplasm of the bad handshake remained. This was, understand, a spectacularly bad handshake.

This one handshake was the genesis of the book. We specu-
lated about it. How could she not *know* she had a bad handshake?
She had been met by other people in the company and they too had
complained of her handshake. Didn't she sense people pulling away
from her when they touched her hand? Couldn't she see their
reactions?

But of course the woman was supremely out of touch
with her hand, and, by extension, with herself and those she was
meeting, too. The initial prejudice against her—because of her handshake—was an accurate assessment of her entire personality.

We began talking about other hands we had known and
loved. We talked about habits and superstitions, about "media
advisors" and Nixon's notoriously bad gestures. Later, in selecting
the photographs for this book, we found ourselves drawn again and
again to unflattering pictures of Nixon. (The chore in photograph selection became one of excluding some of our very favorites, so that
Nixon would not dominate other subjects.) Before the conversation
was through, we were convinced there had to be a book.

Others had been there before us, especially in the seventeenth, eighteenth, and nineteenth centuries, when "chirologia: the
natural language of the hand" was considered a perfect subject for
"scientific" study. There were interesting and *accurate* treatises on
gesture going back to the 1800's, from Canon de Jorio and Cardinal
Newman (in Naples) and Garrick Mallery in the United States, who
studied the sign language of the North American Indian in a series of
erudite, well-written books.

And finally in the twentieth century psychologists and social
scientists have deemed the hand and hand gestures proper subjects
for study. David Efron, in the late thirties and early forties, with his
studies of first- and second-generation Italians and Jews, was the
model of the dispassionate, skilled researcher. R. W. Sperry, with his
amazing studies on the phenomenon of the "split brain," led science
in a new direction altogether, toward a consideration of handedness

Here we see what appears to be then-President Nixon making a rude gesture. We show you this photo merely to alert you to the necessity of taking gestures in context, specifically to see that this is a picture of a man who has just thrown a Frisbee (seen, left foreground). You will notice that Nixon's notorious high shoulders serve him as badly in throwing Frisbees as in gesturing. The New York Times, *Mike Lien*

as a metaphor not only for the organization of the brain, but for the evolution of mankind. And E. T. Hall and Ray Birdwhistle did the serious background work on "body language" that enabled popularizers like Julius Fast, Desmond Morris, and ourselves to write for an eager and educated audience.

There have been other "hand" books before, too, most notably *The Book of the Hand* by Paul Tabori, *The Story of the Human Hand* by Walter Sorell, and *Silent Language* by Macdonald

Critchley—all exhaustive compendiums on an inexhaustible subject. Ashley Montagu concerned himself with tactility in a wonderful book called *Touching: The Human Significance of the Skin.* Other books, some on unrelated subjects, gave us new insights and led us in new directions. We think of Carl Sagan's *The Dragons of Eden,* Jacob Bronowski's *The Ascent of Man,* Julian Jaynes' *The Origin of Consciousness in the Breakdown of the Bicameral Mind,* and Colin Blakemore's *Mechanics of the Mind.* In a different way we also think of Barbara Tuchman's *A Distant Mirror,* Jack Fincher's *Sinister People,* and Laurence Wylie's wonderful book of text and pictures, *Beaux Gestes.* For subjects mystical and medical we are indebted to William A. Nolen's *Healing: A Doctor in Search of a Miracle* and a little gem, Eric Maple's *The Ancient Art of Occult Healing.*

The research for this book could have gone on for years. We found ourselves reading dusty tomes on manners and mannerisms, the mystical arts, fetishes, compulsive behavior, sex, Indian culture, forensic medicine. And we went into the field, studying cave paintings at the Museum of Natural History, having our palms read, being acupressured and Rolfed. We watched hands on television, in bars, at parties, at the dinner table, on stage.

Some of our observations result from hours in the library, some from hours in what social scientists refer to as "the field." We have tried to read, observe, and report our findings in an interesting, lively way. In other words, we tried to read and observe like sociologists, but not write like them. When we found that certain bits of information wouldn't fit into the chapter but were too interesting to leave out of the book entirely, we put them in the forms of "boxes" on such subjects as the hands in funeral arts, table manners, and so on.

In case we seem at times too dogmatic in our pronouncements, we would like here to give the caveat that everything we are about to say should be taken in the spirit of amusement in which it was written. Where we write thumbnail character sketches, where we outline political, ethnic, and sexual qualities as belonging to one hand "type" and not another, we refrain from the repeated "sometimes," "often's," "maybe's," and "could be's" that would otherwise litter this text. A woman is not a liar, for instance, just because she touches her nose while she speaks. Perhaps she slipped and fell on the ice this morning and hurt her nose. Perhaps her nose just itches. But isn't it interesting to speculate? Isn't it useful just to know that nose-scratching is often practiced by people who are telling a lie? It may be that people who fidget with their faces have always seemed to you less than trustworthy. Your intuition then has already singled out what we will be discussing in the chapter, "Let Your Fingers Do the Talking." Just as you do not listen solely to your intuition, you should not listen solely to this book but take it as one source of information and ideas.

You, like us, may find that you see hands everywhere and that you would rather watch a person's hand than his or her face. You may become, as we did, hand addicts. As addictions go, it's not a bad one. It is low-calorie, socially harmless, physically undebilitating— unlike becoming a gourmet cook, a religious fanatic, or a jogger. Come join us.

1/Sinister and Dexter

Part One/The Rise of Right-Handedness

... handedness may have approached the fifty-fifty ratio of pure chance for Stone Age man, then dramatically shifted thereafter in favor of the dextral.

Jack Fincher, Sinister People

Mother Nature, like most of us, loves taking sides. From the largest mammals to the smallest crystals, she has occasionally, capriciously, made some right-handed—or more appropriately and less anthropomorphically, right-sided (dexter)—some left-sided (sinister), and some symmetrical. Those creatures that have a bend, a twist, a skew interest us here because for some reason humans are right-handed, right-sided, right-footed, and right-eyed. Not all of them, of course, but a large enough number to make a discussion of taking sides appropriate.

This taking sides can be seen everywhere: some plants (the morning glory, for example) entwine to the right, some (the honeysuckle) to the left, in what is called tropism. Some bulls hook to the left, some dogs paw on the right, some chickens peck more on one side than on another. Some horses are left-sided (and prefer to canter on a left lead), while others are right-sided. Sometimes sidedness has to do with geographic location: tropical flounder, halibut, are nearly all left-sided, yet the flounder of the Antarctic are chiefly right-sided. Mice, our favorite and cheapest laboratory animal, will usually use their right paw for reaching a lever set on the right and their left paw for reaching a lever set on the left, but there seems to be a go-against-the-grain mouse minority of 8 to 14 percent that will confound researchers by reaching across with the left paw to operate a lever on the right, or vice versa. This percentage is very close to that given for the go-against-the-grainers among humans—the left-handers.[1]

The higher and more complicated the form of life, the more difficult it is to call an animal left- or right-handed. That bull we mentioned tends to hook to the left, but don't count on it in the bullring. The horse may tend toward left- or right-sidedness but can be schooled to be "even-handed." Jack Fincher states, "In the higher apes such as gorillas, chimpanzees, orangutans, and gibbons, even-sidedness appears to be nature's dominant scheme."

But not among humans. Before we proceed, let's test your handedness.

The Handedness Test
Take out paper and pencil.

1. Draw the profile of a dog or horse. Neatness does not count.

2. Blau's Torque Test: With the pencil in your right hand, inscribe a circle. When you have finished, indicate with an arrow the direction of the circle you've drawn. Now, with your left hand, do the same thing.

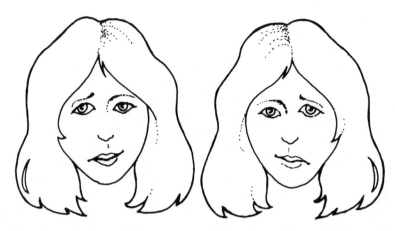

Figure 1   *Figure 2*

3. Jaynes' Test:[2] Briefly stare at the nose of Figure 1, then at the nose of Figure 2. Which is a happier figure?

4. Point at a distant object with your right or left hand. Now close first your right eye, then your left. Which eye lines up with your finger?

For those of you who cannot close one eye at a time (we know you're out there) use the Bausch & Lomb test. Make a hole the size of a quarter in a sheet of paper and sight through it at arm's length. Fix on the object with both eyes. Pull the paper toward you until it touches your face. Which eye is the hole over?

5. Close your eyes. Imagine that you have been locked in a room with your hands tied behind you to a chair. In front of you is a telephone, your only means of alerting the authorities. Which foot do you reach out with, to pull the phone closer?

6. Which side do you chew your food on?

7. Which hand do you use for masturbation?

8. Put both hands in front of you. Interlock your fingers. Which thumb is on top?

9. Bruning and Kaeppel's Test:[3] Hold your arms out in front

of you from the elbows (in other words, with bent elbows, not with arms extended from the shoulders). Point your fingers toward the floor. Now pretend you are mixing a large bowl of batter with both hands, turning both in the same direction. Increase the speed of your "beating" until one hand goes out of control and starts turning in the opposite direction. Which hand has gone out of control?

     10. Pretend to be clapping for a performer. Which hand is "on top"?

     11. Clasp your hands behind your back. Which hand "holds" the other?

     12. Fold your arms in front over you. Which arm is on top?

Analysis of Handedness Test

     1. Right-handers will almost invariably draw the profile facing to the left. Left-handers will draw the profile facing right.

Figure 1   *Figure 2*

If you think about this, you will realize how it makes sense. By drawing important features toward the center of the body, the artist is able to see what he or she is doing. Most people will also draw the profile from the top down. Don't ask us what it means if you drew from the bottom up.

2. Right-handers will draw both circles in a counterclockwise direction:

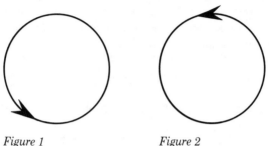

Figure 1   *Figure 2*

If either circle was drawn clockwise, you have some left-handed tendencies. If both were drawn clockwise, you are a lefty.

If you think of the circles as lying flat, you will see that counterclockwise equals left to right, the direction by international law in which we orient our racetracks. Bottles in Western culture open "right-handedly," that is to say, with a counterclockwise twist. We have found at least one bottle, from Japan, that opened the opposite way.

3. The two figures are, of course, mirror images. About 80 percent of right-handed people chose Figure 2 as the happier. That means that if you were in fact staring at the nose, you perceived the smiling side of the face with your left visual field, which is connected to the right hemisphere of the brain. Fifty percent of people who are left-handed chose Figure 1 as happier, making that judgment in their left hemispheres. Of those who are not only left-handed but also left-sided, the percentage choosing Figure 1 is much higher. This test was devised by Julian Jaynes, professor of psychology at Princeton University.

4. If you saw the object with your right eye lined up with your finger, you are right-eyed. About 80 percent of the population are right-eyed; that means their right eye actually sees the object a moment before their left. The left eye, as a result, has to work more since it must turn in slightly so that the eyes can focus.

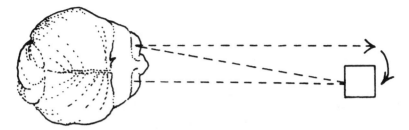

Angle left eye must turn in to accommodate dominant right eye.

You might also notice that your nondominant eye tends to close if you are reading in bright sunlight. It shuts down to give itself a break. Those of you who showed left-eye dominance have at least some left-sided tendencies. Only 2 percent of tested subjects are even-eyed.

5. Again, most people are right-footed as well as right-handed and right-eyed. If you are right-handed and you imagined yourself reaching out with your left foot, you should consider yourself a mixed dominant, a frustrated left-handed, or a left-hander.

6. If you are right-handed you will have a tendency to chew your food on that side also. This may be a result of side dominance or may simply be a function of your right-handed eating habits, that is, your tendency to put food into the right side of your mouth.

7. Many experts believe that the hand you masturbate with is your true dominant hand. This may be because *no one* was standing over you when you learned to masturbate, telling you to "Use the other hand." The masturbating hand is clearly the hand of personal choice.* Men taking this test might now take a look to see which of their testicles hangs lower; it will usually be the one opposite the dominant hand, that is, for most men, the left testicle.[4]

8. This one is a ringer. There is absolutely *no connection whatsoever* between the thumb you habitually put on top and your

---

Except in certain Eastern cultures. The Hindu and Arab cultures, for instance, instruct that the right hand is for use above the waist, the left hand for use below.

dominant hand or side. For an analysis of what this test means, see Chapter 3.

9. The hand that begins turning in the opposite direction is the subordinate hand. Incidentally, if you are right-handed you probably turned both hands counterclockwise. If you were left-handed you probably turned both hands clockwise. You will notice that when the hand goes out of control, first it begins making irregular circles, the elbow starts flopping, and then the hand tries to reverse itself.

10. Your dominant hand will be the active one, clapping into or onto the subordinate hand. Very few adults clap with both hands held exactly parallel in the "patty-cake" position.

11. Your dominant hand will hold your subordinate one. You will also clasp your opposite arm in the same pattern, dominant hand encircling subordinate forearm.

12. Your dominant hand will lead the arm over the subordinate forearm when crossed in front of the body, just as the Alpha wolf will put to the ground the Beta, subordinate, wolf.

Now, let us consider human handedness. Exactly how many of us are right-handed and how many left-handed? Surprisingly, no one knows. Estimates have ranged from 3 to 20 percent left-handers, depending on the type and number of tasks the subjects are asked to perform. Dr. Bryng Bryngelson of the University of Minnesota has claimed that if there is "no interference on the part of parents or teachers, 34 out of every 100 children born today would be left-handed, and about 3 percent would be using both hands with equal dexterity."[5]

Interference has certainly lessened the number of lefties. In authoritarian countries like China and the USSR, left-handedness is not allowed in schools. Recently in New York one of the heads of the French Lycée system stated that it was unthinkable that children be allowed to write with the left hand and that such behavior indicated a lack of discipline. Where these attitudes are established, the number of left-handers will of necessity be low.

Psychologists and statisticians seem to have trouble describing exactly what a left-hander is. Does he or she use *only* the left hand? For all tasks? To be considered truly left-handed, must one also be left-eyed, left-footed, and so on? And then again at what age were the individuals tested for handedness? Could the high estimates of lefties be blamed on data from first-grade students, some of whom had not yet established right-hand dominance?

What would we say of ex-President Gerald Ford, who says he is left-handed when he sits down, but right-handed when he stands up? Is he right-handed or left-handed?

Psychologist Paul Bakan of Canada asserts that left-handedness results from stress at the time of birth, from difficult deliveries, and especially from oxygen deficiency. Such stress, he says, produces a mild degree of brain damage to the left side, thus allowing the right to compete with it for dominance and thus leading to some of the problems of left-handers—stuttering, stammering, and difficulties in reading.[6]

One study, reported in *The New York Times* of August 2, 1959, seemed to indicate that the number of left-handers varied with the social and political climate. Far more lefties were born during periods of war, depression, and permissiveness. Elizabeth Hurlock's sampling of college graduates in 1964 seemed to bear this out: 2.6 percent of those born before 1918 called themselves left-handers; but of those born during World War I (1918–1921), 8.3 percent claimed left-handedness. In the late twenties, the number of lefties born was back down to 5.7 percent; but during the peak Depression year of 1932, 17.64 percent of those in the sample said they were left-handed. The overall average of left-handers born during the Depression was 9.2 percent, decidedly higher than most accepted figures for left-handers among us.[7]

Why does the number of left-handers mysteriously rise during social upheaval? Or are these statistics the result of a testing bias on the part of researchers? Perhaps parents, busy with matters of survival, spend less time interfering with their offspring's habits. Then again, perhaps the tenor of the times drives borderline left-handers into left-handedness, which is often associated with creativity, willfulness and individual (unsociable) endeavors. But *zut alors,* look when those 1932 babies reached their majority and were turned loose on American society: 1950 to 1953. Were *these* the years of creativity? Willfulness? Unsocial endeavors? Generally speaking, most of us would answer no. The mystery is, what happened to all those left-handers in that decade? Did they become the parents of the willful children who took over America in the late 1960's?

Statisticians know some definitive things about left-handers. More of them are male than female (perhaps because girls tend to be more tractable in school and are therefore likely to let their teachers switch them to right-handed ways). We also know that there are many more left-handers among twins; with identical twins especially, often one is a right-hander and one a left-hander.

We also know that left-handedness is a minority condition. Is this because of a tyranny of right-handers, with their skills and rools and prejudices? Would "left-handedness . . . be as common as right-handedness,"[8] if, as psychologist Gertrude Hildreth believed in 1949, no outside pressures were exerted on the developing child? Or is there something in humans that predisposes them to the right?

Let us take a look at the babe in the womb:

In utero we are already taking sides. Paul Yakovlev and his associate Pasko Rakic report that we are anatomically "wired" favoring the right side, even before we are born.[9] There are more nerves leading from the left cerebral hemisphere to the right side of the body than are leading from the right cerebral hemisphere to the left, and these left-brain/right-body nerves seem to have the "right of way." Not only that, but more nerves go directly from the right cerebral hemisphere to the right side of the body than go directly from the left side of the brain to the left side of the body. (Most people have about 80 percent of their neural pathways crossing over

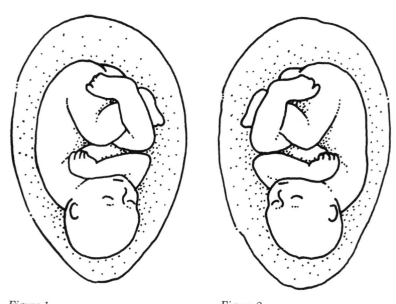

Figure 1   *Figure 2*

and 20 percent staying on the same side. As just mentioned, however, these percentages vary.)

Yakovlev and Rakic also found that newborns only a few hours old showed different levels of electrical activity on the two sides of the brain, with the left usually more active. Roughly parallel to the percentages of lefties in the population, 87 percent of the neurological systems were rightwardly oriented (i.e., left-brain dominant) and 13 percent were not.

Of the babies that present in the above positions, 60 percent "choose" 2 and 40 percent "choose" 1. We offer this as a possible reason for the development of right-handedness, though it could be argued that babies in position 2 receive more stimulation on their right sides because that is the side that is nearer the skin.

The diagram might also demonstrate Gesell's tonic neck reflex:

The earliest manifestations of human handedness are in some way bound up with the phenomenon of tonic neck reflex. The tonic neck reflex is an attitudinal behaviour pattern which figures fundamentally in the mechanics and morphogenesis both of locomotor and prehensor movements. . . . In its earliest form, the tonic neck reflex consists of: (a) the head turning to the right (or to the left); (b) the ipsilateral arm and leg extending, the arm at right angles; (c) the opposite leg and opposite arm flexing. A well-defined tonic neck reflex may be observed in the fetal infant as early as the 28th week after conception.[10]

In newborn infants, Gesell found an "unmistakable predilection toward rightward orientation." Was there a correlation between this early rightward orientation and eventual handedness? In Gesell's sample of nineteen babies, fourteen cases were predictive and the other five ambiguous or contradictory. More important, the four cases that eventually turned out to be left-handers all had shown a strong left tonic neck reflex.

Right-handedness is very strongly associated to left-brain dominance. (The brain is divided into two hemispheres and each hemisphere controls, *in most cases,* the opposite side of the body.) In Carl Sagan's book, *The Dragons of Eden,* we find that "An asymmetry in the temporal lobes in left and right hemispheres of humans and of chimpanzees has been found, with one portion of the left lobe significantly more developed. Human infants are born with this asymmetry (which develops as early as the twenty-ninth week of gestation)."[11]

So it seems, nature has indeed taken sides. Even before baby is born there is something that favors the right side (and left brain). Because nature is often orderly, we should ask this question: When the newborn infant turns to the right, what does the infant find? The answer to that is—sustenance. Over 70 percent of the time mothers hold their babies on the left, which means that when the infant turns to the right he or she is turning to the breast, warmth, protection—everything, it seems, that is important for survival. But why, you may ask, do women hold babies on their left? Certainly there is some right-handed selection going on. If a woman holds a baby on the left, then she has her dominant hand free to work, to defend her child, and to comfort him or her. Studies have proven, incidentally, that almost the same number of *left*-handed women hold their babies on the left as do right-handed women! (The figures are: right-handed women hold and carry their babies on the left 83 percent of the time; left-handed women carry and hold their babies on the left 78 percent of the time.[12]) But again we must ask, why? How could this kind of asymmetry develop? There is something obvious here, something that even our dimmest ancestors recognized about the left side: it is the side on which we hear the heartbeat.

Women, without realizing it, hold their babies to their left breast because it is there that the baby hears the mother's heart, that steady, reassuring beat that has been so much a part of interuterine life. The baby, when carried on the left, is quieter, happier, more at peace, and the mother responds instinctively to this behavior by carrying the child there a disproportionate amount of the time.*

What is interesting is that, with all of this rightward reinforcement, the infant is not immediately right-handed. Lippman's study (in 1927) indicated that babies use either hand indiscriminately up to the age of 4½ months.[13] Another study showed that it was 12 months before right-handedness began establishing itself. Most authorities agree that true right-handedness doesn't exist until the child is 2, and in some children it may not appear until the age of 5 or even 7. During all these months the child will prefer first one

---

*If you think it unlikely that mothers would respond so directly and unconsciously to this kind of conditioning, recall the famous Psych 1 experiment in which a roomful of students were instructed to respond to their professor only when he was to the right of his lectern. In less than a week the students had their teacher delivering his lectures from the right-hand side of the room, and he never once suspected what was going on.

hand and then the other, trying them out, as it were, or will simply use the hand of convenience, whichever hand is closer to the object the child is going to touch. Gesell notes that, at 2 years of age, 92 percent of children are using their right hands but that even so, this is not predictive of eventual handedness.

If humans at conception and implantation in the womb have an equal chance of becoming left- or right-handed (since the blastoderm—a perfect ball of cells—has no left or right, no up or down), why at 28 weeks' growth are humans 60 percent right-handed? Why when they are born do they show a 70 percent chance of being right-handed? Why do they, by the age of 2, turn out to be over 90 percent right-handed? Since ontogeny (the development of the individual organism) recapitulates phylogeny (the race history of the organisms as a group) perhaps we should go back to the muck and the mire for our answer.

The end of the last Ice Age, from circa 17,500 to 10,000 B.C., certainly produced its share of muck and mire. Although this is not the primordial soup out of which the modern man originally emerged, the Ice Age ooze was home to the next great step forward, man's artistic history. Before people could spend time decorating their caves (or defending them with magical symbols, whichever theory you hold to), they had first to invent simple tools: needles, chisels, axes.

Two historians, Gariel de Mortillet and Paul Sarasin, have concluded from stone tools that have been discovered from this period that during the Late Stone Age (or Upper Paleolithic period), *people were as much left-handed as right-handed.*[14] Mortillet studied hundreds of stone tools and concluded that they had been sharpened on the left side (that is, with the right hand stationary and the left hand doing the work of sharpening).

The cows and oxen in the prehistoric African rock painting are running off to the *right,* which is the way a left-hander would draw them. (Look back at Question 1 in The Handedness Test.) In hundreds of cave drawings from all over the world, pictures of bison, horses, bear, deer, mommoth, ibex, and fish show this left-hand,

Typical right-ward running, left-handedly drawn cave painting from prehistoric Africa. The New York Public Library

rightward-running direction. The further back we go, the more often we find this rightward-running direction in cave art. The French explorer Norbert Casteret discovered a number of relief sculptures of horses, bear, and a roaring lion at Labastide in the Pyrenees, and all were in the rightward-running direction.[15] These could not have been life studies, as they were done deep in the cave; therefore we have to assume that these animals didn't just run past the cave from left to right while our ancestral artists painted their pictures. What other reason could there be for this directional orientation?

One explanation could be that our cave dweller ancestors turned toward their right as they entered the caves. Contemporary humans do have a right-turning urge and will veer toward the right in a darkened room or invariably choose to climb a right-hand staircase instead of a left-hand one. When people descend stairs, which seems to require less work, the handedness of the stairs is not so crucial. If the cave dweller entered the cave, turned to the right, and began painting what he or she had seen outside, the rightward-running direction of the renderings would have the animals running out of the cave, toward the light. This answer would have weight if these cave paintings were found only on the right walls, but they are found everywhere, including on the ceilings. Perhaps even then, as now, the left-handers were the artistic ones, the ones whose job it was to paint on walls.

The high proportion of primitive left-handedness is found even in tribes studied in the twentieth century. Jack Fincher states that "A more or less equal distribution of handedness, if not outright sinister preference, still persists among savage cultures as diverse as the Bushmen, Hottentots, Australian aborigines, New Guineans, Bantus, and Pygmies. Judged by their arrowheads and spear blades, furthermore, the North American Indians once were a third sinistral."[16] And in a study of North American aboriginal art, Professor Daniel G. Brinton estimated that one-third of the work had been done by left-handers.[17] Why then, if there were so many left-handers, did those numbers seem to shrink to the levels of left-handers we find today? One interesting theory is that while primitive wood and bone tools (especially chipping tools) wear out quickly, metal tools would survive to be passed down from one generation to the next or from one man to another.[18] These tools were created for either left-hand or right-hand use. It would have made sense, therefore, for metal-tool users to become either left- or right-handed. Also one hand could better master the skilled use of a tool than could both hands. But, again, why the right?

We mentioned earlier that even our dimmest ancestors knew the heart was on the left. (This belief, of course, is wrong. The heart is in the middle, but tips toward the left and can be heard more clearly there.) During battle our ancestors early on began to protect their left side, their "heart," with shields. The shield occupied the left hand, and so the right was delegated to carry the weapon. If we accept this theory, we should perhaps consider the idea that, since men bore weapons on the right, and since women did not bear weapons, therefore there would be more left-handers among women than men. This is not true, as we mentioned before. Men tend more toward left-handedness than do women. And these *left*-handed men must have carried their weapons in the *left* hand, shielding the heart be damned. In Judges 20:16 we read: "And the children of Benjamin were numbered at that time out of the cities twenty and six thousand men that drew sword, beside the inhabitants of Gibeah, which were numbered seven hundred chosen men. Among all these people there were seven hundred chosen men left-handed; every one could sling stones at an hair-breadth and not miss." This source cites 700 left-handed warriors out of a total of 26,700, a figure of less than 3 percent. Note also that the regular warriors are referred to as swordsmen and the left-handers as stone-slingers. Did that mean that the swordsmen were all right-handed and the left-handers had to make do with rocks, or was the reference to stone slinging some kind of physical fitness test required for those called up in the draft? Whatever the reason, this Biblical record makes it clear that by, say, 2,000 or 3,000 B.C., right-handedness had established itself as the norm. Again we ask, why?

There is one striking body asymmetry in addition to right-handedness that we haven't explored at this point. The left hemisphere of the brain, the side that controls the right hand, is also, in 90 percent of cases, the side on which language is processed. In the left hemisphere, Broca's area is responsible for producing speech and Wernicke's area is responsible for *understanding* vocabulary, syntax, meaning, and speech. On the right side, the comparable part to Wernicke's area is responsible for perceiving spatial relationships and music; it, too, however, has some language ability.[19] In fact, if there is a left-hemisphere brain injury to a young child (particularly if the child is younger than 2) the right side of the brain seems capable of stepping in and taking over the functions of Wernicke's area without limiting the child's language ability.

There are other differences between the right and the left

hemispheres: The left hemisphere is orderly, sequential. It seems ideally suited for the acquisition of language. The right hemisphere seems designed for abstract creative thinking and the processing of spatial relationships. With this specialization, each side seemed to proceed in different directions.

And so it was. The left brain, which was for the most part "good" at language, took over the problems of learning how to talk, how to create grammatical constructions, how to cope with mathematics, from that how to use logic and, eventually, how to read. Meanwhile the right, something of an artistic layabout, was free to practice appreciation, not only of music but of theories, of concepts. The right brain, without plodding through all that step-by-step groundwork the left brain was doing, made great leaps of intuition and of understanding. In a situation of growing complexity the brain specialized, one side in orderly thought, the other in creativity, both sides knowing they could consult with the other.

What does all this rather speculative, rather fanciful talk about the two sides of the brain have to do with left- and right-handedness, you say? First let's take a look at a diagram of the brain. This is the motor homunculus, a schema of the amount of control over the body each part of the cerebral cortex wields. Notice the large area connected to the hand and each of the fingers, especially the thumb. The only other part of the body given such a large brain area is the part in charge of vocalization: the lips, mouth, and tongue. Would it not make sense—we are appealing here to your left brain—for the half of the brain that is so well-equipped to deal with language also to be in charge of speaking it and writing it? Both halves of the brain understand language* but only one side produces it. This specialization is true only, as we indicated before, once humans have reached the age of 2 or 3. Whichever side has been chosen to

---

*Think of the people who can understand a foreign language but who never learned to speak it. Strange as it seems, understanding a language and speaking it are two separate language functions.

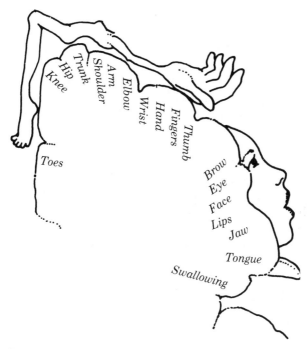

Motor Cortex

generate language, left for most people, right for some, will become the eventual seat for talking, and usually for controlling the writing hand.

One of the ways researchers have discovered this sidedness is in studying patients who have suffered a severe stroke on the left side of the brain and are unable to speak or to write although they can hear and can understand instructions. The unaffected right side of the brain understands but is unable to produce words, except for a few expletives and exclamations of high emotion.[20] These expletives may have been acquired early, before the brain completed its specialization, or may have, because of their "loaded" quality, imprinted themselves on the mute but highly emotional right brain.

A condition very much like that found in stroke victims was surgically produced in patients with severe epilepsy in a series of daring operations and experiments done under the supervision of R. W. Sperry and Michael S. Gazzaniga at Cal Tech. In these procedures the corpus callosum, the part that communicates between the left and right halves of the brain, was cut to eliminate the severe electrical storms that had affected certain patients with uncontrollable seizures. For treatment of this disorder the operations were remarkably successful. But as a by-product of the operation a curious effect was noted. When an unseen object was placed in the patients' left hands, they denied its presence. It was soon found that the perceptive faculties (*knowing* the object was there) and the verbal faculties (*saying* the object was there) had become severed insofar as the left side of a right-handed person was concerned. How did experimenters test whether the patients knew about the object or not? They asked them to pick a similar object out of a box, which the patients did easily. Once they had seen that object with both eyes, they could then say what it was because the right eye could send the message to the left brain, where the speech centers were located. If only the left eye were used, the patients were in the same dilemma. They could pick a similar object out of a box but they couldn't say the word because the knowledge of the object was on the right side of the brain and the word for it on the left.[21]

Let us outline the steps by which speech generally came to reside in the left brain. Primitive people were somewhat left-handed, at least much more so than we are today, and perhaps completely ambidextrous (note: which means with "two right-hands"). With the first appearance of tools, man seems to have begun choosing sides. The tendency toward right-handedness coincides with the first acquisition of language. Because the left brain was better at language than the right, it was the left brain that took over the job of learning how to talk. Simultaneously, people learned to make symbols to represent their transient speech. To do this they had to develop manual dexterity (another of those "right" words). The left brain—

relentless, hard-working, and overachiever—was able to master the three most important developments in human civilization: the tool-using and tool-making hand, the creation of language, and the ability to record that language.

In evolutionary terms these developments were late, almost at the last minute. The rest of the brain was well established when these more recent demands were put on it. As a result, the human cranium grew at the last minute out of proportion to the rest of the body. C. Judson Herrick describes this development in the following terms: The neocortex's "explosive growth late in phylogeny is one of the most dramatic cases of evolutionary transformation known to comparative anatomy." Carl Sagan calls painful childbirth the dues humans must pay for this gift, as the head is the largest part of the newborn baby and is therefore the hardest to deliver.[22] As further proof of this idea Sagan cites the Biblical reference to the acquisition of knowledge and the punishment of Eve for eating of the Tree of Knowledge: "In pain shalt thou bring forth children."

Because of the late development of the neocortex, especially the two areas related to speech and manual ability, we can see why humans sometimes have difficulties with these skills. The old brain, our reptilian brain, had millions of years to evolve. It is not often that the body fails to continue one of its old-brain functions (breathing, swallowing, circulating blood) because of an old brain miswiring. But the neocortex, arrived at so late, wired so haphazardly, has thousands, perhaps millions of opportunities to malfunction. We might say that everyone breathes alike, and that no two people think alike.

Because there are so many different ways of wiring the neocortex, and therefore of thinking, of creating language, and of translating that language into its spoken or written form, we cannot say categorically that all right-handers are left-brained, or that all left-handers are right-brained. You will recall that in most people decussation (the crossing of nerve pathways from the right brain to the left side of the body and from the left brain to the right side of the body) accounts for approximately 80 percent of the nerves. But in some people *over half* of the pathways stay on *the same body side* and in one dissected cadaver it was discovered that *almost all* of the nerve pathways descended directly to *the same side*. Because there are so many ways in which the body can be wired, it is difficult to make a blanket statement about left-handers' and right-handers' brain dominance. Then again some people have what is called mixed dominance: right hand, left eye, right foot, left torque.

A recent article in *U.S. News and World Report* stated: "Left-handers are more likely to have cross-dominant patterns, although many right-handers are known to have some left-sided tendencies as well. Over all, at least 1 out of 4 persons is believed to be cross-dominant. . . . Jon Durkin, of the Johnson O'Connor Research Foundation in Washington, D.C. [says] . . . 'It's bad enough to be left-handed, but being left-eyed and right-handed is even worse. You've got a little war going on inside.' "[23] Theodore Blau, a clinical psychologist, has predicted that a correlation will be found between cross-dominance in children and a later high incidence of schizophrenia.

Not only do we have cross-dominance complicating the picture, but consider this: There are two kinds of left- and right-handers, "straight" and "hooked."[24] This has nothing to do with morality or sexual preference but rather with the way we hold a pen when writing. The straight right-hander holds the pen slanted back toward him or herself and pushes the pen up to the line of writing, the hooked right-hander holds the pen curled around from the top and writes down to the line.[25] The same two variations can be seen in left-handers. Many people believe that *all* lefties write hooked in order to avoid smearing the ink of what they have just written or so that their wrists will clear the spiral binding on their notebooks (notebooks being designed for right-handers). But consider this: Hebrew scribes who are left-handed show the same percentage of hookers and non-hookers as writers of English, even though the scribes are writing *from right to left* and therefore should have no fear of smearing their work.[26]

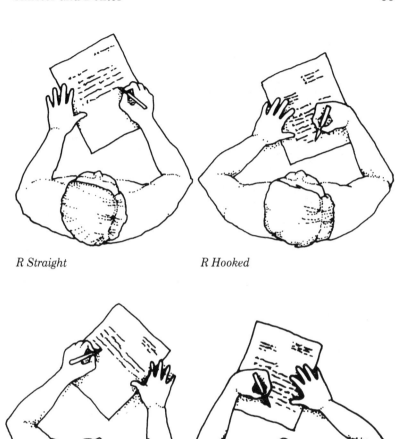

R Straight

R Hooked

L Straight

L Hooked

Jerre Levy, a University of Pennsylvania psychologist, believes that 60 percent of left-handers use hooked writing and 40 percent use straight. The import of this, she believes, is that the hooked left-handed writers "have the brain organization of a right-hander, and may be inclined to use both halves of the brain more equitably.[27]

"What this means," Miss Levy says, "is that most left-handers are probably more verbal and analytic than right-handers. They also would tend to recover faster from result of brain damage, such as loss of speech due to a stroke."[28]

One astonishing finding has turned up in Jerre Levy's comparisons of straight and hooked left- and right-handers. Through tests of their ability to perform on two tasks—verbal recognition of printed words and spatial recognition of dots—a basic division occurred along sexual lines. "In every single group," Levy writes, "*whatever* females are better on, the males are better on the opposite. [Emphasis Levy's] In females the functions of the left side of the brain are enhanced relative to those on the right."[29]

In other words, most women (the straight right-handers) will be better at language (left-hemisphere) than most men (straight right-handers). The men will be better at spatial recognition; the women better at verbal. If you haven't followed us so far, look at this chart, showing where language and spatial ability will fall for our four groups:

	language	*spatial*
right (straight)	left	right
right (hooked)	right	left
left (straight)	right	left
left (hooked)	left	right

Now, combining the above information with Levy's discovery—that no matter what handedness, women's left hemispheres are "enhanced" and men's right hemispheres are "enhanced"—we arrive at the following chart.

| *Areas of Enhancement* | | | | |
	right straight	*right hooked*	*left straight*	*left hooked*
women	language	spatial	spatial	language
men	spatial	language	language	spatial

Since most men and most women are straight right-handers, the above chart begins to explain a basic difference between men and women. If Levy's findings are correct, *handedness* (the fact that most people are the same handed—be it right, as is the case, or left) has determined the basic difference between men and women. If humans had become even-handed, if left- and right-handedness had occurred randomly in the population, as many women would be spatially oriented as men and as many men would be verbally oriented as women.

But right-handed we are, and as a result men watch sports on television (intensely right-brained) while women talk and keep track of children. Men think women are scatterbrained (because women's left-brain enhancement allows them to think about six different things simultaneously); women think men don't listen (and when men's obsessive right brains are going strong, they *don't* listen) and we can blame the entire situation on handedness.

Part Two/The Trials of the Left-Handed

The left-handed personality:
He is overmeticulous in dress and social manner, devotes an excessive
care to useless articles, is either brutal or coldly aloof, accepts and
enforces a rigid moral code, is often secretly superstitious and openly
very obstinate, is with great difficulty diverted from a rigid course of
sternly intellectual thought, constantly experiences the greatest difficulty
in making decisions.
                Ives Hendrick, Facts and Theories of Psychoanalysis, *1941*

One of the authors of this book is a lefty and one a righty; we feel,
therefore, that we represent a small cross section of handedness. The
left-hander of the two of us, for instance, insisted that this chapter be
called "Sinister and Dexter" rather than the other way around,
because left-handers so often come second. The only advantage we
have discovered in being a lefty—other than confounding your tennis
partner, the other team in baseball, or your sparring opponent—is in
throwing coins into the automatic toll keepers on toll roads. Righties
either have to pass the coins from right to left and then make a
pitiful, misdirected toss toward the toll basket, or must heave the
coins more surely, but over a greater distance, with their right hands.
We will assure you that the car six places ahead of you, stopped at
the gate and waiting for someone to come and find the coins that
didn't go in the basket, is being driven by a righty. There now, lefties,
does that make you feel better? Jack Fincher states that lefties also
have an easier time "seeing under water," perhaps "because they
may be better in touch with the more abundant visual receptors of
their non-language hemisphere."[30] Better aim at toll baskets and the
ability to see under water may not be much, but it's something.
    Consider the scorn usually heaped on lefties. Paul Tabori:
"Eugenists advise that two left-handed people should not marry. In
spite of all modern achievements of training and technology, left-
handedness is still a handicap and should be eliminated if at all

possible. Again, eugenics teach that the marriage of left-handed blood relations is especially harmful."[31] This, we hasten to say, was written in 1962, not, as you might have supposed, in *1862.*

Jack Fincher, a lefty, on the subject: "True enough, the left-handed, like the poor, have always been with us. It is perfectly true, too, that a statistically disproportionate number of them have been alcoholics, bed wetters, poor achievers, slow learners and chronic misfits. . . . And . . . a couple of them turned out to be two of the most infamous antisocials: Jack Ripper and the Boston Strangler."[32]

In almost every language the word for left denotes something negative.[33] In French, of course, *gauche* means someone who puts his foot in his mouth; in Italian *mancino* means deceitful; in German *linkisch* means clumsy; *na levo* means sneaky in Russian; *zurdo*, in Spanish, means malicious; and the Anglo-Saxon *lyft,* which became our "left," meant weak or broken in its original form in Dutch. Needless to say, the words for "right" in all of these languages have positive, almost glowing, meanings: justice, correct, truth, and so on. In ancient Greece, however, the beautiful word *aristera* for left also meant aristocratic. (One can only imagine that a lone aristocratic lefty created that neologism.)

The slang words for left-handers in England and Australia say everything. In England one is "cack-handed," from the French *caca* meaning *merde,* and in Australia a lefty would be a "Molly dooker," Molly meaning woman, with the phrase equaling "woman-handed," which in Australia is not a compliment.

Even in our dreams we denigrate the left-handed. William Stekel says: "The right way always signifies the road to righteousness, the left the one to crime. Thus the left may signify homosexuality, incest, and perversion, while the right signifies marriage, relations with a prostitute, etc. The meaning is always determined by the individual moral viewpoint of the dreamer."[35] In almost all religions the right hand is holy, the right *side* is holy, and the left side the side of the devil. And when we give a "left-handed compliment," we do more harm than good.

Interesting exceptions are the Chinese, who, according to

Fincher, treat the left side as an equal to the right, and the American Zuñi Indians, who consider the left the side of judgment and the right the side of action.[36] Some authorities disagree with Fincher's assessment of the Chinese. According to a friend of ours who has traveled in China, the Chinese are just as eager as Western cultures to switch lefties to righties.

The whole concept of "left" and "right" seems arbitrary—useful, but arbitrary. Children before the age of 6 have very little talent for learning left and right. Possibly, until the brain truly differentiates into speech side (usually left) and spatial side (usually right), the two halves of the brain have no fixed reference point. Up until a child is 5 or 6 the right side of the brain has many of the same language abilities as the left. It can learn (and does learn) nouns and adjectives. Its talent, however, stops at verbs and grammatical constructions. Could it be, then, that as the child learns grammar, and the left side of the brain finally becomes the language side, the child's brain specializes its right and left hemispheres and the child is finally able to tell left from right?

If Jerre Levy is correct in her assessment of women as being left-brained and men as being right-brained[37] (and here she is speaking very generally), then we would expect women to do worse on achievement tests in identifying left and right. (The male's right-brained mind would automatically do better on spatial relationships.) As it turns out, more women *do* have problems with left and right.

Because left and right are purely subjective, we often need an outside reference point so that we know which way to face. In theater we speak of stage left and right or, from the opposite point of view, audience left and right. In giving road directions we must orient the driver with something on the order of "Go west and take the first left," and pray that he knows the direction he is heading. Even then some people have difficulty remembering which is left and which is right.

In Western culture we write with a right-hand bias, that is to say, from left to right. The Phoenicians and the Semites wrote the other way, from right to left. We should hasten to add that the percentage of left-handers in these cultures is the same as in Western culture. The Greeks, before becoming inveterate righties, used a fascinating switching system known as *boustrophedon*, as the ox turns, with the first written line going left to right, the second right to left, and so on.[38] For most of us in present times, our left to right writing style is so ingrained that mirror-writing has the appearance of another language. The written word is, in fact, one of the few things in the environment that is truly left- or right-handed. Anyone who has watched a movie being run with a reversed negative and has realized the reversal only when a portion of writing, a headline or a sign, is flashed on the screen, will know what we are talking about.

Even the idea of clockwise and counterclockwise is arbitrary. Most right-handers prefer the counterclockwise rotation; clocks must somehow then seem "righter" to lefties than they do to righties.

But there are more serious problems afflicting left-handers than having a handedness with a bad name and perhaps being alone in identifying with the directions clocks run. Left-handers often have serious problems in getting the world the right-way 'round, especially those pesky rightwardly oriented letters. Left-handers more often than right-handers are "alexic," that is, they read *b* for *d* and *p* for *q*, *was* for *saw* and *tap* for *pat*. Whether or not they have learned their right hand from their left, something in the brain cannot decide in which direction letters should go. There is, in effect, a small war going on between the two hemispheres for dominance, and until that is settled, the brain itself can't distinguish direct image from mirror image.

The same problem affects certain muscle controls—over speech, for instance, or over the urethra. Sir Cyril Burt reported that there is a much higher ratio of stutterers among left-handers than among right-handers: 6.5 percent of left-handed children had a persisting problem with stuttering and 11.9 percent had had a problem with it at some time in their lives, versus 1.7 percent and 3.2 percent respectively for right-handers.[39]

Stuttering is three times more common in boys than in girls (left-handedness is also more common in boys).[40] One authority,

Travis, stated that one percent of the school population stutters. Sir Cyril Burt (some of whose conclusions are now being questioned) and others have mentioned that stuttering is unknown in China. We wonder if that might be because the Chinese language is intoned. It has frequently been found that stutterers can produce a troublesome word or phrase by singing it. (Singer Mel Tillis, who stutters, is an example of this phenomenon.) Does the side that controls music (which is the opposite side to that which controls speech), once it is engaged, give the brain a steady sidedness against which the other half can relate? In other words, does singing occupy half of the brain so that it stops trying to interfere with the speech instructions being sent out from the other side? These are fascinating areas for speculation. For anyone who has witnessed the pain and humiliation of a very young child trying to speak despite a stutter, the thought that there might be an eventual solution is heartening. No wonder lefties (10 percent of whom, to refer back to Burt's study, have at some time had trouble with stuttering) also have problems of wetting their beds. The anxiety dreams alone of these children must occupy a large percentage of their sleep time.

Stuttering and stammering are now considered to be the same thing, although they are, in fact, two different problems. Stuttering is being stuck on a particular letter or syllable of a word, whereas stammering is a momentary inability to say anything. "It is a common observation," say H. R. Beech and Fay Fransella in their book *Research and Experiments in Stuttering,* "that one of the most characteristic features of stuttering is day to day variability. . . . There is no adequate definition of stuttering. . . ."[41] Beech and Fransella also note that there is "more of a chance the child will stutter if a relative stutters," but whether that is because of inheritance, stress, or mimicry is unknown.[42]

Some children grow out of stuttering or learn to control it. Some grow into adults still afflicted by the problem. Sir Francis Bacon prescribed what he thought was a helpful tonic: "Stuttering is caused by a cold tongue which needed to be warmed through the day with frequent doses of warm wine."[43] Stuttering could even be magically eliminated when it affected the presentation of a king. King George VI had his radio addresses edited to eliminate stutters and stammers as, when he got older, they continued to get worse and worse.[44] He was a left-hander who had been taught to write with his right hand but continued to play tennis with his left.

Yet despite all of the implications that switching left-handers to the right can lead to stuttering, some writers still urge parents to try it. Tabori, writing in 1962, says: "The education of the left-handed, therefore, needs special care. Small children must be watched carefully; if they show such tendencies [toward left-handedness] they must be treated accordingly. If the 'change-over' can be effected without any serious upset, all is well...."[45] The idea that there should be *any* interference with such a highly individual and such a crucial event as hand preference should be put to bed at once.

We could recite here the litany of famous left-handers, with Leonardo da Vinci and Paul McCartney leading the way, but we will resist. Suffice is to say that right is not better than left, nor left better than right, but that a clear choice of one hand or the other is the most important choice of all.

United Press International, Inc.

2/ Ethnic Gestures

*Foreigners talk with their arms and hands as auxiliaries to the voice.
The custom is considered vulgar by us calm Englishmen . . . If you
use your hands at all, it should be very slightly . . . you should not be
too lively with your actions.*

The Habits of Good Society, 1870

Isn't it astonishing that when you first meet new people, you can
often tell where they are from by their last or given names? Armenian
names have a final *-ian* or *-yan*. Names ending in *-son* (Johnson,
Swenson, Peterson), or *-quist* or *-vist* (Nordquist, Berkvist) are
Swedish, while *-sen* endings (Jensen) are Danish. Consider for a
moment the problems a Danish postman must have in a country

where half the population share fourteen family names and 60 percent of all names end in -sen.[1] Plan ahead if you have to look up a Nielsen or Jensen in the Copenhagen phone book—there are 32,000 of each listed. At a certain point in German history, some people felt it was important to specify whether your name ended in -man or in -mann, the latter being considered the "pure" German name. Welsh names often show the Saxon appositive, the final s as in Williams, Jones, Evans and Daniels; many Irish names are distinguished by the preceding O, and Scotsmen are marked by their Mac or Mc.

Some last names, however, were recent acquisitions, given through marriage rather than through birth. In America, immigrants' names were often simply assigned by bored officials who had a hugger-mugger system of "sounds-likes." One friend of ours, a Chinese woman, has the last name of Dare, not because of a relationship to the Virginia Dares but simply because, to the bureaucrat filling out the family's papers, the Chinese family name came out in English sounding more like Dare than anything else.

The more recent the immigration, the more likely the name bears some clue to the person's nationality. A gradual process of Anglicization occurs in the second, third, and fourth generations, in both Christian and given names, and it is rarely if ever counterbalanced by a backward move. (We note, however, that Irving Wallace's son chose to return to the family name Wallechinsky.)

In the same way that names become homogenized, so do accents and foreign words and phrases. It is now imaginable in New York to overhear someone saying, "That dumb jive-ass gumbah isn't worth bupkas!" Where Italians and Jews live side by side, they begin to share some of the same accents, words, and habits. Where blacks and Puerto Ricans live side by side, they begin to form more and more a single class. Words, dress, styles, and slang all follow the rule of propinquity. It is exactly the same with gestures. We "catch" them from each other.

We also catch the lack of gestures from each other, as we rise socially. The higher the class one enters, the less likely it is that broad, active gestures will be welcomed. This is true not only of American and English societies (where the English inability to move the body might have some influence) but in gesturing societies as well. Macdonald Critchley states: "excessive resort to gesture is commonly frowned upon by sophisticates, even—be it stressed—in those countries where the inhabitants are notorious for their verbal and motor vivacity."[2]

Mario Pei once had a radio show called "Where Are You From?" on which he identified people's birthplaces, to within 200 miles, he said, based on the small slips they made in speech. Might it be possible similarly to guess a person's place of birth by watching his or her gestures, to catch the small slips that would show the individual to be of Irish or English or German or Italian or Jewish or Iranian origin? The answer is a qualified yes, *if* there were a careful enough system, a codification of gestures, body orientation, interpersonal distance, and rhythm. What an extraordinarily difficult job that would be! Consider, for instance, that there are an estimated 700,000 different gestural meanings[3] and that that is only *one* of the variables to be considered.

The enormity of this task has not stopped anthropologists, sociologists, and kinesiologists from setting up systems and categories of gesturers. Walter Sorell, in *The Story of the Human Hand*, formulates his "Law of the 45th parallel," in which he states that "one could even venture to draw a geographic demarcation line in Europe; people settled between the equator and the 45th degree of latitude combine the language of words and gestures most naturally; these people could hardly imagine themselves talking without gesturing. Only the Hungarians and Finns [note: from *above* the 45th latitude] do not fit into this geographic scheme; . . . both are very lively and temperamental in the gesticulations. . . . Both are of Mongolian descent, a fact revealed by the common root of their languages."[4] We rather like this "rule," though proving it might be a Herculean task. Nevertheless, it does seem that people from Southern Europe, from around the Mediterranean, gesticulate much more than their northern neighbors. Neopolitans and Sicilians are particularly noted for their hypermimia (tendency to gesture all the time; the opposite of hypomimia). In 1282, in fact, the "Vespro Siciliano," the massacre of thousands of soldiers of the French army of occupation by the people of Palermo, was planned and executed solely by the use of gestures.[5]

Probably as early as people of one race started meeting people of another race, there were published monographs concerning strangers' superior or inferior use of gestures. We note that Henry Estienne, a sixteenth-century linguist, blamed Catherine de' Medici for importing "gesturing" into the theretofore fairly staid, formal, correct, and needless to say, unmoving French court. "Frenchmen," he noted, "are not gesturers by nature and dislike gesticulation."[6] This, remember, was written 300 years ago. No Frenchman would dare make such a statement today. It is interesting to consider that, if Estienne is right, and the habit of gesturing appeared first in the French court and then filtered down to the peasant class, it may be one of the few instances in which excessive gesturing became thought of as a sign of class status and not of low peasant birth.

In the 1800's, two ecclesiastical souls wrote lengthy "dictionaries" of Neopolitan gestures, surely the most varied and intricate gestures known to a speaking people. The persistence of Neopolitan and Sicilian gesturing can be seen today anywhere Southern Italians meet and talk. One could watch a silent film of these people and know immediately that they were Southern Italians by the speed and style of their hand gestures. Sorell suggests that Sicilians became gesturers because their country was so often invaded and subjugated that "secret" or coded gestures were the only safe way to converse. One could not, supposedly, bring a man into court because of a fleeting, illusive gesture.

A more likely reason would also be a more complicated one, combining the poor and rather rustic nature of Sicily and Naples and the strong ancient Greek gestural influence, along with both the criminal and nautical business of those cities. These three factors—a remote, inbred place; a strong gestural heritage; and the kinds of businesses in which a great deal of time is spent in cafes and on quays discussing deals and telling stories—probably all serve to promote heavy gesturing.

In Europe the Alps seem to make an impenetrable barrier between the gesturers and nongesturers, with the nongesturers intent on describing those who throw their arms about as uncouth, of low birth, ill educated, and untrustworthy. Some, like V. Hehn in 1867, attributed the gesturing to the Italians' "hot blood." K. Skraup, in 1908, saw five factors that determined how hypermimic one was: intelligence, occupation, temperament, culture, and race; of these, the most important was intelligence. This was obviously the direction of thinking of the day because in the same year A. Gehring wrote that Mediterranean types gestured because they were simple and uneducated and that Teutons were taciturn because of the "wealth and complexity of their thought."[7]

One writer tried to organize racial gesturing groups into shapes, of all things. Rutz (1925) claimed that people were spherical, parabolic, pyramidal, or polygonic. (Germans, Englishmen, the Dutch, Swedes, and Hindus were considered parabolic.) This categorizing of gesture was leading in one direction—toward classifying people for the purpose of racial discrimination. Lenz in 1927 said that Jews had a "capacity for expressing thoughts and feelings by gesture and play of countenance. Jewish volubility and haste contrast with Teutonic taciturnity, quietude and slow-mobility." Lenz also commented that their propensity for gesturing made Jews "born actors."[8]

By 1930 a man named Guenther was stating that Jews, even half-Jews, could be discerned by their use of gestures. In 1933 L. F. Clauss stated that there were six types of easily distinguishable "races," and that the "inclination of Mediterranean types for the dancing profession" was racially determined. How did Clauss arrive at these conclusions? Why, he claimed, by intuition.[9] This kind of thinking—which may have started from a Germanic tendency to compartmentalize, intellectualize, and pedanticize details of daily life (you see how easy it is to generalize in this way, convincingly)—led to outright bigotry and persecution.

An interesting study done in America in 1937 by David Efron was much more scientific and less racially biased than the preceding studies. Efron and his partner Foley studied two groups of first-generation immigrants to the United States—Italians from the South of Italy and Jews from Lithuania and Poland. He noticed marked differences between the two groups. The following chart indicates some of the things Efron found. Keep in mind that these observations are of two small samples of specific groups of Italians and Jews of the first generation, but also notice the interesting comparisons between the two groups:[10]

European Jews	*Southern Italians*
elbows are held close to body, arm bent at elbow	elbows are out, gesture is from shoulder
arms, head, hands and fingers all are part of the gesture	arms are often used by themselves
one arm used at a time	both arms used simultaneously
will gesture with object in hand	usually does not gesture with object in hand
rarely touches own body, except for beard, chin	often touches own body
gestures are erratic and choppy	gestures are rolling, continuous
hands are kept near midline	hands will wander away from center of body
gestures are oratorical and indicate logical processes	gestures are pictorial, descriptive, pantomimic
will often point into the face of another	will rarely ever point into the face of another
gestures are centripetal	gestures are centrifugal

European Jews	*Southern Italians*
palm is held upward and flat	palm is held curved and downward
will stand very close to another	will stand far enough apart to leave room for broad gestures
will grasp, poke, and touch another	will rarely grasp, poke, or touch while speaking
will gesture and talk at the same time as another	will gesture and talk one at a time

But what happened to the *second* generation? Consider Mayor Fiorello LaGuardia, whose father was Italian and whose mother was Jewish. LaGuardia used both Italian and Jewish gestures and switched between the two without realizing it. He more naturally fell into using Jewish gestures when he spoke to groups of Jewish voters and he used Italian gestures when he spoke to Italian voters. Obviously LaGuardia was a man who had moved out of the ghetto and who was comfortable in almost any group of people.

This would hold to what Efron found in his study of "assimilated" Italians and Jews living in "Americanized" environments. The gestural lines became blurred. Both groups had picked up some gestures from each other and from other Americans and both had begun relaxing their hands and using less rhythm in their gestures. In the second generation Efron found what he calls typical American gestures: clenching the hand into a fist, using the fist for emphasis, pounding the table. Assimilated Jews—Jews who belonged in this instance to an exclusive Fifth Avenue club—acted like their Anglo-Saxon counterparts in that their gestures were almost entirely pictorial. They did not poke nor did they gesture with objects held in their hands. Another group of non-first-generation Jews Efron studied, however, a group of Jewish students at an orthodox Jewish school, used the same gestures as the first-generation Jews.[11]

What Efron showed (in the first scientific study of the differences in ethnic gestures) was that the use of gesture was culturally determined. This meant that gesturing was not caused by some inherent racial characteristic, as was believed in the German thinking of the twenties and thirties, and as is still proposed in some contemporary writing that refers to gestures being "in the blood." Walter Sorell, in his otherwise excellent book, falls into this trap, saying that a young British man's emerging use of gestures was inevitable because of his (unknown to him) French ancestry. Sorell insists that "Racial characteristics are connected with 'instinctive' gestures which remain uncontrolled and involuntary."[12]

This, of course, is pure nonsense, of the kind practiced by Dr. Charlotte Wolff, who believed that racial background and mental traits determined hand characteristics. She said in her book *The Human Hand*, "Negroes have smaller thumbs than white men" because the thumb is the symbol of ego and consciousness and this power is "more highly developed in Europeans than in Negroes."[13]

So too can we ignore the kind of race-equals-physical-difference-equals-gestural-difference progression of thought in W. A. Rose's conclusion that in Orientals, because "the extensor muscle [is] weaker ... than the flexor, a great many muscular opposites occur among them; notably in pushing and pulling a saw and the like."[14] Obviously this was before anyone had heard of Bruce Lee.

Those who most strongly believed that gestures could be categorized by race were the ones who felt there was a racial predisposition for gestures. Listen to Clauss: "The Mediterranean soul requires and has a small, slender, catlike body, fit for free motion; both its gestures and postures are theatrical. ... The gestural style of the Orientaloid race ... [is due to] the bodily structure of the race, which is flexible, excessively slender and light."[15] What never occurred to Clauss, Wolff, Guenther, Boehle, Berger, and the rest and what *did* occur to Efron (who relied on observations from the field, not "intuition") is that people gesture like the people they are with. It is not race but culture and environment that shape gestures. Fiorello LaGuardia wasn't using Jewish and Italian gestures because they were in his blood but because they were in his home. Why else would he be able to switch so securely from one to the other when he was in first one, then the other cultural environment? Though there is no racial reason for a difference in gestures, people in one country or in one region of a country begin to share a common gesture language. It is by this *cultural* difference that we can identify Italians by the richness of their gestures or, contrarily, spot suspected Britons by the absence of gestures (the stiff upper lip syndrome).

Consider what we do in a foreign country. First we use more gestures because we haven't learned the words we need. We mime what we want, we shrug, we use our hands to keep people's attention while we grapple with our faltering command of the language. Then we begin using the gestures we see around us. When we use French gestures, body stance, facial expressions, we feel more French and therefore our spoken French feels more fluent.

There are universal gestures, which would be understood anywhere, by anyone. Putting a hand to the mouth to indicate food, putting the two hands together horizontally and resting the head on them to indicate sleep, holding the nose to indicate "something stinks"—all of these would be understood by another human no matter what the language barrier. Gestures that pantomime a basic human activity will, if deftly done, usually be greeted with some kind of recognition. This recognition extends to other primates—the great apes and chimpanzees, for instance. Adriaan Kortlandt, a Dutch scientist, reported that wild chimps make a sign of submission somewhat akin to hat tipping and that the gesture varies slightly from band to band.[16] There are many other instinctive signs among chimps that humans would instantly recognize. It is for this reason, if for no other, that humans visiting zoos stand watching monkeys and chimps with fascination and that chimps are the favorite anthropomorphic substitute. A trained seal may be interesting but it doesn't fascinate us as does watching J. Fred Muggs shake hands, or smoke a cigar, or stand on his head.

It is for their similarity to us that chimpanzees have been taught Amislan (American sign language) in an attempt to learn about nonhuman use of language. Many of the Amislan signs are pantomimes, or what might be called "natural" signs. "I love you" in sign language is indicated by holding yourself with both arms wrapped tightly in front, a sign that would convey its message even if you had never formally been taught sign language.

An incident described in Eugene Linden's *Apes, Man, and Language* is of interest here. One of the first primates to learn Amislan, a chimpanzee named Washoe, wanted her bib and drew an outline of it on her chest. The researchers firmly corrected her with the proper sign for bib. Only later was it discovered that Washoe's sign was a perfectly acceptable alternate. Washoe intuited the sign because it was a pantomime.[17] Although there are many variations in sign language between English and American users, or between French and English users, many of the pantomime signs are mutually recognized.

(Readers might be surprised to learn that sign language is, according to the American Speech and Hearing Association, the fourth most-used language in the United States, right behind English, Spanish, and Italian.)

It is this "natural" usage in sign languge that allowed American Indians of both northern and southern tribes—who used two different systems, the northern tribes gesturing with both hands and the southern tribes gesturing with one hand—to understand each other. Captain William Clark spent three years with the Indians, including the time of the Sioux and Cheyenne wars (1866–1867). Among his 300 Indian scouts there were six different tribal languages spoken: Pawnee, Shoshone, Arapahoe, Cheyenne, Crow, and Sioux. Yet, Clark reported, the Indians could sit around a campfire for hours in silence using only sign language for communication.[18] Those who have expertise in this area say that the Cheyenne developed the finest nuances, followed closely by the Arapahoe.

Says Macdonald Critchley, referring to unassimilated Indians, "Indians can communicate without any difficulty with the deaf of any nationality."[19] Garrick Mallery, writing in 1861, said, "What is called *the* sign language of Indians is not, properly speaking, one

The Apache, Shoshone, and other Indian tribes make this sign for rain, bringing the hands downward a short distance. Tears are indicated by the same sign, made from the eyes downward, with the back of the hands almost touching the face. Heat—the sun's heat—is the same sign held above the head and thrust toward the forehead.

language, but it and the gesture systems of deaf mutes and of all people constitute together one language—the gesture speech of mankind, of which each system is a dialect."[20]

Not only do American Indians and deaf mutes share common signs, but Australian aborigines and women in Russian Armenia and the Caucasus also use many of the same signs. In this sense we can say, therefore, that there is a universal sign language. But once we have exhausted the more easily recognized gestures (putting the hand to the mouth to indicate food or drink) how do we mime the more difficult requests? How, for instance, do we ask, "Where is the bathroom?" No wonder this phrase follows only "hello" and "thank you" in foreign tourist guides. Thank goodness the overhead water tank toilet came along so that the gesture of pulling an overhead chain suffices in many parts of the world for "a flush toilet." This might be what we could call a technological gesture. A similar one would be signing the air, or signing the palm of one hand with the thumb and forefinger of the other to signal, "Where is the check?" If the American Express card is recognized in 140 countries, this gesture is also. Another technological gesture might be the puffing of an imaginary cigarette to signal "Do you have a smoke?" Using the forefinger as a gun, or dialing an imaginary wall telephone are also fairly widely recognized.

One would think we could gesture yes and no securely. But in Greece shaking the head from side to side indicates yes, not no. Their word for yes—*ney*—even *sounds* like no. And the way the Greeks indicate "no"—with a backward toss of the head—can seem to us a way of nodding agreement. Hand signals are sometimes more reliable because in any country a shaking finger or a pushing away gesture will indicate refusal or no. This pushing away, along with table pounding, is the first human "gesture" we see in infants and is universal.

But beyond a few pantomimes and technological gestures, and perhaps yes and no, are there any gestures that are worldwide? Maybe, if we can also read facial expressions. There are pitfalls in making any gesture without knowing if it will be understood, without knowing if it will be considered obscene or insulting. Here is an example from Laurence Wylie's very amusing book, *Beaux Gestes:* "A Haitian told me of a Florida beauty queen who was invited to participate in a celebration in Port-au-Prince. In the parade she sat atop her float, waving innocently to the crowd, unaware that in Haitian gesture language she was proclaiming 'Screw you! Screw you!' "[21] Not even a wave, you see, is safe.

To write a comprehensive list of all the national and regional variations on gestures would require vast resources of time and space. Herewith we would like to show you the more interesting variations we know of in four categories: table manners, gestures of insult, gestures of threat, and obscene gestures—the areas in which you are most likely to run into trouble.

Table manners are taught us at an early age and they are well taught. In America we are told it is absolutely unacceptable to put the elbows on the table. In France and Italy you would be thought a stiff prig if you sat there with your hands in your lap. In France, in fact, it is considered rude to put your hands *under* the table: there seems to be some suspicion here of exactly what you might be doing. In China it is rude to pass a bowl with one hand only, especially a bowl of rice or a cup of tea, as both are sacred. In Arab countries passing any food with the left hand would be the highest insult. The left hand is reserved for body functions of the eliminatory sort, not the alimentary kind. A French peasant might cut the sign of the cross into a loaf of bread as a way of blessing it. Arabs wash their hands, at the table, several times during the meal, especially after eating meat; and at the end of the meal they brush their teeth with a stick, a custom not too far removed from the European and American practice of picking the teeth. In Orthodox Jewish homes, especially during feasts and holy days, elaborate systems are observed involving the ritual washing of hands and which plates and foods are to be touched by specific members of the family. And there is the European custom, dating back to medieval fears of the devil, of throwing spilled salt over the left shoulder.

The Fork

One of the earliest lectures on tableside behavior was written in 1480.[22] It includes this advice for children: "Take your meat with three fingers only and don't put it into your mouth with both hands. Do not keep your hand too long in the plate."

What seems to modern Western man to be an indispensable table utensil—the fork—is relatively unknown in most of the world. As you can see from the above, it was unknown in England during the Middle Ages. Anglo-Saxons had once used the fork—there are references to such an implement as far back as 796—but it soon fell out of fashion. Italians have been using the fork since approximately the eleventh century, and it was an English traveler to Italy in 1611 who brought back with him some of these handy objects. But rather than finding a welcome acceptance of the new-fangled gadgets, this man was greeted with scorn for using an implement so "finicky and effeminate." In the seventeenth century, apparently, the height of manly grace was evidenced by one's grabbing a joint of boar with bare hands and then wiping the grease on the nearest roughcoated dog.

Priests condemned the forks outright; using them, they said, implied that God's creatures were dirty and therefore to be touched only by a piece of machinery, not with the bare human hand. Still, the novelty item caught on. The fork at first was an upper-class affectation and it possessed only two prongs. By the end of the eighteenth century it had filtered down through the social strata to common folk and had acquired three or four prongs. The rich, it appears, are more skilled in keeping food on a two-pronger than are the commoners. The more prongs on your fork, therefore, the lower your station in life.

Making a mistake in table manners might be considered a sign of boorishness, stupidity, or provincialism but it probably won't be taken as an insult. (Except for left-hand offerings at Arab tables.) There are certainly gestures, however, that are universally mildly insulting. We are not speaking here of obscene gestures, which we will discuss later, but of the kinds of insults children might give. "Cocking a snoot" or "snook," or as it is called in America, "thumbing your nose," is probably the world's record-holding insult. Desmond Morris claims there are 22 different names for this one gesture.[23] It is called the "Shanghai gesture," although it was unknown in the Far East until Westerners introduced it. The Germans call it *die lange nase* (the long nose) and the French call it *le pied de nez*. Rabelais was supposedly the first writer to make mention of it, in 1532. The gesture can be performed with one hand, or, to make a highly visible taunt, two hands can be used.

Mallery, in his discussion of Neopolitan signs, explains that the *naso lungo* was meant to imitate the look of an idiot: "A credulous person is generally imagined with a gaping mouth and staring eyes, and as thrusting forward his face, with pendant chin, so that the nose is well advanced and therefore most prominent in profile."[24]

We think the thumb to the nose may have started in imitation of the thumb in the mouth—a way of saying "you are just a baby"—with the added finger wiggle a way of calling attention to the gesture. The transfer of the thumb from the mouth to the nose, a place of greater prominence, was undoubtedly made for reasons of added visibility.

*It's not just the hand gesture, it's the facial clues accompanying the gestures
that give these two signs their power. Notice how our seafaring friend,
Peter Throckmorton, has taken on the look of an idiot on the left and a
sage fellow on the right.*

Making "donkey ears," "horns," or "elephant ears" all mean
the same thing: "You're a dunce, a dummy" to people in Europe and
America and to people around the Mediterranean. The gesture
would not be well-known to people in the Far East or in South
America. Saying that someone is a "donkey" is a fairly mild form of
insult and is often used by children.

A similarly mild gesture is the "He's crazy" gesture of circling
the forefinger at the temple or, as it is done in the Mediterranean,
putting the thumb to the temple and twisting the hand back and
forth. Tapping the forehead (or, in Holland, simply pointing to the
middle of the forehead)[25] is sometimes a sign of "craziness" or
"dizziness," but more often a tap of the temple means just the
opposite: "He's smart." The expression on the gesturer's face is the
giveaway here.

Some insults are merely shows of boredom or disinterest. In America we might feign putting our hands to our mouths and yawning, or we might pointedly pull back a cuff to look at a watch. In Europe the gesture consists of holding the hand palm up under the chin, to show how long one's beard has grown while the person was talking. In France the gesture is done with the finger curled inward, brushing the side of the face, as if feeling for stubble. Wylie calls the gesture *la barbe* (beard) or *"Rasoir,"* how dull!* The gesture acquired this meaning sometime in the nineteenth century. Worldwide, the gesture of yakking hands (the fingers and thumb rapidly closed and opened) is used to indicate someone who never stops talking.

If you wanted to imply that the speaker is not so much boring as stupid, this would be accomplished in Arab countries by applauding with one inverted thumbnail against the other.[26] This says, "What you are saying is worth so much." This same gesture in Spain means, "I squash you like a bug" when the thumbnails are ground together. This latter gesture is surely an insult too, probably related to the Arab gesture.

Stronger insults involve a slur on one's manhood, reference to one's mother, or the implication that one has become a cuckold. Several nationalities have gestures to indicate someone is gay. The French *pédé* or "He's a fairy," a gesture involving a raised little finger, is actually a play on words. *Pédé* is short for pederast and also the sound of the initials for *petit doigt*, the little finger.[27] In England and America this little finger is applied to the eyebrow, after being licked, as a campy sign for "He's gay." There is also the limp-wristed gesture made famous by Milton Berle.

A raised little finger doesn't always mean that someone is gay. In South America it indicates that someone is thin. There the gesture for homosexual is one hand placed on top of the other, with the two thumbs "flying," or the okay sign made with the hand held at

---

The French, apparently, are eloquent punners even in their gestures. La barbe means "shut up" and rasoir *has a close association to* raseur *(shaver) which is slang for a bore.*

the side. In Italy gesturers pull on or touch their earlobes, a reference to earrings, a sign of femininity.

There doesn't seem to be any gesture to indicate *"She's gay,"* or if there is, we've never heard of it. And just as there is no known gesture to indicate "lesbian," there is no gesture women use to indicate a good-looking man (*or* an ugly one). Try as we might we haven't discovered any. Perhaps women simply verbalize instead of gesture about men.

There is one gesture, the *comme-ci, comme-ça,* that can be used to indicate bisexuality or AC-DC. Here the hand is turned palm down, palm up several times. This can also mean any either/or situation, depending on the topic of discussion.

Insulting a man's mother is a fine old custom. The Saudi Arabians seem to have come up with the most elaborate insult in this category: touching the forefinger of the right hand to the bunched fingertips and thumb of the other hand, indicating "Your mother is a whore" or "You have (literally) five fathers," one for each finger.[28]

An even stronger insult is the "cuckold," indicated with the raised first and fourth finger. This gesture originated in Italy and is commonly used throughout Europe, but is less well-known in the United States, where the gesture is sometimes interpreted as "bullshit." (The connection here may be between the idea of "bullshit" and the "bull's horns.") One explanation of the origin of this gesture is that it comes from castrated bulls (oxen), who were so fixed to make them docile and useful for farm work. The sign of the bull's horns then became generalized to mean any male who had lost his virility because his wife no longer needed him sexually.

Another explanation is that the sign resembles a cock's spurs grafted onto his head. In ancient Greece it was the custom to do this with a capon, and the inference is easily taken from there. This is a gesture of high insult in countries where manhood and honor are things you come to blows about. In Italy, where they take their gesturing seriously, a truck driver in Verona was fined $50 for "hoisting the *corna,*" as it is called there, to a driver behind him beeping his horn. The penal code, in fact, could have awarded him

The vicious look on our seaman's face indicates that this cuckold sign was not being given in jest but as part of a sincere insult.

six months in jail for "offending the honor or decorum of a person."[29] "Person" in this case means just your ordinary countryman. For someone in high office, a pope, the Italian President, prime minister, or a senator, the sentence is three years. (Americans can rest easy in the knowledge that a Connecticut court recently decided that giving an obscene gesture—in this particular case, a raised middle finger— was not illegal under the anti-obscenity laws.)

This cuckold sign is not always the sign of a cuckold. In Hindu mythology it signifies Brahma or Dagon and can be found in paintings and statues in Burma and Japan. In the Middle East the sign is the "Kef Myriam," the hand of Mary. In the form of an amulet, a *manu-cornuta,* worn at the neck, it is considered powerful enough to ward off the evil eye.[30] (The belief is that an insulting sign will distract the evil eye from the person wearing it.)

The sign has an even milder meaning in South America when it is held horizontally. This says merely, "Bring me another drink—a double."[31]

Much more serious is a gesture impugning someone's honesty. This one is used frequently in cafes in port cities, where Italians, Greeks, Turks, and Marseillais might gather to discuss shipping and smuggling. One sign for "He's a thief" is putting the hand down, fingers outstretched, and slowly closing them. Another gesture, originally Neopolitan, indicates deceit; it is the hand inserted under the collar with the back of the hand slowly rubbing the neck. And, of course, the all-important sign for bribery is pinching the cheek between the thumb and forefinger while the hand is wiggled up and down. Another Neopolitan gesture of suspicion is the finger placed alongside the nose, which might originally have meant "This deal (or man) stinks." In France today this gesture has come to mean, "You can't fool me" or "I have a good nose" to search out the truth. In either case the gesture means that someone should pay close attention to where the truth lies. We also have "my eye," in which the forefinger pulls down the lower lid of one eye from below. It means "This person cannot be trusted."

In South America, a continent that has seen its share of political turmoil, smuggling, and vice, the sign for taking graft is one hand with fingers straightened, sawing across the other straightened hand. The sign for thievery in Guatemala is a hand in the shape of a claw (called *puños muy largos*) or similarly *tocando el piano,* playing the piano, meaning light fingered.[32] In South America, "my eye" means take care. Or, contrarily, if aimed at a woman, it means "She's a looker."

Such signs as "He's a thief" or "They take graft" are insults if the person being spoken of happens to see the sign being given. On

"My eye."

the other hand, such signs might not be considered insults in certain countries and among certain people for whom bakshish is a way of life and petty thievery a commonplace.

The "chin flick," which is used in Italy, France, and other parts of Europe but is unrecognized in England and America, can indicate anything from a simple no to annoyance to "bug off." Wylie calls this a French schoolyard gesture, used "to taunt a child who has displayed vexation and to make him even more miserable."[33] But Morris has it (as *la barbe*) as a very hostile sign, in effect a false piloerection, or hair-raising, as if readying for a fight—a symbolic beard-jutting.[34]

The thumb bite, followed by the forward flick and accompanied by the sound effect of the thumbnail on the front teeth.

Gestures of insult verging on threat are directed *at* a person. With a curious affinity for inflicting pain on *themselves* during an insult, Italians have perfected the thumb bite, finger bite, and hand bite. This is a strong substitution for "I would bite you if I could." In France the thumb bite is not nearly so strong, and it means "That isn't worth anything" or, according to Wylie, *que dalle,* with *dalle* being a worthless piece of floor tiling or a small coin.[35] Yet in England the gesture is strong again. In Tudor times biting the thumb was an invitation to fight or to quarrel.[36] (By the late eighteenth century the insult sign in England had changed to the thumb to the nose, and in the twentieth century to the inverted "V" for victory.)

Consider the lines from *Romeo and Juliet,*[37] an interchange between Sampson and Gregory, two servants to the Capulets:

Sampson: [urging Gregory] . . . Quarrel—I will back thee. . . .
Gregory: I will frown as I pass by, and let them take it as they list.
Sampson: Nay . . . I will bite my thumb at them, which is a disgrace
*   to them, if they bear it.*
Abraham [Servant to the Montagues—traveling with Balthazar—the
*   other side, you see]: Do you bite your thumb at us, sir?*
[Sampson then checks with Gregory to see if the law would be on the
Capulet side in a case of indiscriminate thumb biting. When Gregory
answers "No," Sampson says:]
Sampson: No, sir, I do not bite my thumb at you, sir, but I bite my
*   thumb, sir.*

Indeed, Sampson and Gregory's cavil on the thumb-biting question may have had more to do with cowardice or prudence than with bowing to the law because seven lines later, when one more of the Capulet party enters (and the Capulets have the Montagues outmanned and outranked), they are suddenly at swords. All this over a little thumb biting? Yes, but it was *Verona,* Italy. Still, Shakespeare must have expected his audience to be familiar with the thumb bite, which, as an ancient gesture may have been brought to England by the Romans. In modern England the gesture means "Up yours," a stronger statement than the French "It's nothing."

There is a specialized threat gesture in Greece, Turkey, and the rest of the Eastern Mediterranean that would scarcely be understood in France, England, or elsewhere. It is the *Sta matia sou* (your eyes) or *moutza,* a savagely insulting gesture: "Go to hell!" or "May the evil eye be on you." Desmond Morris says in *Manwatching* that the gesture harks "back to the ancient practice of thrusting filth in the face of a helpless prisoner,"[38] and Critchley concurs,[39] but our experience is that most people in the Eastern Mediterranean would consider it just one form of the various "evil eye" gestures. *Any* display of the open palm, or the sole of the foot, even shod, is

The moutza.

considered an insult. It is for this reason that the Greeks and Turks wave good-bye with their palms facing themselves and are offended by the sight of the bottoms of Americans' shoes when men sit with their legs crossed in the American style (the ankle of one leg over the knee of the other).

It is one of the great mischances of intercultural relations that the strongest insult (for the Greeks and Turks) and one of the most frequently offered gestures (for the Americans and Britons) are one and the same, the open palm. Because of extensive intermingling between these peoples, insult is usually avoided. Every Greek tourist

The late Nelson Rockefeller's vigor in offering the "American" finger sold this picture to front pages of newspapers across the country. Just for the record, it happened in Binghamton, New York, in 1976. Wide World Photos

book warns foreigners not to use the "facing" wave. Every Greek native has forgiven the inadvertent insult in favor of Touro-dollars and international goodwill. But it is still possible, especially in small towns in the countryside, where the "evil eye" is something to be reckoned with, to create confusion and turmoil with an open palm.

The subject of the cursing hand brings us to threats. The raised fist and the pointing finger will be understood as threatening gestures anywhere. But what about the forefinger and third finger, held stiffly and jabbed at the intended victim? What does that mean? Well, in Italy and other areas around the Mediterranean it indicates a willingness to poke out the other's eyes.[40] And while our "I'll wring his neck" gesture is widely understood in the Western world, an Oriental might wonder what we meant by wringing a rag in the middle of a harangue. A more likely Oriental gesture might simulate karate blows or swordplay.

But threatening gestures have little color or value to enrage if they are not obscene, what Ashley Montagu calls "gestural swearing." One gestural swearword that has retained its shock value for thousands of years is the raised middle finger, the *ditto impuro*. In Latin it was called the *digitus obscenus*; its recorded use goes back to Caligula, who shocked the Romans by presenting his middle finger to be kissed instead of his hand. Approximately 300 years earlier Diogenes flashed the finger to Demosthenes, but since our records are literary we have no way of knowing which version of the finger it was—up in the American fashion, down in the Arabian fashion, or sideways in the modern Greek style. One modern version, which we have traced to the West Coast, is the upright middle finger followed by the sideways middle finger meaning "Fuck you, and the horse you came in on."[41] The dual gesture does not seem to have currency in Ireland or England, but may have originated elsewhere on the continent.

A unique version of the "screw you" sign is the reverse English V-for-victory sign, with the forefinger and middle fingers extended, the thumb folded over the other fingers and the entire hand *facing* the person doing the gesture, rather than *facing away from* the person (as in the well-known Victory V). Winston Churchill made the "good" V sign famous during World War II, although the "insult" V had been used in England as early as 1913. What is strange about the insult V is that it doesn't *look* like an insult. There is nothing overtly phallic about fingers held in a V; the use of the Victory V has made the insult V seem unremarkable-looking, unless you already know the "bad" meaning. Consider how many American youths—especially since the co-opting of the V sign as a peace sign in the 1960's—have inadvertently given insult in England when they carelessly gave the V wrong way 'round. And consider how unre-

For some reason Churchill seems to be giving this cheering crowd the insult V instead of the correct victory V. The Library of Congress

The Churchill Memorial Statue in Washington D.C., showing the properly given V. Andrew Bradtke

warding it would be for an Englishman to give the screw-you "V" while motoring in another country only to have the Italian or Greek or German he was passing wave back at him and smile good-naturedly.

The real obscenity of the insult V becomes apparent if you examine a possible gestural ancestor—the Arab "nose jerk." The same palm-inward V sign is brought up under the nose and the fingers are jerked up against the nose one or several times. This is a pictograph of intercourse, with the woman's legs being the two fingers and the nose taking its accustomed spot as a phallic symbol.[42] One can only imagine that the English soldier class on duty in Arab countries, or perhaps the men building the Suez Canal in the mid-nineteenth century, saw the Arab nose jerk and carried it back home with them. Because of their being English and having a disinclination to touch their own bodies and a similar dislike of overtly graphic gestures, it seems a small step for the men to have eliminated the nose jerk and simply kept the finger V. So the innocuous V—representing only the woman's open legs—has become an obscene insult.

In the spirit of contrariness the English have made popular the "thumbs up," meaning "Everything is all right," when that same gesture to many people in the Eastern Mediterranean means quite graphically "Sit on it." This can lead to trouble—especially for hitchhikers—in a place like Sardinia, where the obscene meaning obtains. The only acceptable form of "thumbing" a ride in Sardinia and in Eastern Europe is by waving the hand at an oncoming car, a gesture that would look like a happy greeting to most European drivers. In Israel a more direct approach to hitchhiking is practiced; there the hitcher simply points down the road toward his destination.

In the United States the thumbs-up gesture, either held stationary or done with a smooth, sweeping motion, is the standard one for hitching a ride. While the thumb point is used by many Americans to show direction—"it's over there"—this gesture is one of mild insult in a number of countries. Pointing with the forefinger is preferred or, as saleswomen in one Tokyo department store were instructed, making a gentle sweep of the kimono to show the proper direction, certainly a most feminine gesture.

The forearm jerk—commonly used in central Europe, Italy, and Greece—has an unmistakable obscene look to it although the French phrase that goes with it, *Va te faire foutre,* while saying "Go get yourself screwed," carries the less obscene meaning of "Go to hell." (*Foutre,* because of its frequent use in French, does not have the shock value of the English "screwed." Perhaps the meaning would be more like "Go get yourself stuffed.") According to Wylie the gesture is not always sexual to the French. The action can be "raising the right arm with the hand tossing something over your shoulder or putting something behind you [indicating] utter disregard for the opinion of the other person."[43]

The French also have two hand signs for "You've had it in the ass" (*Tu l'as dans le cul*), a signal that is not particularly sexually libelous.[44] It means merely, "You've let yourself be had," or as might be said in America, "You've taken it in the ass" (among men) or "You've taken it on the nose" in mixed company. One of the gestures is graphic—the middle finger of one hand inserted into the fingers of the other hand held as a tube—and the other one is schematic—the flat of one hand coming down "boff" against the vertical fist of the other hand. This latter gesture, when done in Italy as the "Italian palm bang," is also considered obscene.

The *fica* or fig sign is an ancient copulatory gesture. Here the thumb is thrust between the forefinger and the middle finger of the same hand, simulating the penis thrust through a woman's labia. The gesture is more often done with the left hand than with the right. It is called the *fica* or fig because the inserted thumb is about the size and shape of the fig, which, being an ancient symbol of abundance, carried with it a sense of virility and fecundity to the *mano in fica.* The fica worn as an amulet is considered a charm against infertility as well as a good way to ward off the evil eye. And sometimes the gesture itself is not considered an insult. In northern Europe it can be used as a sexual invitation, a racier version of the forefinger and middle finger interwined, saying, "You and me, together, yes?"

For sheer power, the best obscene gesture is the *bras*

d'honneur or the "royal shaft," with one hand slapped to the opposite upper arm, and that arm raised with a fist. This is a mixture of obscene—with the fisted arm representing the erect penis—and threatening, a mighty combination. Wylie calls it "the most *macho* of gestures."[45]

In many countries, several "I want to grope you" gestures are employed, either as a sexual come-on or as an insult. The grope gestures become more obscene as eye and tongue flashes and descriptive phrases are added. Perhaps the most overt form of grope is the male crotch grab in which a man grabs his *own* crotch. This is a sign of supreme male assertiveness and is usually practiced by a man in a group of men as a form of male display to a passing female. A woman walking past a construction site might be subjected to this gesture, accompanied by a called-out statement like, "Right here, sweetheart." Desmond Morris claims this gesture, which he calls the "crotch scratch," is "most commonly found in Mexico."[46] Maryse Holder seconded this in her *Letters from Mexico*: "Studs here finger their balls a lot, a disgusting habit." Richard Pryor, in his film *Live in Concert*, demonstrates how deftly black men perform the crotch clutch while simultaneously maintaining a loose and easy walk down the street.

It would be unthinkable for an Englishman to do the crotch grab, or for a Scandinavian. It is not a part of Northern culture and therefore it is not a part of the Northerner's personality. This difference in the Northern Hemisphre, between those above the 45th parallel and those below (what we called in the opening of this chapter "Sorell's Law"), might be extended to "Lee and Charlton's Law": namely, those in the south of each country gesture more than those in the north. Sicilians and Neopolitans gesture much more than Milanese. Those who gesture a lot in Paris are considered not just hicks, but hicks from *the south*. In America, too, those in the north (New Englanders, Midwesterners, Pacific Northwesterners) tend to be reserved in their gesturing while those in the Sun Belt tend to be more expansive. Even within ethnic groups known for gesturing—

Italians and Jews—from the second generation onward those in the south gesture more than their northern cousins.

The extremely active gestures of the revival preachers, the backslapping Texan, the "warm Southern hospitality" would seem to be too physical for anyone living in a hot climate. It would make much more sense for people in a *cold* climate to move about, hug and touch each other, and generally be more active, but touching and gesturing seem to follow illogical laws. In the same way that the hottest (spiciest) foods are eaten in already hot climates and the brightest colors are worn, so people in hot climates touch each other.

Which is more remarkable—that different cultures have different gestures, or that any cultures have similar gestures? In the same way that cultures can be analyzed and compared through a study of their grammar and syntax, so can cultures be compared by a study of their gestures. It is always surprising to learn that French cows don't moo, and that French horses don't neigh, but instead cows *ova, ova* and horses *henni*. It is just as amazing to find out that Europeans, Americans, and South Americans have three different systems for counting one-two-three with their fingers. An American will (generally) count (1) forefinger, (2) middle finger, (3) ring finger. If asked to count up to five, Americans will count (4) the little finger and (5) the thumb.

To a European this system is crazy. One is obviously the thumb, 2 is the forefinger, and 3 is the middle finger; if a count of five is required, the ring finger is 4 and the little finger is 5.

To a South American both of these systems are cumbersome. The forefinger of the right hand is used to count on the fingers of the other hand, from the inside finger outward. So in South America, the little finger is 1 and the thumb is 5.[47]

The subject may seem academic until you are faced with this dilemma: try to gesture to the bartender for one more beer in

Germany. A friend of ours, an American girl, complained of gaining ten pounds in Germany alone just because she couldn't remember that the thumb was 1 and the forefinger 2. When she held up a forefinger, meaning bring me one more beer, she invariably got two steins.

Or consider how we indicate that something is *this* tall. In most of the world, a flat hand held a certain distance from the ground would say "this tall." But if you were talking about someone's child and were on a trip in South America, the gesture would be considered an insult because a flat hand is used only for animals and inanimate objects. A person's height is indicated by a vertical hand.[48]

Even something as simple as crossing the fingers is done differently in different countries. Crossing the fingers is actually a Christian gesture, symbolizing the cross, of course. In Mediterranean countries the forefingers of both hands may be held perpendicular to each other to form a cross, either to repel vampires, or as protection from the evil eye. In South America the sign of the cross is frequently made by the thumb and forefinger, with the thumb the upright "timber" and the forefinger (actually its first two joints) making the "crosstimber." Both of these crossed-finger gestures can be made more effective by kissing the fingers, a pledge or oath gesture meaning "I swear this is the truth."[49] But in northern European countries and in the United States the fingers are crossed with the second finger tightly wound around the forefinger. This gesture is often performed not when we are telling the *truth* but in fact when we are *lying*. The crossed fingers are also a sign for good luck, a use that bears much closer resemblance to the original intentions of the cross and that might have accompanied "God be with you."

The subversion of a Christian crossing gesture to a sign to be made while lying seemed a curious one to us until we considered this. The "Christian" sign was not always a safe one to give. When Christians were being persecuted and fed to the lions, who could blame them for making the sign of the cross covertly, behind their backs, instead of in full view. It is not too much of a leap to suppose that they may have likewise told a white lie or two to protect them-

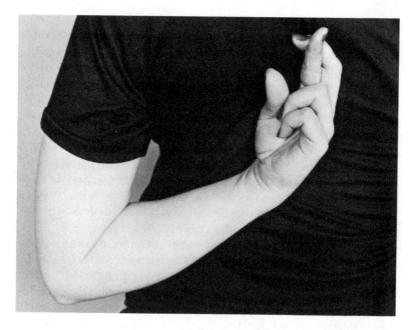

selves from the consequences of being an avowed Christian and thus, it must be that the sign of the cross was expected to protect you when you told a lie.

If there is one gesture that could be called purely American it is the OK sign, which has gained currency anywhere American troops have been stationed, with the same meaning as in the United States. OK means something stronger than just "all right"; it means whole-hearted approval. The sign supposedly originated from the initials of Old Kinderhook (New York), the home of President Martin Van Buren. So powerful was the Old Kinderhook party that its imprima-tur, the OK sign, was enough to get a candidate nominated and was therefore much to be desired.

Although the sign is well-known in its American meaning, in France the same sign would mean either *au poil*, "to the hair," perfect, or, if held in front of the eye, "zero," "It is worth nothing," two rather contradictory meanings. Those in the south of France are more likely to use the sign at the eye meaning "zero," a sign that, in context, most Americans would understand to mean *not* OK.[50]

Despite the Japanese passion for things American, the OK sign in Japan still carries its Japanese meaning—money, most likely yen.[51] If there had been no similar gesture already in the Japanese culture, the OK sign meaning approval would undoubtedly have become as common as baseball.

De Jorio in 1832, in his dictionary of Neopolitan gestures, shows the OK sign being given with the palm held downward meaning "justice" or "a just person," a meaning not unlike the American OK of approval.[52] In Latin America the same gesture, with the hand held down but more at the side, means "It is exactly right," almost a combination of the Neopolitan meaning, the French *au poil,* and the American OK. Yet in Colombia almost the same gesture means a gay person. In Malta, the sign means a male homosexual, a *pooftah.* In Sardinia, Greece, and Turkey it is an obscene gesture when made to either sex and refers to the anal area. In Italy and other parts of the Mediterranean the OK sign, slightly squashed, is the symbol for the female orifice and is considered a sign for copulation. There is even a variation on this, done with two hands held in front of the male genital area, a sort of double-handed obscene OK.

But even in Italy and Greece the OK sign made with the palm facing outward is recognized as a sign of blessing. In the Roman Catholic Mass and in Hindu and Buddhist mythologies this gesture symbolizes perfection and completeness. And according to St. Jerome, the sign when done with the left hand in classical times was called "the kissing of the thumb and finger" and symbolized union, in particular, marriage.[53]

So the OK means Old Kinderhook, all right, gay, female genitalia, blessing, marriage, insult, and obscenity, depending on the country it is used in and the way it is used.

The "hand-purse" is another multi-meaning gesture. It is done with the thumb and four fingers all touching and the hand held palm up. It can be used casually as an emphasizing gesture, in, say,

With the thumb touching only the first two fingers, this gesture means,
"How much?" But with the thumb touching all four fingers, the meaning
changes to "Worth it at any price, que bella.*"*

"How much does it cost?" In the United States, you might see it
being used when someone is groping for a word, with the gesture
being almost one of pulling the desired word out of the mouth.

In some countries, however, it has other specific meanings.
Whenever this gesture is used, it is performed with a certain beat,
sometimes in time with the words, sometimes in silence. The more
urgent the use, the angrier the use of the hand-purse, the more beats,
and the more violent the beats. With the softest use, the French
gesture of appreciation, the hand-purse is brought to the mouth,
kissed and then in one beat extended in the direction of the admired
object. In Greece and Turkey it also means appreciation. It is used
similarly in Italy as "que bella." In Spain the gesture indicates
quantity, probably in the same sense that "handsome" as in "handsome price" meant a "handful of money." With this meaning there

might be two or three beats. Two or three slow beats of the hand-purse in Tunisia will advise "Go slowly." The Maltese use it as a gesture of scorn and derision;[54] there the hand is pulled once downward, almost in an obscene manner, as in "Go milk yourself." Almost any gesture done slowly has a derisive quality. In Italy the scorn gesture is done rapidly and violently, usually in someone's face. It means, "What's the matter with you?" or "Give me the story straight." And in Iran the gesture takes on an even stronger edge when, in some places, it means "Cut the crap." It is interesting that in France the hand-purse when held in front of the body and pulled downward with fingers opening and closing slightly is a sign of *la trouille,* which Wylie calls "a common expression meaning 'fear.' " He suggests that the gesture might mean being so scared that one dirties one's pants, because of the etymological background of the word *trouille.* (*Trouille* is from the Flemish *drollen,* to defecate.)[55]

There is one area of gesturing that seems strangely under-represented—gestures to indicate ethnicity. We might mime an Oriental by pulling at the corners of our eyes, but there are almost no other "ethnic" gestures. The one gesture that would seem to be missing, considering the volatile racial history in the United States, is a gesture to indicate blacks. We know of only one country where there is such a gesture—in Cuba, where, John Nordheimer reports in *The New York Times,* some whites indicate that a person is black by rubbing the top of the forearm with the index finger, a simple gesture apparently drawing attention to the skin. Cuba has one of the most varied and racially gradated societies in the Western Hemisphere and this gesture is probably used to distinguish a nearly "pure" black from one with more mixed blood.

The only reason there is no gesture for blacks in this country is that there is no use for such a gesture. Either a person's race is obvious or it can be stated openly, without fear, and therefore a "secret" sign is unnecessary. There is little likelihood that such a gesture will develop or that any gestures to indicate ethnicity or religion will now appear.

Shakespeare said in *A Winter's Tale* that "there is language in every gesture." It must be, therefore, that our language is becoming poorer and poorer. With global television and the blending of national characteristics, we have fewer and less interesting gestures today than we had 50 years ago. And as gestures are lost or fall into disuse (like most of the two-handed gestures), they will be forgotten. Gestures are transient, ephemeral. Photographs of them, while catching the moment, are artifacts, mounted butterflies of what was once inscribed on the wind. The wonderful range of ethnic gestures, if unused, unrecorded, and unrecognized, will become as extinct as the *Glaucopsyche Xerces.*

3/ Let Your Fingers Do the Talking

We respond to gestures with an extreme alertness and, one might almost say, in accordance with an elaborate and secret code that is written nowhere, known by none, and understood by all.

E. A. *Sapir* Selected Writings of Edward Sapir
in Language, Culture and Personality

If you are reading this book sequentially you have just finished the section on ethnic gestures and should be able not only to recognize a person's ethnic background by the kind of gestures he or she uses but also to make the person feel comfortable by using the same gestures, or at least ones that won't be insulting when you are talking together.

But beyond ethnic gesture-language there is a whole other level of meaning: the psychological language of hands. What we are saying verbally can be either underlined or undermined by what we are doing with our hands. When we speak we are a multi-media happening: sound effects; rising and falling inflections; gestural illustrators, comments, and emphases; changes in skin color and eye openings; and postural adjustments. It is much easier to observe and critique someone else's orchestration of these skills than it is to be able to pull it off ourselves, just as it is easier to listen to a symphony than it is to write one. The best of us in this field become actors, preachers, politicians, or simply people who always seem to be able to get a job, win friends, influence people, and tell stories that keep the rest of us spellbound. Contrarily there are those of us who, despite expensive educations and high scores on Scholastic Aptitude Tests, seem always to lose out on jobs, have trouble keeping friends, rarely influence anyone—even the scraggly coleus on the window-sill—and lose an audience the moment we start telling a story, even the one we know is guaranteed boffo.

Now, we're not saying that polishing up your hand language is going to help you if you still think it's funny to wear your Mickey Mouse ears, if you invariably do your famous Steve Martin imitation, if you drop ice cubes down ladies' dresses, if you consistently have "just" five drinks too many, if you bitch and moan nonstop about mundanities, if you don't bathe or change clothes for a week, or if you think Don Rickles is a scream. But if you have *any* capacity for self-improvement, a terrific place to start is with your hands.

Probably the single most objectionable use of the hands in public is for masturbation. It follows then that masturbation substitutes—striking yourself, scratching, nervous jigglings, biting your nails, and so on—are also unattractive in public. Some of them might be borderline acceptable, depending on the circumstances (an athlete, for instance, might rub his arm in public; a politician could never pick wax out of his ear during a public debate), but all of them should be avoided when you are trying to come across as someone who is in control, a top-drawer candidate for an upscale position (as they might say in advertising), what is called a one-one at Princeton admissions, or someone "with his shit together." Here are fifteen things never to do in public:

1. Don't stick a finger or a hand into an orifice, especially someone else's. Remember that little ditty:

You can pick your friends
and you can pick your nose
but you can't pick your friend's nose.

Nor can you pick your own nose in the presence of your friend. So keep those hands out of orifices—and we mean all orifices—at least until you are at a stage not dealt with in this chapter. (See "The Hands and Sex.")

2. Don't diddle, fiddle, or twiddle. Little antsy gestures like drumming your fingers, flicking your thumb over the other fingers, or diddling things, like Queeg with his steel balls or Greeks with their worry beads. Also, do not tumble coins between your fingers. Leave carrots and breadsticks alone too.

3. Never goose anyone. You should have stopped that by the time you reached fourth grade.

4. Do not pop zits. This is strictly a solitary occupation. One of us remembers a zit-popping contest at a weekend religious retreat during the fifties, but public zit popping is probably frowned upon even more than public sex. They do not, for instance, encourage public zit popping at Esalen. Enough said?

5. Don't floss your teeth or use any other instrument in contact with your mouth, nose, ears, or body parts, except for a discreetly used good old-fashioned white cotton handkerchief (or fresh Kleenex) to the nose. Included in this category: even if you have a piece of cauliflower stuck in your teeth, a hemorrhoid that's been around so long you've named it George, or a raging yeast infection, in polite company you *don't let on* by applying any sort of twitch, itch, or pluck to the affected spot. This rule is inviolate.

6. Do not apply the pecking forefinger to anyone's shoulder

to get his or her attention or use the pecking forefinger to reinforce a point you are making. There is a tendency to use it after a few drinks, in a spirit of bonhomie, and it has been responsible for driving people away in droves. It is the sign of an authoritative, pushy, insistent personality. Can it.

      7. See the soldier over there
         with the stripe down his pants.
Never repeat the above ditty in public while wiping your nose with a forefinger and cleaning it off on a pants leg.

      8. Never take out your contact lens and reapply it by spitting into it in public.

      9. Never play a drum solo with a pencil on your teeth, nor should you take your teeth out in public.

      10. Do not groom your fingernails, clean them, file them, bite them, polish them, or buff them in public. Blowing on the nails and buffing them against a sleeve as a wry gesture of "I'm pretty terrific, aren't I?" is allowable no more than once every six months.

      11. Needless to say, you must not comb your hair in public.

      12. Knuckle cracking is out—even if you can do all ten simultaneously.

      13. Do not fiddle with jewelry—earrings, necklaces, bracelets, eyeglasses, rings, or pins. Leave them where they are applied. Do not call attention to your jewelry. It's ostentatious and unattractive. Slipping your wedding ring on and off your hand is an especially objectionable gesture. If you've put it on, wear it. (One friend has told us that men wearing wedding rings have much better luck getting girls to talk to them in bars than men without rings. The reason? Apparently, women suspect that any man not wearing a ring has deviously just removed it.)

      14. Lint picking is a sign of obsessiveness, compulsive self-grooming, and possibly, of disapproval. Women might pick lint off themselves as a sign of insecurity. They pick lint off a man's collar, say, as a sign of caring, possessiveness, and mothering, or as a tie sign to show they are related. It seems that men rarely pick lint off themselves and see the act of picking lint off a woman as a form of

criticism, almost a slap in the face, a way of saying, "Look, can't you keep yourself neat?" Both men and women might pick a piece of lint, perhaps even imaginary, off their own sleeve or skirt or trouser leg as a tacit way of saying, "I don't believe what you are telling me for a minute, but I'm constrained by the situation and propriety from saying so."

15. Finally, don't use obscene gestures unless you are in a position to beat a safe retreat. (We feel, incidentally, that as the purpose of obscene gestures is to be shocking, women are far better than men at giving a really good one. The more demure and stylish the lady and the less often she resorts to these gestures, the more effective they are.

All right, at this point you may not be David Niven or Dina Merrill, but if you follow the above fifteen rules you have eliminated some of the most egregious habits in your repertoire. Now let's move to the positive side by talking about things you *can* do: to get a job, to become everyone's favorite party guest, or to seduce a mate.

Part One/Hands and the Art of the Interview

The word "interview" comes from the French *entrevoir,* to have a glimpse of, to see imperfectly, and that is precisely what happens at an interview: we see each other imperfectly, that is, sometimes at our best, often at our worst. Some people have what we call *judicaphobia,* the fear of being judged by others. (The opposite condition, *judicaphilia,* is most often found in hot doggers, stand-up comedians, and overachievers of all stripes.) Judicaphobia can be suffered as much by the person *giving* the interview as by the person *going* for one, and the only solution is to become Superperson or to learn how to hide your problems. Your hands can help you both to look like a better prospect than you are and to cover up those problem areas, like your nervousness, your insecurity, and your awkwardness.

First, let's talk about the person giving the interview, and by interview we mean any daily or weekly situation in which you are

Henry Kissinger fussed and fidgeted at his face incessantly, some people think as a sign of his frequent rearrangements of the truth. Wide World Photos

meeting and judging people, or in which you are negotiating for goods or services. Included would be talking to the garage mechanic down the street, meeting your roommate for the first time, talking to a fellow club member about the luncheon next week, hiring a baby-sitter, or any other encounter of this nature.

In *Essentials in Interviewing* by Anne F. Fenlason, the following rules are outlined: An interview (1) cannot be dull or dreary, (2) cannot be too talky, (3) cannot be aimless or vague, (4) should have one or two dramatic high points, (5) should have a summary to tie up loose ends, and (6) must have a natural, reasonable ending.[1]

For each of these rules we propose a hand rule equivalent.

1. During an interview, don't let your hands drag down the conversation. Hands that lie limply on the lap, as though the tendons have been severed at the wrist, bespeak a dead personality. Use your gestures to make an attractive, vibrant, three-dimensional person of yourself.

2. Just as the conversation can be too talky, so can your gestures be nervous, jumpy, fussy, and distracting. The person who will be working for you wants to respect and trust the person over him or her. Moreover, antsy gestures on your part might make the other person feel you don't know your own mind, can't make decisions, and would be a horror to work for. Keep a clean desk, if you are in an office, so that you won't be tempted to fuss over it.

3. Using gestural substitutes, especially the single or double wrist rotations in the air, instead of clear verbal descriptions, makes the whole flow of the interview almost impossible and leaves the person you are talking to feeling you are ill-prepared. If you find yourself doing this, practice what you are going to say beforehand so it will come out smoothly.

4. Don't overuse big, dramatic, or expansive gestures. A hand to the heart used once to show sincerity, or arms held out at the shoulders to emphasize the size of the job or the organization, will be enough for any close encounter.

5. As you summarize, use the appropriate gestures—enumerating on your fingers, marking each point with a downbeat of the

hand—so that there is a clear understanding of *what* you want done, *when*, *where*, and *how*.

6. Finally, signal the close of the talk with the proper leave-taking gestures that will prepare the person for the good-byes. Preparatory gestures can be grabbing the arms of the chair as if to stand, checking a watch for time, stacking or organizing papers on the desk, dusting your hands off—anything to signal a natural close.

What we've been talking about are rules for the person running the interview. If he or she bungles running the interview, the worst that can happen is that a highly desirable person will be lost for the job. If that "interview" was with your prospective son-in-law you may have some extra-nasty ramifications to deal with. But you'll still have a daughter, now, won't you?

The person on the other side of the desk has a much harder task: to cover all of her faults, emphasize all of her strengths, to look calm, collected, and presentable while doing so, *and* to be *hired*. First let's talk about hiding those signs of nervousness, what Desmond Morris calls "miniaturized-locomotion actions." These include strumming the fingers, tapping the hand or foot, or slapping your thigh like Gene Krupa. Watch people in line at a bank, a movie, a fast-food restaurant, and notice the number and variety of hand-to-hand, hand-to-head, hand-to-thigh, and just plain hand gestures. Dr. Anthony Pietropinto, the Director of Mental Health at the Lutheran Medical Center in Brooklyn, New York, commented that all of these nervous twitches are unattractive to watch and more often than not turn people off. These gestures, Dr. Pietropinto says, simply broadcast that the person has no control over himself, which can only worsen what may already be a bad impression. Not only are these signs of nervousness, but they might well be interpreted as signs of boredom. Take particular care not to check *your* watch, or to gaze around the room while the interviewer is talking. Don't lean your head on your hand or cover your mouth while you are talking or listening. No matter how boring the interviewer is, he is *fascinating* to you.

This is not the time for self-conscious grooming gestures. Do not fidget with your beard, hair, nose, or chin. Women, if hair-pulling

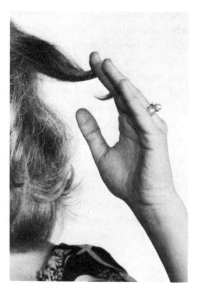

A basic no-no for interviewers. Don't look like Jack Benny waiting impatiently for some exasperating event to pass, and don't fall asleep on your hand during the interview.

This should be saved for study hall and very private parties. Otherwise don't play with your hair.

is a habitual gesture, get your hair cut. As a general rule don't raise your hands above your collarbone. If you can do it well, and consciously, a slow, brief chin or beard stroke to indicate thought and deliberation can be effective. Check yourself first in front of a mirror, though, to see what you look like doing this.

Keeping your hands clasped in your lap is always good form. One hand reinforces the other; you are, in effect, holding hands with yourself. Very reassuring. When you clasp your hands together you might keep one thing in mind, because you never know what kind of books the interviewer may have been reading: When you intertwine your fingers, the right thumb clasped over the left thumb indicates a person who is rational, realistic, and aggressive—in other words, executive material—according to Walter Sorell in *The Story of the*

Human Hand. Left thumb over right indicates, contrarily, a person who is intuitive, instinctual, receptive, passive, and imaginative.[2] If the interviewer seems to be watching your thumbs closely, take care to fold your hands in a way that makes you look qualified for the job you want. This kind of interviewer might also want to know your birth sign, or might suggest that the two of you throw the I Ching to see whether or not you get the job.

A word about left- and right-sidedness. Many authorities claim that the right side of the face is the public side and that the left side shows true emotions. The same might be said for your right and left hands. "Those who gesticulate freely during their small talk and in their colloquy usually display to some extent a manual preference. Ordinarily the right hand is more in movement than the left."[3] And the left hand, sneak that it is, is waiting for the right moment to slip in a sign of the way you *really* feel. Two-handed gestures, for instance, are usually reserved for strong statements, pleas, and the like. If you catch your left hand out there on its own, and you are usually right-handed, stop to think whether or not you are telling too much. Put your best hand forward.

There are certain gestures designed to show confidence in yourself. When you sit opposite the interviewer, lean forward to show attentiveness and alertness. Once you feel the situation is under control, you can lean back and do the classic Sylvester Stallone gesture of clasping your hands behind your head. Now listen carefully: Do not clasp your hands and put them *on top of* your head. That makes you look like a dunce, as though you don't know what to do with your hands and have to hold yourself down so you don't float away. Hands placed *behind* the head throw the chest forward and display the entire ventral area. This looks like a tremendous show of confidence in a man. He is literally saying, I am relaxed, I have nothing to fear. It is *not* acceptable business practice for a woman, though, whether the person doing the interview is a man *or* a woman.

Confidence is one thing; power plays are another. Such threatening power gestures as the imperious point, the hand chop, and the table pound—especially if the table you are pounding be-

This man looks like the type who would steeple his hands.

longs to the boss—will not endear you. Associated with power plays are signs of arrogance, which are not to be tolerated in either the interviewer or the interviewee. Buffing the nails on the jacket is forbidden. And don't cross your arms in front of your body. Then there is steepling the fingers, or what might be described as a spider doing push-ups on a mirror. This gesture says, "I'm not listening, I've got better things to do with my time," certainly an insult to anyone. Macdonald Critchley takes a strong stand on this posture: "This is scarcely a gesture, nor for that matter is it a symbol; nor an item of pantomime of even rhetoric. It is no more than a mannerism— out-moded, almost Dickensian. One finds it perpetrated by the serious-minded during a discourse loaded down by pretentious gravity. It is an irritating habit, made even more so when the speaker slowly abducts his hands horizontally a few inches only to bring them together again. This manoeuvre is usually repeated several times. It is ugly and unpleasing and should be rigorously inhibited."[4] (So strong is Critchley's condemnation that we wonder if he in fact spent endless schooldays with a finger-steepling headmaster. Perhaps it was the church vicar.) So fussy is this gesture, we're not sure if even the clergy or psychiatrists can now get away with finger steepling. It used to be taken as a sign of omniscience and patience. No more. These gestures all say, "I don't care what you say," or "I disagree with what you say." You can disagree *after* you get the job.

One more thing: sit comfortably in the chair. Don't grab the arms as if you're being electrocuted. You may cross your legs, if you're a man, in either the American or the European fashion, but it is preferable to use the European, with the knees close together. This keeps your shoes and socks down near floor level and away from your fidgeting hands. You will also be less tempted to pick lint off your cuffs. However, if you feel that the European leg cross looks too "effeminate," you can use the American style, with the ankle of one foot at the knee of the other.

Women can cross their legs at the knee or at the ankle. Hands can be comfortably held in the lap with the legs crossed. A word in general about women who are being interviewed. Yours is the hardest job. You have to appear business-like but not tough, cold, or ruthless. You have to appear somewhat womanly (attractively groomed) but not simperingly feminine. The hands can be of value to you here: they can show your feminine, open side (you might try cupping one open palm inside the other on your lap, a common female hand-rest position, to signal subtly your openness), or they can show your strong, business side (with crisp, well-executed gestures of emphasis). No clanking jewelry (especially bracelets) allowed. Wear only one ring. Cut the number of gestures in half to avoid looking flighty.

Whether you're a man or a woman, don't smoke, unless your interviewer lights up first, not even if an ash tray is brazenly displayed. For all you know, it might be there because one of the boss's oldest and dearest colleagues smokes in this office even though the boss detests smokers. Also, although you may feel that a cigarette would give you something to do with your hands, it may well give you too much to do. Remember, any prop increases the strength of a gesture, and a burning prop increases the strength that much more. You might come off too strong, or you might simply drop ashes on the Oriental rug or start a fire in the drapes. The smoking/no-smoking controversy is the Vietnam War of our time and is almost as divisive as the pro-/anti-nuclear power issue. It's too political an area to enter during so important an event as a job interview. If, however, the person giving the interview offers you a cigarette and lights up herself, and if you smoke, of course, you should do so. The sense of shared sin might well work in your favor.

     You should never light up a cigar, *unless* you are trying to get a job as a tout. If, on the other hand, the interviewer opens his humidor and produces a four-dollar Havana beauty and if that is your thing, you should do the whole act of appreciation: rolling it between your fingers, bringing it to your nose, listening for the crackle, graciously taking the cutter when it's offered (or, better yet, pulling out your own), leaving the ring on, and finally, lighting up and pulling it away from your face so you can appreciate the wafting odors.

     Perhaps the most obvious thing to avoid is any sign of nervousness. At the same time this is sometimes excruciatingly difficult because nervousness can seep out in so many varied discreet units. We develop "tics" to keep ourselves under control: fidgets, scratches, rubs, and pokes at ourselves of which we are totally unaware. Here's Ashley Montagu on the subject:

"The use of the skin as a tension-reliever takes many forms, perhaps the most familiar in Western cultures being head scratching in men. Women do not usually behave in this manner; indeed, the sexual differences in the use of the skin are marked. In states of perplexity men will rub their chins with their hand, or tug at the lobes of their ears, or rub their forehead or cheeks or back of the neck. Women have very different gestures in such states. They will either put a finger on their

lower front teeth with the mouth slightly open or pose a finger under
the chin. Other masculine gestures in states of perplexity are: rubbing
one's nose, placing the flexed fingers over the mouth, rubbing the side of
the neck, rubbing the infraorbital part of the face, rubbing the closed
eyes, and picking the nose. These are all masculine gestures; so
is rubbing the back of the hand or the front of the thight, and
pursing the lips. "[5]

Although Montagu states that women are the ones who put a finger in
their mouths against their teeth during times of stress, we have seen
men do likewise. The difference is that women will use a forefinger or
thumb, while men will use only their thumbs. The echo here is of
sucking the thumb during times of stress as a child, something that
little boys do more often than little girls. Men and women have also
been known to tap a pencil or a capped pen against the front teeth.
One of us has seen a man push his loose dental plate back and forth
as a nervous gesture whenever someone else was talking.

On the subject of women and long nails: We feel that long
nails, if they are immaculately manicured, are no hindrance to a
woman applying for an executive job, assuming that the job doesn't
require the use of the hands for fine work, like surgery. If the woman
is applying for a secretarial job, obviously her nails should be short
enough to enable her to hit the keys accurately. Fingernail polish is
all right for either men or women, but it should suit the rest of the
look.

If you're going to Batten, Batten, Curry & Smith law offices in
Boston, don't turn up in your Chiquita Banana look-alike outfit with
crimson nails. If you're seeing the manager of the local supermarket
for a job as a checkout girl, don't arrive without the polish, preferably
a different dark shade for each nail.

A woman who is wearing conservative but stylish clothes and
is coiffed to the limit, who has long, elegant nails and beautiful
hands, can probably get away with even the most vivid shade of
polish, although she should be aware that some men abhor the look
of bright nail polish on their wives or girlfriends. It's part of the

Anglo-Saxon heritage to prefer muted, subdued colors. Judge the sophistication of the office before you make any decisions about clothes, jewelry, or makeup.

Men's nails can be buffed and polished discreetly. A man's hands can look rugged and tanned, as if he skis, plays tennis, and sails on weekends, or they can look elegantly manicured. Either approach works.

In the West and Southwest United States, silver jewelry, turquoise, and the like are perfectly acceptable on a man. In the Midwest and South, at least for the job interview, men should limit their hand jewelry to a Masonic ring, a service ring (if you're a "ring knocker" from West Point, Annapolis, or the Air Force Academy), a school ring from one of the better schools, or a wedding band, period. In the East, particularly in New York, the choice is simple: wear a wedding ring or wear none. You should wear a watch. If it's an analog watch, make it a real Cartier tank watch or a Patek Philippe. If it's a digital it should have more than one function. It's bad form to have your watch set to beep at any time during the interview.

There are five basic things any interviewer is looking for in a candidate and there is an appropriate gesture for each of these qualities.

1. Candidates must seem confident. In addition to the overall sense of assuredness, you might try to project confidence by keeping your hands far back in your lap and your elbows naturally at your sides. This will throw your chest out and high, a desirable posture for either a male or female job applicant.

2. Sincerity is highly prized. Putting a hand to your heart is a little too obvious, but subtler forms of self-touching, in the chest, breastbone or collarbone region, accompanied by statements like, "I've always thought so," or "That was a very important moment in my career," can be effective. The hand on the heart signifies "on my honor" and is a duplication of old pledge gestures. It can also mean "I really mean it."

3. Honesty, obviously, is one of the things an interviewer wants to find. You can increase the appearance of honesty if you

refrain from touching your nose or face and if you limit all nervous gestures. An interesting study of nurses' successes in lying revealed that when the nurses were asked to tell a patient a lie they decreased the number of simple gesticulations while increasing the frequency of hand-to-face contacts. When they were telling a lie, the nurses touched their chins, covered their mouths with their hands, touched their noses, rubbed their cheeks, scratched their eyebrows, tugged at their ears, fussed with their hair or caps. The most-favored gestures were covering the mouth and touching the nose. The nurses who ranked highest in the class scholastically also turned out to be the best (most convincing) liars. So show your talent by lying without touching your face.

4. The interviewer should feel that you are being open with him or her. Don't close off your body by putting your hands in front of your face and don't cross your arms over your chest. Critchley reports in *The Language of Gestures* that "people feel 'covered' if so much as one finger touches the nose."

5. Most important, the interviewer wants someone who will be dependable. Your best chance to prove your solid-as-a-rock character is in the opening and closing handshake. Make it firm, but not too firm. Don't make it either too short (you have something to hide) or too long (you're desperate). In other words, try for the ever-illusive "normal" handshake. Ask your friends to practice with you. If all else fails, take a course as a salesman where they *teach* you the correct handshake.

Everything we've said about the job interview should be true also of your general office behavior. If you are going to work this hard preparing yourself for the interview, the least you can do is to practice the art of the well-thought-out gesture for the rest of your time on the job.

Part Two/Hands' Night Out

There are three reasons for going to a party:
1. To have a good time.
2. To please the host.
3. To meet new people, often those of the opposite sex.

If the host happens to be your boss, the order of your three reasons should be numbers 2, 2, and 3 (particularly those with whom you might make business deals when you are back at the office). "Having a good time" (number 1) has nothing to do with parties like this. Often people on the outside think publishing is a glamour industry because of the endless dinner parties, drink dates, and publication parties. There are those—often boyfriends and wives—who think these events are *fun*. Wrong. These are no more than extensions of the office, and anyone who thinks otherwise will find him or herself shortly out of that office. If the party is indeed a business party and you are the type who can think only of reason number 1, and your idea of a good time is chugging a bottle of Chivas and then throwing up in the punch bowl, torturing the family pets, putting Saran Wrap on the underside of the toilet seat, throwing lighted matches at the couch in the den, spending the entire evening watching the Knicks on the upstairs TV, or seducing every female there, whether or not she is a relative of the boss, then please stay home. The only way your hands can help you, my friend, is if you've got a great right hook.

If this is a friend's party, you can order your priorities as numbers 1, 2, and 3. If it's your own party you can concentrate on numbers 1, 1, and 1, because that will cover all contingencies.

What produces anxiety in most people in connection with giving or going to a party is the possibility of the big R, rejection. Hands can help you meet people, get you into interesting conversations, and better yet, out of boring ones, help you circulate around the room, get you another drink, get your food to your mouth, filch nifty ash trays, among other things. Whether you are in someone's home or at Studio 54, if you have any awareness of hands and body

Here we see a Half-Macho with mantle prop being used with great success on a woman who is using the appropriate broken-wristed gesture of entreaty. L. Lee

types you can size up people in the first 30 seconds and avoid getting stuck with someone who is going to make your evening miserable. For your convenience, we have divided men into seven categories, women into nine categories and offered one ambi-sexual type. Women first:

Bernice Bombshell: She seems to arrive with one hand delicately attached to her body at the collarbone, perhaps clutching a little something her escort gave her in the limousine. Usually blonde, sometimes redhead, occasionally dark-haired, her coif is always long and elaborate. Her dress will show off cleavage and bare arms. She is, needless to say, statuesque and taken. You can, however look and fantasize. When she uses her hands, it will be almost always in gestures that bring attention to herself. These gestures will never be extravagant except on the disco floor, where she will often raise her arms over her head elbows slightly bent. She specializes in self-touching.

Suzi Perki: She's bouncy, peppy, and waving "Hi" as she enters, and she's *short.* She circulates around the room by hopping from foot to foot. Her gestures are on the order of "See that basket, see that rim." She may not be intellectual but she's probably quick. She's never at a loss for short words or silly animations. Don't assume she reads.

Flamboyant Leonore: Picture this: She weighs 40 pounds more than she should, dresses in primary colors, wears jewelry that always makes noise. She wears costumes or caftans and nothing about her is understated, especially her gestures. Leonore is a *toucher* and usually enters the room in hand-over-hand hellos. She can admire your jacket, pinch your rear end, and wave hello to her friends across the room at the same time. Leonore works in people-oriented businesses—public relations, advertising, agenting, and so on. In private, with her clients, she can be sensitive and quiet, but when she hits the party circuit, it's boogie, boogie, boogie.

Inez the Intellectual: This one you're not going to notice coming in the door. If the party is in a private home you'll find her looking at the books or records. If it's in a club she is looking lost. Inez wears sensible, honest clothes and carries a Peruvian cloth bag. Her hands move slowly and deliberately, usually to emphasize a point she is trying to explain to someone who doesn't quite understand. Although she owns contact lenses, she often wears her hornrims to parties and occasionally takes them off for use as a pointer.

Mom: She's already there when the party begins because she arrived early to "help out." She comes in all shapes and sizes and you'll recognize her by her nervous gestures of picking up, scraping, and straightening, both animate and inanimate objects. She's trying to make herself indispensable. She cossets, she comforts, she cleans. When she can't find something to clean, she organizes. You may see her carrying a bowl of "something she whipped up" before the party. If you have a loose button, lint on your clothes, or a spot, look out for her. She will mother both men and women.

The Kook: She is ultrafeminine and comes in all sizes but reaches her peak in the truly anorexic macrobiotic space pilot. The Kook's hands continuously grope the air for words long lost in a drug fog. She's never had a job to speak of, tends to be a sucker for the wrong kind of man, is a leftover from the Sixties, and, if you ask her, will tell you she's saving up for a trip to Findhorn. A conversational gambit with the Kook: discuss whether "holistic" should really be spelled with a *w*.

(Wish They All Could Be) California Girls: Hers are *tan hands*. Let's face it, she's tanned everywhere. Needless to say, she is also a naturally sun-streaked blonde. What makeup she wears is natural-looking. The body is as sleek as a Masserati. She is tall, well-honed, *healthy*. In short, she's a goddess. She's not embarrassed to arrive with a man a full head shorter than she and considerably darker. He will be stricken with Shiksa Madness, the same disease that afflicted King Kong. California Girl's grip will have been learned on a tennis racket and she will give an honest, athletic, enthusiastic, and natural shake. California Girl is the most at-ease person at the party. She'd better be because the women either envy her or hate her on sight. No one is unmoved by her. California Girl's hands will often serve to draw attention to her perfect health, her perfect body, her

He is a camera; she is Flamboyant Leonore; he an eccentric Moneybags; she Suzi Perki.

perfect teeth (see her bite the celery stalk), her perfect hair, her perfect . . . oh, you get the idea.

Suburban Jennifer: You'll see her at the door taking off her Burberry. She is wearing a gold locket with pictures of her two-point-three children. As a nervous gesture (her divorce papers just came through and this is her first night out Alone) she keeps one hand on the locket at all times. If you ask, she will be only too quick to crack open her Etienne wallet and show you her children's school pictures. Jennifer is dressed in Suburban Mufti—tweed or velvet hacking jacket, stylish pants or skirt, boots. She looks as if she left her horse with the doorman. She's sooo WASPy (grew up in Locust Valley) that she doesn't eat. She nurses one drink the entire evening, so she won't get drunk in public. Her gestures are tense, well-bred, reserved, and moderate. The only thing excessive about her is the divorce settlement.

The Humorless Frump: Every party has one. She sometimes comes equipped with a do-or-die political stance and she doesn't see anything funny about it. All of the Frump's reactions and gestures are out of place at a party. She can't do anything freely or spontaneously. She will either be sullen or will laugh loudly and nervously, at the wrong time. She will spill something and then spend the rest of the evening in the bathroom. Mom will consider her an asset because she's always willing to be first in the food line. Give her credit for showing up but, for your own sake, avoid her at all costs—unless you want to work at reforming her. The Humorless Frump, despite her political strength, has perfected clinging: to the wall, to the couch, or to you. Take your pick.

Now for the men.

Macho Man: The Big Guy comes in two types, city dandy and country boy. The country macho look is L. L. Bean—plaid shirt, work pants or jeans, boots. He's carrying at least one pocketknife, which will be useful for cutting the brie and opening the wine. He looks as though he's done some time at pistol practice.

The city dandy variety has seen *Saturday Night Fever* one time too many, and though he's given up the white suit/dark shirt/white tie he used to wear, he'll still sport a mostly unbuttoned shirt (the better to show off that manly chest), well-cut pants, and the better breed of footwear, be it fine Italian shoes or Ostrich leather cowboy boots. Both Machos make strong, assertive, masculine gestures and are catnip to women.

Macho Man will pull both elbows back until his entire body from knees to collarbone is in a position known as the genital-dorsal display. There is no question about which side Macho Man dresses on. He isn't going to waste any gestures; he's made of granite. (If he does make a move, though, keep him away from glass tables.) In general you will find him poised in the two-hip thrust, with both hands at the hips or fingers looped through the belt, or in the one-hip thrust, one hand at the hip, one leg casually cocked, like a horse at rest. His eyes, however, will never be at rest and he will manage to give a flattering glance to every woman in the room at least once during the evening.

Junior Jock: He would like to be Macho Man but can't stand the pressure. Instead he has chosen to concentrate on his career in high school football. When he walks into the room, he doesn't take the macho stance but instead keeps shifting from foot to foot like he is standing on hot playground pavement. He trades feints, fake passes, arm pounds, and punches with fellow jocks during their evening-long discussion of who played third base for the 1950 Phillies. He seems uncomfortable with women. His athletic ease leaves him when he is in their company and he looks almost boyish. He has come to the party (as long as it didn't specify "black tie") in his Adidas and a Washington Redskins jersey. The only women in the room who will appreciate him are Suzi Perki and Suburban Jennifer—Suzi because she understands him, Jennifer because she can afford to keep him in tennis shoes and isn't ready yet for a "serious" relationship.

Freddie Fashionplate: He's elegantly built and if he's not tall, he *looks* tall. He also looks like he could go either way. People invite Freddie because he is the ideal extra man. His hands seem permanently affixed to his lapels or to the white silk aviator scarf he wears on the outside of his jacket. He stands in a perfect tableau. Perhaps he's so stoned he can't move, because if anyone's carrying heavy drugs at this party, it's going to be Freddie. Go up and ask him for some. He's generous, because he's rarely paid for them himself. People are always giving him things. Freddie is built to wear clothes, which means he has the smallest buns in the room. He will occasionally bring attention to this fact by slowly drawing one hand up his leg and over his hip. His other gestures will be theatrical, self-grooming, or involve the taking of drugs. He will dance with absolute abandon on the disco floor, and look good at the same time. Freddie has lots of woman friends, so don't feel awkward about starting a conversation with him.

Carl Critical: His arms are crossed over his chest and he's wearing a beard. A copy of the *Paris Review* and a pipe will be poking out of his old corduroy jacket. People think he's unconcerned about his appearance but it has actually taken him years to get his look just right. He will be standing back, making mental notes on the other guests when you see him. If you engage him in conversation, which you do at your own peril, you will find that he gestures like your old college professor. He uses one arm at a time and makes lots of batons, or gestures to accentuate or punctuate what he is saying. He keeps one elbow tightly alongside his body in a self-protective gesture, and in moments of high passion he will use whatever is in his hand to make his point—his pipe, his glasses, or a carrot. You might notice that while you are talking he listens with one elbow cupped in the other hand. This means he is only waiting for you to pause for breath before he pounces. He was trying to be polite when he asked you what you thought. After your first three words he is merely readying his intellectual overkill.

Though he looks and acts forbidding, he's one of the most interesting people there. If you don't make your move early on, you may find that the California Girl has left her date and settled in with Carl. He's not looking for an intellectual equal after all, but for someone impressionable. Pretty doesn't hurt.

Sensitive Sinclair: He's the one about whom "still waters run deep" could have been written. Sinclair is totally right-brained: he's a musician, a poet, or a painter. He may be sitting there getting quietly sloshed or quietly high. The only gesture you'll ever see him make is a pensive left hand to his lips. He will spend the party listening to people compliment him about his last work or telling their life stories. Because he's a listener, he's a wonderful target for Leonore, the Intellectual or Mom. He may also pair up with the Kook, who came over to compliment him on his "terrific" work clothes.

C. D. Moneybags: This is the diametric opposite of Sinclair. He undoubtedly came with the Bombshell or the California Girl, neither of whom can understand him when he talks debentures, exchange rates, or tax shelters, which he does throughout the party. His hands are constantly in motion, physically describing the layout of his new shopping center, while he clears the area immediately around him with his cigar. The East Coast version has pale, pink, and pudgy hands. He may be wearing a pinkie ring. If he participates in any sport it will be racquetball. The West Coast version is tanned from playing tennis in the backyard but that hasn't kept him from developing the distinctive C. D. Moneybags paunch, the result of all that good eating and drinking. The West Coast version has the same gestures as his East Coast cousin because that's where he came from. He may have gone to a speech therapist to lose his Nu Yawk accent but he'll never get rid of those aggressive gestures, no matter how "mellow" he thinks he's become.

The Nerd: His gestures are pretty awkward, always inappropriate, and often involve old high school *shtiks*, like giving "nuggies," shooting rubber bands, and catching peanuts in his mouth. Nerds have big appetites and don't mind talking with their mouths full. Nerds are never directly invited to parties, they just come with someone who *was* invited. If Mom is on her toes, she'll spot him and put him together with the Humorless Frump so they can annoy each other. Nerds can be spotted by their plastic shirt-pocket pencil holders. Think of Bill Murray as Todd on *Saturday Night Live* and you're getting warm.

They Are a Camera: As we mentioned before we began this list, there is one party type who is ambi-sexual, a type we call *They are a Camera*. You will recognize the Camera the moment he/she comes in because you suddenly stand up straighter, put a public smile on your face and pose. It doesn't matter to *you* whether the Camera is a man or woman. What matters is that the Nikon is pointed at *you*. The Camera never goes to a party without his or her equipment. It is a great excuse for being there, the sure way to avoid conversation, a way to look like he/she belongs. (Incidentally, the Camera doesn't always carry a camera. You might recognize the same type carrying a guest register, a clipboard, or some other emblem of official business.) The Camera, if he or she ever takes a peek over the viewfinder, will have a glazed look from having seen an entire party in 35-millimeter.

If you are at this party, you've already picked the one you want to meet. Consider for a moment how your hands can work to your advantage. Say you want to talk to Suzi Perki; get your energy level up first. She's used to leading pep rallies, so if you're not up to enthusiastically responsive gestures, let her go until another night. If you're trying to come on to the Kook or Inez, get ready your ideographs—gestures used to illustrate the flow of ideas. You can rest on your oars, gesturally speaking, when you talk to Leonore. If you're going to try for the Elite Two—the California Girl or the Bombshell—you've got to have it all together: the self-assured stance of Macho Man, the easy way of wearing good clothes of Fashionplate, the boyish charm of Junior Jock, and a dollop of cynicism from Carl's corner. You've got to look like you have as many cash assets as C. D. Moneybags but the good taste not to mention it. If you want to come on to Mom, just rub your tummy and say, "What good dip! I wonder what's in it?"

Women, every man in the room is going to go for the Direct Feminine Display. This means self-grooming gestures that draw attention to your breasts, neck, face, and hair. Lick guacamole off a finger. Touch him on the shoulder and say, "Why, Rhett, that's the funniest thing I ever heard." You've got to build up a man's ego so he will feel he can risk rejection when he asks you out. (This may sound like the old feminine creed but it's the New Feminine Creed; the tactics are almost identical, but the objective is not to find a man to support you the rest of your life but to find a man who won't be threatened by your ambition and success. Human intellectual machinery changes a lot faster than old gut response. First let him fall for you, *then* let him glimpse that indomitable spirit of yours.)

Now, if you're going for Macho Man you've either got to challenge him sexually as the Bombshell or challenge him physically, turn him into Petruchio to match your strong-willed Katherina. For the first role an evening gown is required, or a plunging neckline.

Macho Man is elemental, not subtle. You can make the Femme Fatale display gestures for a while (hand to the back of the head, picking a few artfully arranged stray curls up off the nape of your long, elegant neck; lots of self-touching in the chest area; finger your necklace, your earrings; hold your glass up to your mouth and, lowering your eyes, give him a direct Stare of Interest), but eventually you're going to have to go over to him—if he doesn't come to you— and lay on the hand. Touch him on the hand, arm, or shoulder. Take a cigarette out of his mouth to light your own. (Bombshells have all the traditional vices—they drink, smoke, do amusing drugs—which gives them lots of seductive hand gestures. If Bombshells eat, they eat only "fun" foods like caviar and oysters, good, sexy prop foods.) The other alternative (the *Kiss Me, Kate* routine) dictates that you out-macho him. Wear tight pants and hook *your* thumbs through *your* belt loops. Put your hand, fingers outspread, on your waist (this not only shows self-assurance, it shows off a good figure). Think of this as a showdown at the OK Corral. Use the direct Stare of Interest, but imply that he can't have you. Then, when he makes his move, engage in a little hand-to-hand combat before you give in, this time.

For Junior Jock you're going to have to spend a lot of time either watching sports, playing them, or talking about them. Junior Jock won't mind a woman who crosses her arms in front of her chest while he and the boys patter on, as long as she indicates with other body language that she's merely sitting this conversation out. She should touch him reassuringly from time to time. Junior Jock needs a lot of love and an audience, but he also wants to hang out with the boys. Give him the room and you'll find him coming right back to you.

Freddie Fashionplate is himself a toucher, but he may not want you to touch *him*. He will appreciate good, stagey gestures and listen to long, long stories, amusingly done, if he can be standing in a prominent position in the room while he listens. Freddie is here to be seen, not heard. Show him off and he's yours.

Revive those gestures you used to use in English 101 and the Critic will consider you not totally hopeless. Bite your forefinger thoughtfully as he talks. Scratch your cheek (self-touching to any part of the face or head makes him think of that little brain of yours, just spinning to keep up with him). Tap your front teeth with a fingernail when you're about to say something. Use your hands in little gestures of appreciation for his wit: clap them together, separate them to show "wait a minute," then clasp them again in rapt attention.

Sensitive Sinclair has to be drawn out. He's not going to respond much to you physically, so you have to be encouraged by the smallest flicker of interest. He may be startled by big, aggressive gestures, but on the other hand Mom and Leonore often seem to sweep him up. The Intellectual may be able to approach him properly: glasses held in right hand, one bow to the mouth, appraising look, quiet questions like "Aren't you the one who. . . ." The Intellectual has the brains to look like she is following him even when he starts talking about color fields and tectonics and chthonian statements. She must, however, when he finishes, summon up a few lively gestures, like clapping her hands together, and say "Why don't we get a drink and talk about that some more," or they will both sit there the rest of the night, getting progressively soberer, with their legs falling asleep.

If you want to meet C. D. Moneybags, you're going to have to ask someone to introduce you. He's so interested in what he's saying that he's never going to notice someone signaling to him from across the room. If you don't know anyone who knows him, just walk up and introduce yourself with a handshake. C. D. always enjoys a good handshake; it allows him a chance to size people up before he puts them down or buys them out. Because C. D. is so busy talking and gesturing, you might endear yourself by bringing him fresh drinks (to replace the ones he has set down somewhere) and ash trays for his cigar. If he still doesn't notice you, turn to him and do something overt, like straightening his tie. This is a blatant sexual gesture (the two-in-hand tie, with its wider base and knotted top, is a precise representation of guess which part of the hidden male anatomy) and if he fails to respond to it, forget him and talk to Freddie Fashionplate for the rest of the evening.

Women will often rather meet *other* women at parties than spend their time looking for the one decent single man there. This is an understandable result of the women's movement. For one thing there seem to be an excessive number of intelligent, original, funny, attractive women around, and for another some of them are only now beginning to discover one another.

But what about the future of mankind? What about mating and reproduction? Women, you mustn't give up. Men can be brought along. It's *not* hopeless. Therefore we have given instructions only for meeting amorous companions. We assume that men will find it relatively easy to meet and talk to other men in the room, and that women will always find it easy to meet and talk to other women. As for the gay readers, any of the above character types and descriptions works for gays as well as straights. For anyone you want to meet—male, female, straight, *or* gay—try the "meaningful glance." It works for puppies in store windows; it will work for you. If you get any response, Mom excepted (she will respond to anyone), figure you're on the right course.

Now that you've begun circulating at the party, you might notice that your hands have taken up party props: cigarettes, drinks, finger foods. Each person has a Basal Hand Movement/per minute quotient; some people move their hands five or six times a minute (5 BHM/pm), others can keep their hands relatively still for minutes at a time (.56 BHM/pm). Everyone's BHM/pm increases in times of stress; parties are definitely times of stress. Let's say that at home your BHM is 2 BHM/pm. At an important party it will increase to 4 BHM/pm, or double the normal rate. The reason this is important at parties is that food, smoke, and drink are maximal users of BHM's. A drink alone will keep 2 BHM/pm occupied in sips, shuffles, and the basic clasp of the glass. A cigarette will occupy one hand *full time* for that minute, if you hold the cigarette continuously. A bowl of chips will occupy both hands nicely for five minutes, but at the end of that time, calculating 4 BHM/pm and 10 calories per chip, you have consumed 200 calories, or the equivalent number of calories in two glasses of wine. And you are sober, which may or may not

Here is a typical party stance, with her holding something in each hand, the modern version of sword and shield. L. Lee

be desirable. The real killers at elaborate parties are cashew nuts, with 20 calories a nut. Five minutes of noshing at the nut bowl and you are in for 400 calories. Drink a glass of beer at the same time and you have consumed another 110 calories. This is the first five minutes, and you haven't eaten anything yet, but already you've packed on 510 food units. And that's not counting the avocado dip.

You begin to see the problem. What's worse is the drinking compulsion that seizes some party-goers, simply because they don't know what else to do with their hands. If you're not smoking a cigarette and you're not eating nuts and chips, you are going to want to bring a glass of something to your lips with some regularity. One of our friends, a publishing party regular, has solved this problem by alternating glasses of wine with glasses of Perrier, increasing the ratio of Perrier to wine as the evening goes on. You may wonder why he doesn't just drink spritzers. It's because he doesn't *like* spritzers. Another friend, who has great self-control, simply has one mixed drink to start, makes that drink last the first hour, and then switches to soft drinks.

Beer provides a neat compromise—lots of volume, meaning it uses plenty of Basal Hand Movements, with relatively few calories and much less alcohol per volume than mixed drinks. Beer is making a deserved comeback from its shady image as the drink of jocks, rednecks, and truck drivers. Still, at a party, the jock is more likely to have a beer in his hand than is Suburban Jennifer. The jock would prefer to drink beer straight out of the can or bottle, but if you give him a glass, he'll hold the glass and the beer bottle in the same hand so as to free the other for those fake ball-passes.

We suggest the pinkie prop grip on a glass at a party. You never know, when you've had a few drinks, just how securely you are holding that glass. Better to keep the pinkie there as a support of last resort. C. D. Moneybags will be gesturing with his glass, whether it's full or not. This may be a way of keeping his audience spellbound. You are not to fear. C. D. rarely, if ever, spills a drop.

Mr. Suave, the offhand drinker, will use a low cupping grip as if to say, "I don't really care if I have a drink in my hand or not." Women sometimes run a finger reflectively around the rim of a glass. Men will never do this unless they are about to start telling you of their recent divorce. Women who are trying to project softness and sexiness will hold the glass with what we call the feminine arch: the glass will be held by thumb and one or two fingers, the entire hand is arched gracefully from the wrist, with the ring and little fingers held gently curved toward the bottom of the glass.

Oenophiles will say that chilled white wine must be held by the stem only, an admirable rule at the dinner table where a glass of wine might last half an hour or more. But on the stand-up party circuit we believe a firm grip is better than a baptized rug. Your wine will be disappearing at a fairly fast rate, so your hot fingers won't be doing too much damage. Also, with the wine cooling your fingers, you are better prepared for a cool, civilized handshake. The fact that the room is twenty degrees too warm won't matter as much.

The mechanics of getting another drink gives you an opportunity to use hand and body language to meet someone new. Say you are standing on the edge of a circle of conversation. You are finishing your drink (either because you were about to finish your drink anyhow, or because you see that a handsome person of the opposite sex is about to finish his or her drink). You look up, make eye contact, gesture with your glass to ask if the other person wants another drink too. A nod and a smile are your answer and you are on your way. It is a much more natural way to begin to talk to someone than the standard openers like "Hi, what are you doing here?" (A stupid question.) "What's your name? I'm so-and-so." (Boring and ineffectual, because once you know the name, which you will immediately forget, where are you going next? To some inane comment about how cute the name is, or to a reminiscence about your cousin Betty who, by gosh, had the same name?) Worse yet is the old "Having a good time?" One woman of our acquaintance uses "Are you rich?" as an opener, and gets away with it, but she's a special case. Better than risk verbal rejection, just use those hands, in combination with eye contact and the right kind of friendly, but not sloppy-friendly, smile.

We've talked about two ways to use up Basal Hand Movements—eating and drinking. Let's talk further about the greatest BHM-user of them all, smoking. Neither of the authors smokes. Perhaps because of this we have noticed a great range of variations in the ways people hold their cigarettes. The standard American grip, also known as the two-fingered scissors-grip, works equally well for men and for women. Women who have learned how to operate a cigarette holder can use it to tremendous advantage. Among grasps, the hand held with all fingers extended and the cigarette grasped between the first and second fingers is an oddity. This works best when the hand is at rest or gesturing. When the hand is brought to

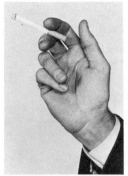

*Three grips: the basic American, the backward French pinch, and the
Russian covered hand.*

the mouth, however, it looks like you are stifling a yawn or covering
your face. The opposite extreme is the French thumb-and-forefinger
pinch, where there is only the smallest grasp and where almost none
of your mouth is covered. This allows for the sensuality of the lips
reaching for the end of the cigarette to be seen.

We also have the Mediterranean thumb and two-finger grasp,
used by Italians, Greeks, Arabs, and North Africans, and there is also
the Russian covered-hand gesture, where the cigarette is all but
obscured by the hand. As this is used in mountainous Bulgar areas as
well, it might be considered a way to keep the hand warm during
smoking. Macho Man might use this grasp. The Critic would undoubtedly use the French pinch. The *backward* French pinch should
only be used by Hercule Poirot, Charles Boyer, El Suavo, or Freddie
Fashionplate. What is important to remember is that your hands
always have *some* style when you smoke. It may be good style or it
may be bad style. At the very least be aware of it and if possible,
change it to go with the image you want to project.

We should also mention ash acrobats, people who let the ash
on their cigarettes grow until the person whose couch they are sitting
on is ready to have a heart attack. These people are sometimes
exhibitionists, sometimes absentminded, sometimes just drunk.

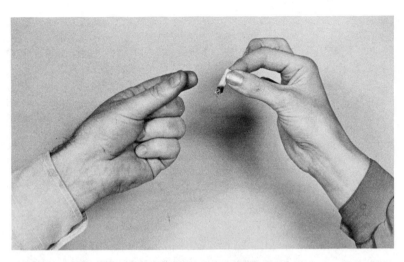

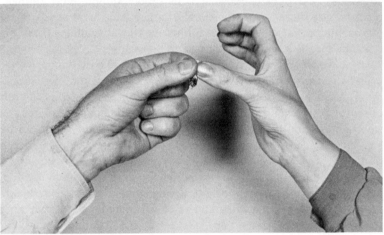

The California Thumb Pass. Work here on your overhand thumb stroke. Cooperation, communication, and understanding between you, the passer, and whomever-it-is, the passee, are crucial.

Psychologist Sandor Feldman wrote of one patient who had the opposite problem: ash-knocking-compulsion. He "flicked his ash whenever it appeared. He was from 'low' origin and did not want to be identified with that group."[6] And then there are the flagrant ash-tray smokers, people who light a cigarette only to let it sit burning in the ash tray. These types enjoy the ritual of lighting a cigarette but want to cut down on their smoking. The result is that the cigarette smokes itself and the nonsmokers in the room get to inhale an additional lungful or two.

Marijuana consumption in the form of joint-smoking at parties calls for one grip and one grip only—the Mediterranean thumb-and-two-finger grasp. With a little proficiency you can master the perfect Thumb Pass. Practice at home is essential because, as the evening wears on, as you get high and the joints get low, expertise in this one area is the only thing between you and the humiliating Roach Burn. Clips are barely acceptable. They do aid in passing roaches but have a clinical and predetermined look about them. Women are far better than men at polishing off roaches without the aid of a roach clip. Whether this is because of women's natural dextral superiority or because of their longer nails has not yet been proven.

Part Three/The Hands and Seduction

Have you had a good time at the party? Did you meet someone special? Now you are ready for hands and the art of seduction. The second most important use of the hands in seduction is for dialing the telephone. This is an often-overlooked step. Men, *if* you have met a woman at a party and *if* you have asked for her number and *if* she has given it to you, you *must call within three days*. This is a strict requirement, unless you have already informed her that you will be in Novosibirsk for the next three weeks. A woman *might* speak to you if you call her after the three-day limit, and she *might* go out with you, but you will already have one black mark against you. You may call her the next morning and find that it is too much of a push too soon or you may call the next morning and find out that she was hoping

Some self-grooming gestures are flattering. Fluffing the hair is one of them.

you would call. You've got to use a little initiative and common sense here. Let us repeat, though; use the telephone or, even better, drop her a note with a paperback book you thought she would like, or an invitation for a casual date. Women are constantly being tortured by men who don't call and don't write.

Women, you have almost the same opportunities, if not the same responsibilities. In order to make calling the man a lighter occasion you might want to have a good excuse: you just bumped into an old friend and you discovered that he was also a good friend of *his* and you just had to call and let him know, or you wondered if he remembered seeing where you left your scarf at the party because you can't seem to find it. These are pretty pathetic excuses, but if he wants to hear from you, it won't matter. Ideally you are inundated with invitations to screenings, lectures, dinner parties, cocktail parties, and so on and you can simply call him and ask if he would be your "escort" for the evening.

Now you are together for an evening. We come to the single most important use of the hand in seduction—the meaningful touch. You will have already touched each other casually. He has helped you on with your coat, or handed you a drink, or lit your cigarette, or brushed your shoulder to get your attention or to show you something. She has touched your arm, walked alongside with her shoulder occasionally touching yours, been generally friendly and receptive to you.

Dr. Gerhard Nielsen, in his book *Studies in Self-Confrontation*, listed 24 separate steps between initial physical contact and the coitional act, in American adolescent males and females.[7] Somewhere among those 24 steps is the Meaningful Touch. It could be taking the woman's hand, which Dr. Nielsen says must be followed by her warm response before the male can take further steps. (Her response would be a softening of her hand to accept his touch or perhaps even a return pressure. She might respond by tracing her fingers on the back of his hand, or her fingernails in his palm or between his fingers, if she is bold.) Only then, says Dr. Nielsen, can the fellow go on to the other steps: entwining fingers, putting an arm around her shoulders, moving his hand down her back, approaching her breast from the side, kissing, returning to the breast, and so on and into bed.

"Skipping steps or reversing their order is fast," says Dr. Nielsen, and indeed it is. It is also the waste of a delicious moment— that of doubt and anticipation. Sexual desire does not diminish with the time you spend waiting; it expands to fill it.

Then again, Dr. Nielsen's study was referring to *adolescents*. As adults you may have found many happy opportunities to approach a new person more creatively, not on a pre-programmed one-and-a-two-basis. Because the entire body is an erotogenic zone, as Freud has reminded us, one has first to be an explorer before one can be a conqueror. As long as the other person reacts favorably to your touch, you may continue.

Let's talk about what we mean by "reacting favorably." If she clamps both of her hands into fists, stiffens her entire body and

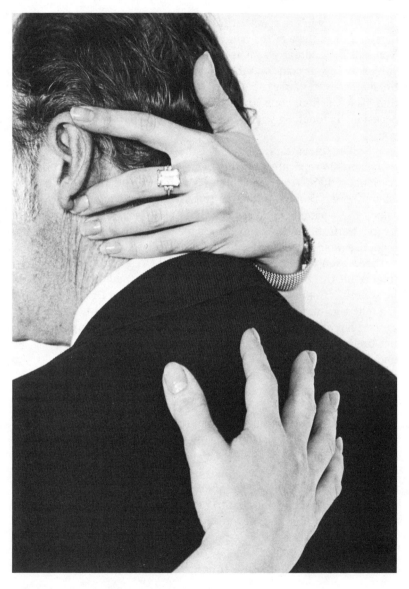

the cords stand out in her neck, one might comfortably surmise she is not enjoying being touched. If he flinches, moves away, and calls for the waiter, you might guess he is not "reacting favorably" to being touched either. A gentle acquiescence to being touched is indeed a favorable reaction. Your partner doesn't have to proclaim, "That feels so good, do it again" every time you touch him or her. If you are sensitive to your partner's personality you will have some idea of what to expect in the touch department. Macho Man may need no more than your brushing of his hand for him to sweep you out the door and back to his place. Sensitive Sinclair may need to be *taken* by the hand and tugged into bed. Both men are "reacting favorably" to being touched, however.

You may find ploys helpful. Kinesthetic sexual gambits don't seem nearly as obvious as verbal sexual gambits like "Do you live nearby?" or "What do you think of vibrators, anyhow?" Any excuse you can find to touch the other person's body—helping her with her tennis backhand, giving a massage, tieing a scarf, holding his hand as he lights your cigarette—will bring you closer to ground zero. You might study a point chart for fencing to get an idea of the sexual hotspots in casual touching.

These are some of the things we have found electric: undoing the top button of his shirt and saying "this looks much better"; coming up behind her unexpectedly and touching the back of her neck, her shoulder, or arm; stroking his thigh; touching her ear or sweeping a strand of hair back behind her ear; brushing something from his cheek or, especially, his lips; examining her bracelet or watch, letting your hand linger on the inside of her wrist; picking lint off his sleeve or lapel; teasing the skin on the top of her hand with your fingertips; feeling his tennis muscles, especially his *sore* tennis muscles.

If your attempts to seduce your partner have been successful you may want to stop reading this book for now, or you may want to turn to Chapter 8, "The Hands and Sex," Part II. If you have been unsuccessful in your evening's attempt, we recommend you turn to "The Hands and Sex," Part I.

4/The Hand
in Coming and Going

As a species of primate, we are remarkably rich in greetings and farewells. Other primates do show simple greeting rituals, but we exceed them all, and we also show farewell displays which they seem to lack entirely.

Desmond Morris, *Manwatching*

Throughout the primate world there is a recognizable ritual in greetings. First the apes or men make eye contact, which includes an act known as the "eyebrow flash." You might think such a term would be self-explanatory, but kinesiologists, who take this kind of thing very seriously, have quantified and qualified this short-lived event as follows: "In the first phase the greeter looks at his acquaintance, raises his lids slightly, and sometimes puts his head back a little. In the second stage—an instant later—the eyebrows are raised and the eyes opened widely."[1] Having defined what constitutes an "eyebrow flash," researchers such as Eibl-Eibesfeldt have filmed it among all peoples around the world. To state it simply, when you see someone you know and like, whether that someone is fellow ape or fellow human, you open your face to him by opening your eyes.

The next stage of greeting is shared by all mammals: the salutation. Prairie dogs bark, horses nicker, cats hiss, pigs grunt. Humans do all those things, and more, given the right circumstances.

Finally, primates present their palms either by raising them or by clasping them with each other. Some sociologists have insisted that ritual hand-clasping among men was a holdover from earlier times when it was necessary to display the empty palm, that is, a palm free of weapons. But the greater apes, chimpanzees, and monkeys also present the palm in greeting. Could it be that this gesture is actually a show of fondness or bonding? How much nicer to think the showing of the palm means, "Come here, I want to touch you," instead of "Look, I'm not going to kill you."

If we observe young children we see that the first attempt to wave "bye-bye" is usually an opening and closing of the raised hand, in a grasping movement. Beginning usually in the ninth month, babies practice this gesture not only when someone is coming or going but at their stationary toys or to the room in general. With shaping of these initial movements by the resident adults, waving bye-bye becomes a consistent, recognizable, and appropriately used gesture.

Of course humans, being prone to props and social stratifiers, have expanded upon this basic list of recognition, eyebrow flash, and presenting the palm, and have made greeting somewhat more complicated. We use the ritual greeting to establish station in life and to show honor by total abasement and prostration, genuflecting, clicking heels, kissing hands, hems, or rings. We salute—with cane, sword, or

hand—and we tip our hats with a nod. In addition, we have verbal
salutations to accompany each of these moves. Some greetings, like
tipping the hat, have gone the way of the nuclear family, but this
practice once was not only considered nice but required. The Cheval-
ier de la Barré was decapitated in July 1756 on two charges, one of
which was failure to doff his hat when a religious procession went by.[2]
Not even kings considered themselves above tipping their hats;
Louis XIV tipped his hat to every woman he met, including chamber-
maids, although, of course, the degree of tipping was directly propor-
tional to the lady's rank.[3]

The hand is also used to announce arrival by knocking on a
door or doorsill. For general home use, we feel that a four-knock is
standard, although some people use and prefer the three-knock. In
offices a short double-knock (knock-knock) might be used because
the distance from door to office occupant is small and two short
knocks should be audible in all but the grandest of offices. One friend
of ours, an imposing man, had a formidable, distinctive knock. It was
one very loud, very singular KNOCK, which when practiced on a
solid wood door in a large house, had the sound of a sonic boom.
Because he was not only an imposing man but a nice one, the BOOM-
knock was always a welcome one.

If confronted with a push-button doorbell, you should restrict
yourself to two or at the most three rings. Four rings has an impatient,
imperious sound. If you are so lucky as to find a twist-ringer on the
door, a single twist will do, no matter how tempting it is to give
another.

Your style of interpersonal greeting reveals your social and
your ethnic background, your feelings about yourself, and your
attitude toward the person you are greeting. Orientals traditionally
fold their hands and bow their heads in greeting, Hindus touch the
forehead with the right hand, Arabs fold the arms across the chest,
Europeans generally make a light movement of the right hand. Some
greetings were shared by widely divergent cultures: for example, the
straightened right arm of the Romans and Nazis. We can't help but
make judgments about people based on the way they greet us. It is

the very first move we see them make, and perhaps the most revealing.

The Continental Wave (often seen at Cannes, Gstaad, and the Polo Lounge): This "wave" comes in two varieties, the French and the Greco-Roman. The basic wave is made by holding the right arm up and having the hand imitate a set of chattering teeth. The French perform this wave with the palm *facing* the person being greeted, but the Greeks and the Italians, with their superstition about the open palm and the evil eye, perform this wave facing *away from* the person being greeted. Both waves seem odd to exuberant Americans because they are small gestures that look not so much like waves as like grasping at the person being greeted. This gesture is actually the closest one to the first attempt at "waving bye-bye" in a very young child.

At the Polo Lounge one can often see a bastardized form of the Continental, with the waver simultaneously giving the French wave, making little gourami kisses, and shouting "*Ciao*, baby!" Like several other waves, this is suitable for both coming and going.

The WASP Wave: As with all things Anglo-Saxon, moderation is the key word. The typical WASP wave is the mildest of events: fingers of the hand are either held straight or allowed to curl slightly, there is some relaxation of the elbow and wrist, movement is first away from the head and then back. The basic image is of one gently polishing the flank of a Rolls-Royce Silver Cloud.

The Window Wiper (the Pinto version of the above): This wave can be done comfortably in a double-knit leisure suit. There is a tendency with it to get carried away and look like an idiot. No sexism here: this wave is used equally by men and women. It is seen often in Kansas, Missouri, and South Dakota.

The Single Wipe: This wave consists of one move of the raised hand, from in front of the body to the side. It is favored by wise guys, and usually accompanied by "See ya." One version has the hand held flat and skating out from the body. This might be accompanied by "later."

The Scout Salute: In North America this wave is used only by socially inept women; in South America both men and women use this wave.

The Mock Salute: Done almost entirely by men, this gesture uses the Girl Scout fingering above, but with the hand touched to the brow and then smartly removed. The mock salute reached its epitome in Casablanca with Bogie. To work, it has to be accompanied by a suitably wry face.

The Peremptory Point: This sign of greeting is often used in a crowded room. One finger is held aloft and may be inclined once toward the person being spotted. The finger says, "I see you," or "I'll get to you in a minute." The peremptory point is done either by an executive or by, perhaps, the leader of a discussion—in other words, someone in power. It is simultaneously a greeting and a check. You'd better be able to pull this one off if you're going to try to use it.

The Vegas Point: Comedians or other entertainers use this gesture to recognize colleagues or regulars in the audience. It is often used to self-interrupt patter or even a song, accompanied by "Hey, good to see you." (What is meant for the audience is "Look who came to see me.") As the forefinger is leveled at the person being recognized, a nod or ducking of the head should accompany it. An entertainer who is charged up that night might also give a finger-snap with the Vegas Point.

The Pistol Point: This is a simulated drawing of a pistol, done close to body—cool, Clint Eastwood rather than Tom Mix. A male gesture, it is done by young men rather than old as a subconscious expression of virility. Odd, isn't it, to greet someone by pretending to shoot them?

The Dave Garroway: Here we have the old "How" sign. Utterance of the word "peace" is optional. This is a greeting for the laid back, not overly friendly man or woman. It connotes a calm and pleasant personality. Don't *say* "How" unless you were at Wounded Knee.

The Black Power Salute: This became associated with the black movement in the mid-Sixties and peaked on the victory stand at the 1968 Olympics. It has now become generalized from its

The eloquence of this gesture is not only in the raised fists but also in the simultaneously downcast eyes. Wide World Photos

original Black Power use and is seen on athletic fields and elsewhere as a way to say, "Go get 'em" or "Right on" or "Lookin' good, Mama." The Black Power salute can be delivered with the arm either vertical or horizontal.

The "V": A nostalgic salutation, the "V" for victory or "Peace Sign" is usually done by a person still lost in the Sixties. There is a high correlation between giving this sign and listening to old Melanie albums. (The sign was once used by politicians but, since Nixon, has fallen into disfavor.)

The Windmill: This wave is most often seen on audience-participation game shows. It consists of a full rotation of the arm in the shoulder socket. The hand may be either clenched or open, and the wrist is sometimes loose, giving the arm and the hand separate

The Single Wipe; the Pistol Point; and the bastardized Continental, with Gourami Kiss.

motions. "Woo-hoo" is sometimes heard accompanying this wave, if done by women, or "hey-hey" if done by men.

Beckons are specialized salutations that can range from the informal and familial to the imperious. The most common beckons are probably the signals we use for calling a waiter. We can give the peremptory point or a raised hand or we can be much more elaborate, with pictographs to make specific requests: mimes of writing up the check, pouring more coffee, turning a pepper mill. The head waiter or floor manager in a department store might have a ruder way of summoning an employee: the staccato clap.

There are professional beckons: the traffic cops' gestures (more binding on us than mere beckons, these are outright commands, sometimes punctuated with sharp blasts of a whistle), the beckon of a doorman hailing a cab, standing like the Statue of Liberty. There are the teacher's here-there beckons, which say, "*You,* move over *there!*" These can be delivered gently or emphatically, and can even specify the numbers of people being addressed by using points and numbers of fingers. The most all-encompassing here-there beckon is the roundup; it involves the use of the entire arm in a huge sweep and says, "*All* of you, get your asses over there."

Then there is thumbing a ride, an entreaty beckon. It should always be performed while one is standing and facing oncoming traffic or while walking backwards with the flow of moving cars. This way you can fix approaching drivers with a sincere look and make them feel guilty for passing you by.

Kindest is the come-hither beckon, which involves only the forefinger, highly and suggestively arched, calling man or beast into its physical or emotional range.

Many waves of greeting are used interchangeably with those of parting: the Mock Salute, the Vegas Point, the "*Ciao,*" the "V," the Black Power Salute, and others. Some waves of greeting do not demand a reply; they are casual, almost desultory in nature. Other waves are indeed salutes; they demand an answering, sequential, mirror reply.

All good-bye waves, on the other hand, require of us some form of answering wave, usually done simultaneously. If we don't have some more eccentric way of waving good-bye, most of us will resort to the Granny Wave, with the head usually bobbing and the hand held aloft, flapping up and down or switching from side to side.

Then there are the Morganatic Farewells, done by a person of higher station to a group or an individual of lower station. Included in this category are the Dinah, which is a one- or two-handed kissing the palm and flinging the kiss at the audience; the Harry Chapin, a two-fisted salute done with elbows tight to the body; the Rocky, a generic victory sign in boxing; the Christian Blessing of the sign of the cross; the Greek Tycoon (two hands held palm downward and bounced); and the Papal Acknowledgment, done at shoulder height, both hands held with fingers touching thumbs, back of the hands to the audience, and moved in a gentle bob.

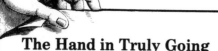

The Hand in Truly Going

No discussion of the hand in coming and going would be complete without a discussion of the weird and fascinating rules for placement of the hands on Final Parting.[4]

The subject of the placement of hands of the dead comes up in the most primitive of societies and in the most complex. France, Australia, England, Italy, the Scandinavian countries, for example, do not view the body of the deceased, or they view only the face. However, in Africa, in Bali, in India, in Iran, in rural Balkan countries, among native American Indians, and in American death palaces, the placement of hands is rigidly outlined in custom and in religious law.

African burial traditions are fascinating. In Ethiopia the placement of the hands in death signifies station in life. Laymen are buried with their arms meeting at the abdomen, thumbs tied together with white string. A monk, priest, or once-married nun is buried with the arms crossed over the chest, and a celibate monk or virgin nun is buried with the arms folded so that the fingers rest in the mouth.

Among the Annang tribe of Nigeria, the right hand of the deceased, if he is the firstborn son, is raised and held up by a string tied to the ceiling of the hut in which he lies in state.

Iranian Zoroastrians fold the arms over the chest and leave the body to the vultures, the preferred form of "burial."

In India, Moslem law instructs that the right side be washed before the left and that the body be laid out on its right side with its head to the north (facing Mecca).

The Dakota Indians *painted* a hand in black over the lower face of a great warrior.

In Rumania the hands are laid across the breast with a candle, a small icon, and a coin between them. In Yugoslavia the hands are crossed over the chest with the right hand uppermost. In Poland the hands are placed over the heart; in Hungary money is put into the deceased's hands. These traditions have much to do with (1) the fear of vampires (thus the *crossed* arms and icons); (2) providing

money for the transport of the dead soul to the beyond. In rural areas in these countries, it is the relatives, mostly the women, who wash and lay out the body.

Judaic law has many instructions for the treatment of the body after death, but the only reference to the hands is that "the limbs should be straightened." Thus in America, at a Jewish funeral or memorial, if the coffin is open the arms and hands will be at the sides.

There is one exception to the generalization that the dead are not viewed in England, or, if viewed, that only the face is shown, and that is in Lancashire, where traditionally the open portion of the coffin allows the hands to be seen. Hands there and in America are arranged depending on the deceased's religion and the preference of the mortuary. Catholics will often be buried with a rosary held in the clasped hands. Hands folded on the stomach are most common, hands at the side second, and, rarely, the hands will be crossed over the chest. Because in this country such concerns are mostly a matter of "funeral arts," we have no particular customs, beliefs, or reverence for the hands of the dead.

One of the most bizarre funeral customs flourished in Europe and America in the nineteenth century, when it became fashionable to be buried in a coffin equipped with a pull-chain which was attached through a copper tube to a little bell above ground. Coffins so equipped offered the only-seeming-to-be-dead a second chance—*if* they could find the pull-chain in the damp dark, and *if* anyone chanced to be passing by, and *if* the person passing by were not frightened out of his wits by the sound of a little bell tinkling in a deserted churchyard.

*These hands, in their distinctive pattern of thumb apart and fingers divided
in a V, illustrate the mark of the Kohainim, the priests of Israel. The hands on
gravestones identified descendents of the priests, as seen here on a stone
in the old cemetery of Prague. The sign has been adopted in modern times
by Leonard Nimoy in his Mr. Spock's Vulcan greeting in* Star Trek *and in
Mork's "na-nu na-nu" handshake. © Jim Feldman.*

Alfred Adler said the perfectly normal handshake was so rare as to be almost immediately suspect if it is encountered.[5] In *The Human Hand*, Geza Revesz says, "The handshake is a symbolic manipulation . . . it points to an equivalence of worth and right."[6] In other words, offering a hand is in a way offering yourself for testing. The handshake we offer the world is as much put on as the clothes we wear. Skin has an expressive value, which we all instinctively respond to, whether it's moist or dry, hard or soft, cool or warm. This element is lost, sometimes purposely concealed, when the hand is sheathed in a glove.

The late J. Edgar Hoover believed that wet skin was an expression of bad character and refused to admit any candidate into the FBI who had sweaty palms. As a result, all FBI men carried handkerchieves with which to dry their hands in case they should meet the Boss.

A cool handshake is recognized as a sign of ladylike or gentlemanly, polite character. Young Southern belles recognized this and stood just outside the parlor with their hands held over their heads, so the blood would drain out and they could present their callers with the cool, pale handshake that bespoke femininity. Hand models do the same thing to reduce puffiness and redness in the hands before they go in front of the camera. In Victorian times, glass hand coolers served the same purpose.

Femininity requires soft, pampered-feeling skin. Billions of dollars are earned each year by cosmetic and pharmaceutical companies to achieve just this image. Men physiologically have thicker skin (which information will not surprise many women who always felt that men were thick-skinned), and that is why most of us expect men to have calloused hands. Men can get by with either soft or calloused hands. Women, even if they work as stevedores, are somehow expected to have doe-soft hands.

So far we have described various waves and beckons, but haven't listed the different types of handshakes practiced in America.

Here is a marvelously manipulative handshake, delivered in Sioux Falls, South Dakota, in 1960. Paul Schutzer, Life Magazine © *1960 Time Inc.*

Each of the following types has variations depending on the exact strength, warmth, and moisture of the hand as well as on the length of the handshake. People from the Midwest, especially people of German background, love giving a long, five or six-stroke handshake. Easterners, both because of busy schedules and because of an Anglo-Episcopalian inhibition against lengthy touching, give the shortest handshakes, either one beat (down and up) or, occasionally, only half a shake (down).

The Basic: First we have the so-called normal handshake that Adler warned us about. This is a restrained, noncommittal, relatively brief clasping of hands with one or two up-and-down moves. This shake reflects an Anglo-Saxon heritage and is of shorter duration than a normal handshake would be in South America or in Europe. It is, however, the handshake ideal for businessmen and salesmen.

The False Macho: This is the hand-wringer, bone-crusher shake done by the guy who equates pounds of pressure with degree of masculinity. Beware of these types; they're out to prove *something.* They usually climax too early or not at all.

The Finger Shake: In this one a person offers one, two, or at most three fingers. Finger-shakers come in two types: the timid, who want to avoid any physical contact and get it over with as soon as possible; and the Total Woman, who has been schooled to present her hand this way so that it can be kissed or at least made free with in any way the man wishes. This, however, is the surface reading. As with many facets of "Total Womanhood," this act on the woman's part requires of the man either a courting, fostering, or paternalistic reaction. He may do with it as he will—kiss it, clasp it, fondle it—but he is not allowed to be neutral. Total woman requires total man. Get ready to become a male stereotype before you take her hand.

The Protocol (The Regal Handshake): There are special rules for handshakes with dignitaries, who must suffer through hundreds of handshakes an hour. If you are about to meet a V.I.P., remember: let him or her take your hand first. The Queen, dignitaries, wives of politicians, starlets, and violinists all give this soft, quiet clamp to proferred hands.

The Dead Fish: This is the bad one. Avoid doing it yourself, and avoid anyone else who does it. It is cold, it is clammy, it is weak and indifferent—it is a hand locus of a devastating low energy field. The person giving the dead fish can't seem to summon the energy or the interest to give you a real handshake. When you've been given the cold fish, you walk away feeling less a person than you were just a few minutes ago. You are drained. The person delivering a dead fish is probably lazy and undependable, sullen, absentminded, and emotionally limited. It is amazing that someone can have this terrible handshake and not be aware of it.

It is worse than halitosis. If your best friends won't tell you to stop giving the DF, you may not have any friends at all.

The Politico: This is a two-handed, overly sincere shake. The right hand grabs yours, but, as in the disappearing coin trick, it is the left hand here that tells the story. The left hand is manipulating—pushing, pulling, covering, directing—as it takes its place somewhere on your body. The most common positions for the left hand are clasping your hand, your wrist, forearm, elbow, bicep, shoulder, or neck. The higher the left hand goes, the more you are being controlled, and when you are being clasped by the neck, there is a presumption of intimacy or ownership. Anyone who wants to be in a winning, manipulating position—the clergyman, the shingle salesman, the boss—will use the politico. It is meant to imply sincerity, but it is nothing less than winning through intimidation. Lyndon Baines Johnson's famous "pressing the flesh" was perhaps the best-known Politico handshake.

The Squeeze: This is another handshake of control. The person giving the squeeze is not responsive to your handshake at all. He wraps his fingers over the top of your hand and starts squeezing, like a farmer at the udder. Politicians sometimes use the squeeze with both hands as they work their way through a crowded room.

The Bonding Tie: This affectionate clasp either follows or stops short of the full embrace and gives the appearance of completing the circle between two people, to the exclusion of all others. It is two-handed, two-sided, with the hands laid over as large an area of the other person as the situation will allow. When it is not reciprocated—as with, say, a hostile child—this is not a Bonding Tie but a Politico.

The Athlete's Slap: This is not really a handshake, but a double or single-handed slap. It can be one- or two-handed and, in a social situation, the active one (slapper) is of a higher station. In sports, however, the one who has hit the home run or scored the touchdown receives congratulations as the slappee. He will offer his hand or hands to his teammates to be slapped. In addition to the palm-to-palm version, this can be done fist-over-fist, a variation that may have originated with boxers.

The Athlete's Slap, also known as the Soul Slap because it seemed to be the blacks who used it first in sports, has become generalized far beyond the playing field, probably because of the exposure of athletes on television. Actually this slap long predates the NBA; it most likely originated as a sign of agreement. References start appearing in eighteenth- and nineteenth-century literature to the slapping of palms to seal a bargain, especially among the French.

The Brother: The Athlete's Slap/Soul Slap has now been replaced by a stronger, two-part handshake and clasp, which requires a longer time for execution and better understanding and synchronization between the two people greeting each other. It can be used for hellos and good-byes, as well as for congratulations.

Two-part handshake/clasp that has replaced the Soul Slap on the playing field and off. Fellowship of Christian Athletes.

All About Clapping

Psychologists and mothers have observed that children in their first year of life use hand clapping as a greeting, a joyful expression of hello. It appears that they are reaching out to be held, especially by Mother. Usually she reacts by picking the infant up and patting little him or her on the back in a reassuring way.

The adult hand clap appears to be an extension of the child's clap combined with the mother's back pat of approval and reassurance. When we clap in a theatre or at a sporting event we are, in effect, patting the performer on the back. If we could, we would be on the stage to do it literally but instead we do it from a distance. So the clapping is a sign of affection and approval. Russia is one country in which the performers, politicians, or cosmonauts clap back to the audience. When that happens, the performer is symbolically clapping them on the back, having them join in his or her success or triumph as a partner—a nice touch when you think about it.

Circus performers and others, after completing a difficult feat of skill, will hold out their arms in a poised-to-clap motion, almost as if they want to embrace the audience for sharing in that precious moment.

When we clap hands, we don't clap each hand equally, no matter what our style or speed. Whether we cup both hands, trapping the air in a resounding explosion, or just tap two fingers together in a reserved clapping gesture, one hand still does most of the work. Usually this is the dominant hand, with most of us the right hand. This is the hand that is on top; it is patting the performer on the back, the other hand acting as a substitute for the performer.

As natural as it seems to us now, clapping did not always mean praise and approval. Even now it can be used to summon a servant or a child. In Job XXVII hand clapping is said to mean disapproval. Indeed, the Latin word *explodo* meant "to drive an actor off the stage by clapping hands."[7]

It is hard to say just where or when the switch occurred (was there a particular production?) and performers started seeking out "the sea of clapping." Actors certainly have since learned how to milk a response from an audience. The word "claptrap" means literally to trap a clap, to get that extra round of applause by using any method. Rousseau, in his *Confessions,* mentions that when the King was present there was never any clapping in the theatre, a practice that seems to have been abandoned somewhere in the last century.

These are only a few of the hundreds of rituals people around the world use for greeting and parting. There are hundreds of secret and fraternal handshakes, most of them involving turning one or more fingers under as the hands are clasped or adding a complicated preceding ritual or follow-up to the handshake. Try as we might we couldn't get a Bonesman to break down and show us the secret shake. Several Phi Beta Kappas offered to show us theirs, but it somehow didn't seem as interesting. Among political groups, subcultures, and groups outside the law, there are additional signals and "hi" (or sometimes "high") signs, and there will continue to be more of them as specialized language and interests create larger groups of people who can speak only to each other.

As for ourselves, we prefer the old, homey hand greetings—the "pull your whistle" sign, for instance, known to every small child who has lived near a railroad track, a sign now becoming obsolete as trains go faster and noise-abatement laws keep engineers from gratifying a child's hunger for power over a speeding locomotive.

Even more long-gone, except perhaps for certain Europeans, is the beautiful ritual of hand kissing. The custom became fashionable in England in the late sixteenth century, having been imported from the Italian and French courts. (This timing was long enough after the time of the Black Death to ensure that such unsanitary intimacy had nothing to do with spreading the plague.) The Italians were passionate about kissing a woman's hand; they actually kissed it. The English, however, chose to follow the French fashion, that is, to bring the hand to the mouth and bow over it.[8] The hand we are referring to was *never* that of an unmarried girl, who would have been scandalized by such liberties. Here are the instructions for hand kissing, from a manual of etiquette in the eighteenth century:

Always kiss the right hand. Never touch the hand to your lips but keep it somewhat distant. Bend the hand a little, do not keep it straight. When raising the arm and bringing the hand toward the mouth, keep your

wrist and hand curved inwards. Bring the lady's index finger [then the
favored ring finger] nearest the mouth.[9]

If you envisioned doing something racy with the hand so near the
mouth, like *breathing* on it, remember that the woman was undoubtedly wearing gloves.

Even women needed instruction in hand kissing for one con-
tingency: being presented at court. Instructions for this operation
were given in *Manners: A Handbook of Social Customs,* published in
1888 and written anonymously by a woman later identified as Elizabeth Marbury. If the book's world seems distant to you, keep in mind
that the book was endorsed by Mrs. Theodore Roosevelt:

The Lady advances and bows very low, extending her right hand,
palm downwards, and the Queen places her hand upon it, which the
lady kisses.

No word here about whether you actually kiss or not. Our best would
be "not," else Victoria would end up with chapped hands. You might
be interested to hear what one was required to wear at court:

Full dress . . . , unless a certificate from a medical man is forwarded to
the Lord Chamberlain, giving satisfactory reasons why a lady should
not wear a low bodice. The dress consists of a low bodice without
sleeves, a train of from three to four yards in length, and a head-dress
of feathers (white are preferred) and lappets, with whatever ornaments
and other appointments of a grand toilet that the wearer may select.

All this seems somehow beyond the Americans, who *tried,* God bless
them, but rarely succeeded. Better we concentrate on perfecting a
normal handshake than try to master hand kissing.

Ring Magazine

5/The Hands and Power

Power! What do we know about it? We don't know anything about it. We have sex education—why don't we have power education? You can train yourself to handle power.
Rev. John J. McLaughlin, The New York Times, *June 2, 1974*

"Power is the ultimate aphrodisiac," said Henry Kissinger, and he wasn't necessarily talking about the power of men over women. Genetic researchers may some day discover that there is a "power gene," some inherent reason why certain people seek and wield power and others merely stand, watch, and follow. If such a gene were discovered, it might be found to be sex-linked—appearing almost exclusively in men—and to produce as a side effect short stature. This coincidence of shortness with power craze has long been noted as the Napoleon Complex.

You might be wondering why we are talking about *shortness* and power when the subject of the book is the *hands* and power. The explanation is simple: there are two types of hand gestures. People taller than five-foot-eight (women) or five-foot-ten (men) can carry off the *grand gesture*; those shorter than that must rely on prop-supported gestures. In hierarchical groups—offices, college campuses, churches —short power-seekers can often climb to the highest ranks by using the small, prop-supported power gesture. In large-scale politics— national office, nonhierarchical churches—the taller candidate usually wins with grand gestures.

But a smaller person, properly equipped, with a keen awareness of power gestures and how they can be manipulated, would have a chance against the bigger individual. In power gestures, David's rock is the power prop that can slay Goliath.

Egon Von Furstenberg says that power shows in the cut of a man's clothes; Michael Korda, in the placement of one's desk; John Malloy, in the appropriate wardrobe of dark suits and muted vests for the women executive. We say power shows in the way you hold a cigarette or a telephone, the way you call for a waiter, the way you open and close your briefcase, take notes, dismiss someone. You can gesture weakly, sloppily, and inefficiently, *or* you can gesture consciously, elegantly, and powerfully. Which will it be?

The telephone, the pen or pencil, cigar or pipe, the ruler, the telescoping pointer are not powerful in and of themselves, but used well, with style and panache, they can become power props. You have to live up to your props, though. If you are going to splat yourself with ink, don't bother carrying a Mont Blanc pen. If you can't handle smoking a Havana, don't smoke. Power props are only as good as the hands they're in.

Some props are totems of power. Their proper use can help you ease your way into a new position that might not yet fit comfortably. Say you have just been made department head at your college. Now is the time to take up a pipe, which will signal maturity and pensive reflection—just the thing for a department head. You will soon live up to your pipe. You will learn to use it as a pointer. You will learn to fondle it, stroke it, bathe it in nose oil, clean it, and even tamp it and light up. During any of these activities your underlings will not think of you as a malingering, indecisive old toad but as a serious man, a good listener. This pipe would work as well for a teacher under you (beware an underling who suddenly takes up the pipe habit), a psychologist, an authority figure of any type. Gerald Ford was advised to begin using a pipe to give additional weight to his public persona.

A cigar, because it is so distinctly objectionable, makes a terrific power prop. Only someone in a position of power can get away with burdening those around him—and we use the pronoun "him" advisedly—with the noxious vapors of a lit cigar. Cigars carry with them connotations of Daddy Warbucks, back-room deals, ostentatiousness, diamond pinky rings, and arrivist mercantile-class leanings. In other words, the cigar is a most volatile power prop. It should be wielded with a certain degree of respect.

When a teacher picks up a ruler or a pointer, it is obviously being used as a power prop. A busy executive with a phone at his or her ear is using that phone to unnerve a determined petitioner. That too is a power prop. Although eyeglasses are the opposites of power symbols—they symbolize, in fact, a weakness—they too can be used by power wielders to profitable effect. The idea is to make a show of *not* using them: take them off at a dramatic moment and tuck them in your breast pocket (men) or let them remain in your hand (women) to be used as a pointer. Use Churchill's trick: look over the tops of them. Think of them as a prop, something to be used *dramatically,* not just as a stationary part of your wardrobe, and, magically, they will become a prop.

There is one power prop that seems almost exclusively a

woman's—the fan. In the hands of an imperious dowager aunt or an achingly pretty Southern girl dressed in antebellum finery, a fan can be used with devastating effect. In a man's hands—even a man *en travestie*—the fan cannot be used to exert power, unless the man holding the fan is so powerful already (Yul Brynner in *The King and I;* Yul Brynner in anything; a plantation owner) that not only a fan but also a dead chicken, a bunch of grapes, or a kielbasa could be used successfully.

Let's face it: some people can turn anything into a power prop, and for them this chapter is not required reading. For the rest of us there is an important rule to be remembered: powerful gestures can be strengthened by almost anything that extends or emphasizes the line of the hand; if the object is itself a power totem, the strength of the gesture is doubled.

Women have a particular power domain, as well as a repertoire of gestures to go with it. We speak of the domestic power gesture, the refinements of mothers and wives. Men often use these same gestures to get *their* way at home, but let us, for the sake of arbitrary neatness, refer to these as women's domestic power gestures. Traditionally it has been the mothers who wielded the broom and the frying pan at home.

If you will excuse the alliteration, we've called these gestures the Six Power P's: the Pat, the Pinch, the Push, the Point, the Pal, and the Projectile. The Pat as a power gesture is actually the Patronizing Pat. It is performed in public or in private, often to the shoulder of the spouse, accompanied by something like, "You must be proud of yourself, the way you beat that little boy in Miniature Golf." This is the deadly False Congratulation. It can be used with a child also, but the child must be old enough to understand the meaning of ironic understatement.

The Pinch, when applied to the husband, is covert (under the table it is done to the upper thigh, on the street to the back of the arm) and a warning device. It says, "Shut up, Fred, you're on dangerous ground." When applied to children, the Pinch usually takes a more active form. The worst cheek pinchers are aunts and grandmothers. No infant, toddler, or child has ever enjoyed having one or, usually, both cheeks seized in a pincher grasp and jiggled, but adults persist in this. Since the pinchee doesn't enjoy it, the pincher must—otherwise the gesture wouldn't survive. We think the cheek pinch is a ritual exercise used to introduce the young to women's real power and to keep those pinching muscles in shape for the more serious pinches to the ear and to the arm. Both the Katzenjammer Ear Pinch and the Propelling Arm Pinch are used to force children to go somewhere they don't want to go. The particular grip, and the tender parts it is applied to, enable a mother to get a kid moving again with the least actual physical effort. More effective than dragging, tidier than pushing, the Pinch is Mom's ultimate weapon. If you think you have escaped this particular power gesture, try this experiment: close your eyes and pinch the soft flesh on the back of your arm. *Deja vu,* right?

Mom uses the Push like a jockey uses the whip in the home stretch. When she is driven to pushing the children toward their rooms, toward their dinner dishes, in the direction of the garbage, she *really means it.*

Mom's Point is a noncontact version of the Push. It is usually delivered in two parts, the first toward the child being addressed (intimidation through pointing), the second toward the job to be done (directive pointing, the push substitute).

The Pal is Mom's one chance to use the old LBJ gesture of a protective arm around the shoulder, her one chance because it is effective only if the one performing it is taller than the one being Palled. Mom usually is relegated to pulling a Pal—the gentlest of power gestures—on her children to persuade them to get on with whatever they are resisting doing.

You might think that Mom reserves the Projectile for Dad and for Dad only, but if a child has driven her far enough, and if there is a relatively soft article at hand, and especially if that child can now outrun her, Mom has been known to throw things at Junior. More

"GO!"

From An Hour with Delsarte *by Anna Morgan, illustrated by Rose Mueller and Marian Reynolds.*

frequently, Mom throws things at her husband, as a way of catching his attention (a signal to him that this is an *important* conversation) or, more often, in complete frustration over his inability to understand what she is talking about.

The woman needs split-second reactions to be able to throw something at the right moment and yet have time to check first to see if it is the wedding china or just Melmac in her hand. The more dangerous the object being thrown (Sabatier knife instead of a pillow), the stronger the statement she is making. If she chooses the knife, she had better be on her toes from here on in. Something happens to men when they have knives thrown at them; it sets up their adrenaline; they get mad; they soon may not be responsible for what *they* do. Sound effects are good. We know one good argument that was settled by the violent pulling out of a dresser drawer, which subsequently broke. If a woman chooses the shotgun technique—throwing something that will scatter on impact, like a bowl of hulled strawberries or a jar full of peanuts—she should remember that whichever is the more fastidious of the two will end the argument by cleaning up.

These Six Power P's refer only to those power gestures of American women; other countries' women have their own power ploys. (The British woman's resort is compulsive gardening; she won't come back in the house until everything is settled. The Italian woman adds a seventh P: calling the Priest—and so on.) Within American women's domestic power structure there are two subgroups—Jewish mothers and Catholic mothers—who have their own *spécialités de la maison.*

The Jewish American Mother (J.A.M.) has perfected the power gestures of outright aggression, gestures only dabbled in by other American mothers. J.A.M.'s channel aggression into two kinds of gestures, those of outright physical aggression and those of guilt aggression. Physical aggression is reserved for children who weigh under a hundred pounds, or those who stand less than two-thirds their mother's height. One gesture of physical aggression that is not confined by this height/weight rule is the Schizophrenogenic Spider,

Here are three instructive Delsarte poses: 1. My back hurts from typing your (a) term paper, (b) business letter, (c) new book. 2. The classic "not tonight, I've got a headache" pose, especially effective in a John Kloss nightgown. 3. Good for "You mean you left a jelly sandwich in your jeans in the wash?" From An Hour with Delsarte

the J.A.M.'s version of the Persuasive Pinch. The Schizzy Spider consists of sinking two, three, four, or five perfectly manicured, sharply pointed fingernails into a son's or daughter's hand or arm. To the outside world it might appear that Mom is giving her child a love pat. What she is saying under her breath might give the observer a clue to the real meaning of what she is doing. "I'm sure *we'll* be getting into medical school, *too*, just as soon as we *work on* our organic *chemistry.*" This gesture is particularly effective because it is two-sided. It *looks* like, and *sounds* like, warm, loving concern. It feels like hate. It says simultaneously: I love you and I hate you—thus the term Schizophrenogenic. Because of this particular bind, many J.A.M. *kinder* go directly from mother's house to therapy.

Guilt aggression leaves scars that are just as permanent.

J.A.M.'s delight in loudly running the vacuum cleaner, banging pots and pans in the kitchen, noisily chopping onions, and running up decibels on the Cuisinart, all the while saying, "You just go ahead and enjoy yourself. I'll be finished with this *sometime*." Many J.A.M.'s have studied Delsarte and have adopted the best moves— forearm to the brow, a hand clenching the heart, flexing stiffened fingers, pinching the bridge of the nose with one hand—just in case the family has failed to notice her sacrifices.

Catholic mothers hit, and *only* Catholic mothers hit. This is our own theory. We don't mean to imply that *all* Catholic mothers hit, but whatever hitting is being done is being done by Catholic mothers. (We are not talking here about child beating. We speak instead of the hit or "rap," a blow of more psychological than physiological damage.) It is handed down from generation to generation, like an old family missal. Why, you may wonder, do Catholic mothers hit? Are you kidding? Have you ever heard of the Papal encyclical aginst birth control? After the fourth or fifth child, hitting becomes a welcome form of physical release. And as for self-expression, hitting has everything: it is cheap, quick, efficient, and unambiguous. "You had toast before you went to *Communion*?" Bam! Since nuns are by extension Catholic mothers, nuns too hit. It is the experience of every parochial school child to have been whomped at one time or another by the Sisters, usually with a ruler. "What was that you were saying, Francis?" Whack!

About women and public power gestures: women should resist making the grand gesture (arms outspread at shoulder height) because it only draws attention to their breasts. This may or may not be what they planned but it almost always works to their disadvantage. Many of the typical men's power gestures simply look too big for women. Consider the case of Bella Abzug. Bella was thought of as a loud, aggressive, pushy woman, not only because of her voice, which was as dulcet as a jackhammer, but also for her assertive physical style. Little did it matter that she was an excellent congresswoman, effective and well respected by her colleagues. To the "fly-over" people (Hollywood's term for anyone not on the two coasts) she was a symbol for all that was wrong with the women's movement. The lesson for women politicians and executives is that they should use moderate gestures or no gestures at all, at least for the next generation.

Women who are in the public eye for physical accomplishments, whether those accomplishments are in sports or in entertainment, should use their bodies in whatever way they like. We can't imagine telling Tina Turner or Suzy Chaffee how to use their hands. These women, like men in their fields, have a professional acquaintance with their bodies, a familiarity and skill with their bodies the rest of us have every right to envy.

The men and women who practice powerful gestures will become the leaders for the rest of us, while we will end up performing manual labor and paying too many taxes. Manipulators—people who consciously use power gestures—*extract* deference, they extort it from others. The best manipulators succeed wildly; mediocre manipulators succeed only well. That may be a cynical statement; it's not an inaccurate one. We think of power as something that affects only corporation and political candidates, but the fact is that in any grouping of two or more, one person will always take the lead over the others. Let's see how that person gets and keeps that position of power through the intelligent use of gestures.

As you read the next few pages, keep situational criteria in mind: Are you big enough to carry off a particular gesture? Are you watching your posture and projecting self-confidence? Are you using the appropriate eye contact and speech patterns for the situation? Can you do that gesture gracefully, without inadvertently knocking something over? Practice the gestures we are going to tell you about, at home, in front of a mirror. Look at yourself ruthlessly. When you are ready, start small, with your bridge or poker club, your group therapy session. Only when you have succeeded there should you go on to conquer the PTA, a cocktail party, or your spouse.

Here is Lyndon Johnson giving a grand geste to the assembled. Compare his style to the style of that other tall politician, Charles De Gaulle. The Lyndon Baines Johnson Library

De Gaulle speaking from a balcony of the government house, Algiers. Life *Magazine © 1958 Time Inc.*

Gestures are going to help you get the maximum mileage out of your words, but they will not help you if you have absolutely no ideas at all and a terrible way of presenting those ideas verbally. However, if you have something to offer, you can be powerful even if the very word "power" frightens you. Think of these gestures as gestures of effectiveness. The important thing is to *think* of them.

For each of these gestures, think of how you can fit the gesture to yourself. If you are tall and forceful, you can use the large-scale gestures freely. If you are small, concentrate on the power props. Tall men and women like to stand up when they gesture because their height puts them at an advantage. Short men and women often prefer to sit, because their height is less noticeable when everyone is seated. Short power seekers are not above having their chairs slightly higher than those of the others at the table. A short person risks looking pugnacious when using the same active, forceful gestures that the taller person carries off easily. Put a fork in his or her hand, a pen, a ruler, or any other power prop, and the short person can cut his or her gestures in half and still be effective.

For a graduate course in the use of the power gesture, turn on your television set one Sunday morning to the local Evangelical preacher, turn off the sound, and watch. Here is a master politician, convincing you to vote not for him but for God. The religious and the secular politicians share common grounds: they both face large audiences; they are both in the business of convincing you through words and deeds (remember that gestures are perceived as deeds) that they are reliable, trustworthy, and honest; they both mount campaigns, one for votes, one for souls.

A campaign is, according to Webster II, "a connected series of military operations forming a distinct stage in a war." Clearly, politicians' gestures are those of a warrior: attack, aggression, and assertion. Remember what happened to Ed Muskie on the campaign trail when he behaved like a mere human being. Even in the church, where humility is said to be prized, no successful religious leader would admit to *weak* humility. No, in the church even humility is a

Here is Billy Sunday beat-the-beat-the-beating with the best of them.
The Library of Congress

strength. Church leaders learn the *lesson* of humility and are the stronger for it.

The religious politician gets away with using larger gestures than the secular politician because his audience isn't just mammon but the Big Guy in the Sky. The higher a religious leader rises through the ranks, the smaller his gestures become (because he is that much closer to God). The ultimate example of this is the Pope, who makes the microminiest of blessings, sometimes with only a finger. Outside of the Catholic religion, which is extremely hierarchical and which therefore allows one man to be at the top, religious leaders must "win" their audiences with each performance and they persist in their larger than life gestures. These ministers are in competition with each other, and with other good news, revival, old- and new-time religions.

No one can match the Southern Evangelist for power gestures. They, like the Jewish American Mothers, have stolen some of their best gestures from the Delsarte technique—the exaggerated theatrical flailings popular in America in the late nineteenth century. There is a peculiarly exuberant gesturing style known as Southern, and it owes everything to Delsarte. The style seems as natural to Big Jim Folsom as to a Baptist preacher and a born-again Christian. Southern politicians' gestural styles were undoubtedly formed at the age of three as they sat on their mothers' knees in the front pew watching that authority figure of all authority figures, the Southern preacher, dishing out hell-fire and brimstone.

Both sacred and secular politicians use the gesture known as the *Point*: it is a direct, antagonistic, decisive gesture. As children we were told never to point because it was considered "not nice." There is a historical reason for this. Early Christians and Jews prohibited pointing because pagans worshipped their gods by pointing at them. Politicians are apparently not interested in "not nice." Pointing is politically *de rigueur,* whether it is a point at the new sewer treatment plant, *up there,* or at you. Uncle Sam's point carries with it more than an invitation. It is a threat, a patriotic command: YOU!

One form of the Point is particularly demeaning: the *Thumb*

I WANT YOU
FOR U.S. ARMY
NEAREST RECRUITING STATION

Point. It is in effect the back of the hand. A Thumb Point is often directed over the shoulder, as if to say, "Get in back of me." It is particularly insulting if the person giving the Thumb Point is looking the other way when he says "Go out and bring me a cup of coffee."

The *Junior Politician's Crowd Punch* (JrPCP) is a short, up-from-the-shoulder, outwardly directed sock that accompanies such phrases as "Get out that vote!" or "Let's go sell *cookies!*" It was stolen from the pom-pom girls because it is used to get up pep and spirit. You might see an advance man doing the Crowd Punch, or a leader of the Methodist Youth Fellowship, but you will never see a senior politician or the Methodist minister doing it.

For emphasis the junior politician might test the waters with a Crowd Punch followed by a pound into the other hand for emphasis. What he is sampling is the power of the *Senior Politician's Pound.* The top man will skip the air punches entirely and move directly to the *Pound en l'aire* or the *Pound Concrete.* The Pound *en l'aire* is self-explanatory. It looks something like the old children's game of "One potato, two potato." When the Pound *en l'aire* is done by a full-grown male, however, it can look suspiciously close to the gesture for "jerking off." If you can't successfully do the Pound *en l'aire,* drop it from your repertoire. If the jerking-off gesture is even hinted at (the secret is in the wrist: let the wrist break and you're in trouble), you will implant in your audience a subtle subconscious area of doubt about your ability to perform.

The Pound Concrete is a strongly emphatic gesture. You can pound into your other hand, on your thigh, or on any horizontal surface. A prop in hand makes the Pound Concrete even more effective. Khrushchev's shoe pound may not have been immensely effective in the long run, but one thing is for sure: no one ever forgot it. This gesture must not be overused or else all the strength is lost and you will end up looking merely like a child who is having a tantrum.

In the *Bandmaster* the politician orchestrates the points with one or both hands. He or she can use an imaginary baton or actually clutch a pencil, pen, pointer, cigar, or cigarette. When so used, the props seem to take on an energy of their own. There is a propless version of the Bandmaster that is much favored by tall power-wielders. It is a large expansive gesture known as the Stokowski. Both arms are held at or above ear level. The gesture says, "Let us all be one," and it is properly used for the grand finale.

For small groups, or when the camera moves in tight, the small gesture of the *Finger Count* or the *Finger Hop* is effective. Here you use your other hand as a prop (the Finger Count) or hypnotize people with your forefinger going over those imaginary hurdles (the Finger Hop). Both techniques allow you to hold the floor while you make point after point of a long series of points. As long as your finger stays in motion, everyone else will feel it rude to interrupt you. Take care, however, not to lose count (to call two different things point number three) or you will lose credibility.

For oratory, nothing beats the *Chop,* which falls into three categories: the *Kennedy Chop,* the *Benito Chop,* and the *Karate Chop.* The Karate Chop is useful for illustrating "Let's cut the bullshit," or, in public, "Let's cut through this bureaucratic nonsense." There is a two-handed version, in which the hands make an X in front of the body, in effect X-ing out whatever is being discussed.

The Kennedy Chop is a smaller, less violent gesture that was created for television debate. Like the Finger Hop, it indicates a progression of ideas but on a stronger, more stately scale. The hand is held bent into a 90-degree angle with the thumb as the hypotenuse. This hand is then moved in steps diagonally away from the body. Because it is a more majestic gesture than the Finger Hop, it is even harder to interrupt; that is what makes it ideal for debates and press conferences. As long as the hand keeps progressing—even while you pause for breath—the floor will be yours. The diagonal direction seems perfect for television. It gives a feeling of depth to the picture without making the camera pull back as it would have to for a lateral gesture out from the shoulder.

The Benito Chop seems to have derived from the two-handed Papal gesture of imploration. Mussolini obviously knew his audience. Unlike the Karate Chop, the Benito Chop does not eliminate a problem but defines it. Much favored by small politicians, the Benito Chop gives them a chance to start out a large area for themselves by Benito Chopping with parallel hands far outside the middle range of most gestures. Stiff wrists and good displacement of the two hands give this gesture its power. In private the Chop can be used by civilians in its modified form, hands held parallel near the midline of the body.

Another form of power gesture is the *Straight Arm*, used to order someone to keep quiet, or to interrupt someone who is trying to take the floor. It is like a football straight arm, used to ward off would-be tacklers, and it owes a lot to the evil eye. Three things are necessary for an effective Straight Arm: (1) the straight-armer must be in the position of control; (2) the arm must be held absolutely straight, otherwise the gesture's power is lost; (3) the raised hand must be directed at eye level of the person being stopped. As with the Thumb Point, a look in the other direction as you deliver this gesture is a real show of contempt and power.

In addition to these oratorical power gestures, there are power gestures to symbolize the winner, the king, Der Fuehrer. One of the oldest is the raised arms and the clasped hands overhead. There is something in the human spirit that wants us to raise our arms in triumph. Not only does it feel good, it makes us visible to those around us in the crowd. Other emblematic power gestures are the raised fist of the Black Power Movement and Churchill's "V for Victory," both of which have been discussed previously. The most powerful emblematic gesture of all is the Heil Hitler, which looks singularly aggressive and is a sign that those giving the salute are willing to protect the person they are saluting. The origins of this salute go back to the Indian Abhava gesture of protection associated with Shiva. When Hitler's legions faced him with upraised arms, they

Italian Fascists salute as Hitler leaves Italy, 1934. Notice the range in the height of salutes. The Library of Congress.

were pledging to fight for him and to protect him. Again we find that the higher in the hierarchy—as with gestures in the Catholic Church—the smaller the actual salute. Hitler's closest associates barely flipped him a "Heil," and Hitler's Heil was perfunctory at best.

Not all power gestures require you to be front and center stage. There are also effective ways to wield power through *passive* power gestures. Engaging in grooming behavior when someone else is talking is a fine way to intimate that you are not riveted by what is being said. At its most discreet level such grooming might include lint picking, nail buffing, nail cleaning, and manicuring. The more personal the grooming behavior, the more insulting it is. Suit adjusting, "two-blocking" the tie, and cuff straightening are relatively mild. Using a tooth pick or applying lipstick is less discreet, as is brushing your hair. Using a matchstick to clean the wax out of your ears is a pretty strong statement. This is your way to keep those boring speakers under control, but it may be going too far.

Another sign of overt restlessness is timekeeping. Dorothy Parker felt that the ugliest gesture on earth was a man checking his watch. It is equally unattractive in a woman. Checking your watch, especially if it needs two hands to activate, is a superb insult. It has lost some of its bite now that these electronic marvels have fallen in price until they are in the range of almost everyone.

If all else fails to catch the speaker's attention, try drumming your fingers. You can also use your finger power to operate a pocket calculator or a cassette recorder. Nothing unnerves a speaker so much as seeing someone in the audience checking the speaker's figures on a calculator, or, even worse, pointedly turn *off* a tape recorder just as the main point is coming up. The calculator is not a power tool for the top executive. It is found instead in the hands of middle-level employees—the treasurer, the bookkeeper accountant, the office manager. These are just the kind of people who most resent the hot-doggers up on the speaker's podium. We remember one man, a product director at one company, who carried a calculator in a case with a noisy Velcro strip. At crucial points in the boss's presentation, rrrr-iii-ppp, out would come the calculator, just to run up a few figures. After the calculations were over, the machine would be fastidiously put to bed, only to reappear a few minutes later with another rrr-iii-ppp. Everyone was terrorized by him and no one dared fire him just in case he decided to reveal whatever those figures were he was working on.

The judicious note-taker can also wield power from his or her spot in the audience. Small note cards tucked into a pocket are preferable to a large notebook. Each card can be taken out separately, no more than two words written on it, and then reinserted, a process that will drive everyone mad. This implies that you need no more than a brief notation to remember everything that was said. The corresponding secretary who is taking detailed notes on a yellow legal pad has no power at all. The secretary is merely a scribe. You are a critic.

For those of you who are not above deception, might we

suggest the fake pocket secretary, a small beeper that you can activate yourself at opportune moments during the meeting. Leave the room as if to call in. Return to the room looking distracted, slightly worried. Beep yourself again, leave the room, and this time return looking positively delighted. Everyone will think you've just acquired General Motors. Even more deceitful, beep yourself again and this time choose not to answer the beep. Everyone will be listening now for the next beep, and you can sit back resting in the sure knowledge that there won't *be* another call. You are now the center of attention, widely admired, well recognized by your frequent trips in and out of the room—and the speaker will have been entirely forgotten.

The person who uses a fake beeper will probably also write a few words on a note card and send his or her secretary out of the room with it. Two power seekers can play this same game by passing a note across the table. Both of you must be able to take this seriously—no overreacting, no giggling, no nonsense. Take a brief look at the note and give your co-conspirator a single solemn nod. That's all.

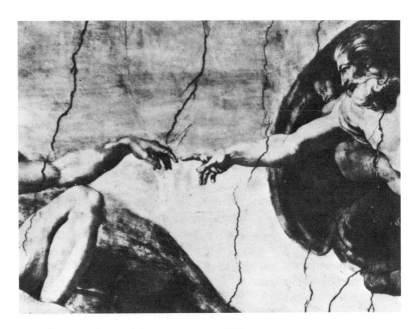

6/ The Touch Test

For touch,
Touch, by the holy powers of the Gods!
Is the sense of the body.

De Rerum Natura, Lucretius

The idea that it was desirable, even necessary, to encourage people to touch each other has been with us in America only since the early 1960's. Until that point, touching was subject to more restrictions than was international trade. One could briefly touch a person's hand during a formal introduction, and then with gloves on. One never touched a person in public above or below certain points. At a formal dance the placement of the hands was carefully prescribed. We were

told "a gentlemen never . . . a lady never . . ." until almost all desire
to touch another person had been squelched. We were even instructed
that "too much" handling of babies "spoiled" them.

It wasn't until the results of Harry F. Harlowe's ground-
breaking experiments on infant monkeys were published in 1958 that
the subject of touching—especially the warm comfort of a mother's
touch—was discussed accurately and scientifically. Briefly, what
Harlowe did was supply newborn monkeys with two surrogate mothers, one warmed with a light bulb and covered with fuzzy terry cloth,
the other merely a bare wire frame. The monkeys were divided into
two groups, one given a nursing cloth mother, the other given a
nursing wire-framed mother. What Harlowe found was that the
monkeys fed from the wire-framed "mothers" spent only enough
time on those wire frames to stay alive. The rest of the time they
spent clinging to the comforting cloth-covered "mothers." Harlowe
wrote of the experiment: "We were not surprised to discover that
contact comfort was an important basic affectional or love variable,
but we did not expect it to overshadow so completely the variable of
nursing."[1]

Although Harlowe was surprised by this finding in 1958, it
seems so obvious to us today we are a bit confounded at those early
scientists' thickness. Couldn't they see the obvious? Touching is
good. Babies need touch, and without it they will die. The more love
and affection available to people, the better off they are. These
beliefs are part of the 1970's credo, the product of the Human
Potential Movement, Primal Scream Therapy, all of the movements
of the 1960's known as the "touch-feelies," the belief that natural
childbirth and the Leboyer method of delivery put a child in touch
with his or her surroundings. But none of these things was generally
understood before Harlowe (and before him, Spitz) began testing
just what part touch played in our lives.

Unfortunately, the way we feel about our own bodies and
about being in contact with other bodies is deeply ingrained in our
self-perception. That is why many of us must submit ourselves to
marathon weekends, therapy, encounter sessions, childbirth classes,

compulsive self-help book reading. We are desperately trying to revise rock-bound feelings about "the most personally experienced of all sensations," our sense of touch.

We would like you to take the following Touch Test. Don't worry about getting right or wrong answers; there are none. What we are trying to help you find out is what you really feel about touching and being touched. You may be surprised to see your score and your answers. Once you know what your score is, you may be better equipped to decide if you want to change.

Mark your answers on a sheet of paper numbered 1 through 17. If, as you answer a question, you feel you need to explain your answer, please do so. Note: if you feel that more than one answer applies, *write down more than one.*

For those of you who routinely skip the instructions, here they are again: you may mark more than one answer if you feel that more than one answer applies.

Remember, there are no right or wrong answers.

1. When visiting your parents do you
A. Hug or kiss them on arrival and parting, but not at other times during your visit?
B. Hug or kiss them frequently and freely throughout your visit?
C. Hug or kiss only your father but not your mother?
D. Hug or kiss only your mother but not your father?
E. Not hug or kiss either your mother or your father?

2. Referring back to question 1, do you
A. Take their hands from time to time?
B. Ever stroke or pat their faces?
C. Ever put an arm around their shoulders?
D. Usually keep them at arm's length, except for when you greet them or part from them?
E. Do none of the above?

3. At work or in public do you touch people when giving them instructions or asking them questions?
A. Often
B. Sometimes
C. Only those of the same sex
D. Only those of the opposite sex
E. Never

4. Has a boss, teacher, or authority figure ever made you feel uncomfortable by touching you in one of these places?
A. Top of the head
B. Shoulder or arm
C. Back
D. Posterior
E. Leg or knee
F. No

5. When walking with an amorous companion do you usually
A. Walk arm in arm?
B. Walk hand in hand?
C. Walk shoulder to shoulder?
D. Walk with arms around each other?
E. Not touch?

6. When in bed with a sex partner do you usually
A. Roll over and face away from him or her, without touching?
B. Snuggle into the "spoons" position? [See illustration]
C. Curl up alongside, resting your arm over some part of his or her body?
D. Rest your head against your lover's head or shoulder?
E. Sleep side by side without touching?
F. Prefer separate beds?

7. Do you often
A. Shred paper, crumple it, or roll it between your fingers?
B. Play with your hair, nose, or chin?

C. Pick lint off clothes?

D. Caress and enjoy your body when you are alone?

E. None of the above?

8. Do you think a crying baby should be

A. Picked up?

B. Left to "cry it out" until it is time for the next scheduled feeding, changing, etc?

C. Picked up at some times and left to "cry it out" at others?

9. Have you ever

A. Asked someone to hold you?

B. Told a person he or she was holding you or touching you the wrong way?

C. Told a person with whom you were intimate *not* to touch you?

D. Touched a person when you didn't know what to say or couldn't express what you were feeling in words?

E. Not touched a person when you wanted to because you knew *they* didn't want to be touched?

The Spoons Position

10. In an intimate relationship, how important is cuddling?
A. More important than sex
B. As important as sex
C. Not as important as other things, like compatibility, shared interests, good conversation, and so on
D. Less important than sex

11. When with a friend on a quiet street do you talk
A. Face to face, sometimes touching, less than two feet apart?
B. Face to face, not touching, less than two feet apart?
C. Face to face, sometimes touching, less than a foot apart?
D. Standing side by side?
E. Further than two feet apart (further than touching distance apart)?

12. Have you ever experienced a special thrill, a feeling of electricity, when someone touched you?
A. Yes
B. No
C. Not sure

13. Have you ever
A. Read an instruction book on giving massages?
B. Had a professional massage?
C. Given a massage that was not a prelude to sex?
D. Given a massage to a stranger?
E. Not reciprocated a massage when you knew it was expected?

14. In your main love relationship, do you
A. Touch your partner more than your partner touches you?
B. Touch your partner less than your partner touches you?
C. Touch each other about the same number of times?

15. Do you cry easily?

A. Yes
B. No
C. Sometimes
D. Only if no one is watching
E. It doesn't matter if someone is watching

16. Do you consider yourself

A. A toucher?
B. A nontoucher?
C. A toucher or a nontoucher depending on the people you are with and the circumstances?

17. Were your parents touchers?

A. Yes
B. No
C. Only my mother
D. Only my father

As you were answering the questions, you may have found yourself thinking about the subject of touch for the first time. You may have thought that you didn't touch enough, or that you touched too much. You may have been thinking about the way your parents touched you, or you touched your own children. If that is all the test does, it will have already served its function.

Before we go on with the scoring, you may want to take a moment out to hug your pet or child, your lover, your pillow, or yourself. Don't feel inhibited about it. There's nothing wrong with it. Do you feel better? Let's begin.

Scoring for women: (You will notice that there are two different scales, one for women and one for men. This may seem sexist, but we are simply being realistic. In our society there is still a clear difference between men and women insofar as when, where, how, and why they touch.)

1. If you marked ____, give yourself ____ points.

A	+7
B	+10
C	+2
D	+4
E	−2

2. If you marked ____, give yourself ____ points.

A	+2
B	+3
C	+2
D	0
E	0

(If you marked 1E and 2D or 2E, take away 5 points. If you marked 2A, 2B, and 2C, award yourself 2 bonus points.)

3. If you marked ____, give yourself ____ points.

A	+6
B	+3
C	+2
D	0
E	−3

4. If you marked ____, give yourself ____ points.

A	−1	
B	−2	
C	−4	
D	+4	
E	+3	for outside of leg or knee
	+5	for inside of leg or knee
F	+5	

5. If you marked ____, give yourself ____ points.

A	+3
B	+3
C	+3
D	+3
E	−5

(Add a 3-point bonus for marking A, B, C, and D. Add a 2-point bonus for marking three of the four.)

6. If you marked ____, give yourself ____ points.

A	−2
B	+3
C	+3
D	+3
E	0
F	−3

(Add a 3-point bonus for answering B, C, *and* D.
Note: If you marked F and *you* are the one who gets up and goes back to her own bed, subtract 7 points. Add two points if you initiated the encounter.)

7. If you marked ____, give yourself ____ points.

A	+1
B	+1
C	+1
D	+1
E	0

(Score a bonus of 3 for A, B, *and* D. Score a bonus of 4 for A, B, C, and D. If you marked C, however, and only pick lint off others, subtract 1 point for unaesthetic possessiveness, invasion of territory, and using a touching substitute.)

8. If you marked ____, give yourself ____ points.

A	+5
B	+1
C	+3

9. If you marked _____, give yourself _____ points.

A	+2
B	+2
C	+2
D	+1
E	+3

(If you didn't mark D, subtract 5 points. If you marked A, B, C, D, *and* E, give yourself 5 extra points. In regard to question E: If you went ahead and touched someone who you knew didn't want to be touched, if that person was a man, and if you were right to touch him at that point, give yourself 3 extra points. If that person was a woman, and if you were right to touch her at that point, score 4 extra points.)

10. If you marked _____, give yourself _____ points.

A	+6
B	+6
C	+2
D	0

11. If you marked _____, give yourself _____ points.

A	+3
B	+1
C	+4
D	−1
E	−2

12. If you marked _____, give yourself _____ points.

A	+3
B	−5
C	−20

13. If you marked _____, give yourself _____ points.

A	+1
B	+4
C	+2
D	+4
E	0

(If you marked A, B, C, *and* D, give yourself 3 extra points. If you marked E, but gave the person in question a verbal rain check, give yourself 1 point for awareness. If you answered E, but simply left the person hanging, subtract 3 points for mental and physical cruelty.)

14. If you marked ____, give yourself ____ points.

A	+6
B	0
C	+4

(If you answered C and you consider both of you touchers, give yourself 4 extra points for choosing a touching partner. If you answered C and you consider both of you nontouchers, penalize yourself 8 points.

Reality check: If you have marked A and your partner disagrees, subtract 4 points. If you marked B and your partner disagrees, give yourself 5 extra points—4 for touching and 1 for not knowing it. If you have marked C and your partner disagrees, subtract 2 points for being with a tactless person.)

15. If you marked ____, give yourself ____ points.

A	+4
B	−6
C	+1
D	+1
E	+6

(Questions 16 and 17 concern background and self-perception and are not to be scored.)

Scoring for men:

1. If you marked ____, give yourself ____ points.

A	+7
B	+10
C	+4
D	+6
E	+2

2. If you marked _____, give yourself _____ points.

A	+2
B	+2
C	+1
D	0
E	−2

(If you have marked A, B, *and* C, give yourself 2 extra points. If you have marked 1E and 2D or 2E, take away 5 points.)

3. If you marked _____, give yourself _____ points.

A	+6	
B	+3	
C	+3	
D	0	(that's not touching, it's lechery)
E	0	

4. If you marked _____, give yourself _____ points.

A	0
B	−2
C	−4
D	+3
E	+1
F	+4

(On answer E, if it was the inside of the leg or knee, give yourself another point.)

5. If you marked _____, give yourself _____ points.

A	+3
B	+3
C	+3
D	+3
E	−5

(If you marked three out of A, B, C, and D, give yourself 5 extra points. If you marked all four, A, B, C, *and* D, give yourself 7 bonus points.)

6. If you marked _____, give yourself _____ points.

A	−1
B	+3

C	+3
D	+3
E	0
F	−3

(If you marked B, C, *and* D, give yourself 3 extra points.)

7. If you marked _____, give yourself _____ points.

A	+1
B	+1
C	+1
D	+1
E	0

(If you marked A, B, C, and D, give yourself 4 bonus points. If you marked A, B, and D, give yourself 3 bonus points. Plus, if you marked D, give yourself 1 more bonus point for not being put off by the word "caress.")

8. If you marked _____, give yourself _____ points.

A	+5
B	+1
C	+3

(If you marked A and pick the baby up yourself, give yourself 5 extra points.)

9. If you marked _____, give yourself _____ points.

A	+3
B	+3
C	+3
D	+1
E	+3

(If you marked all five, A, B, C, D, and E, give yourself 5 extra points. If you did *not* mark D, *subtract* 5 points from your score.)

10. If you marked _____, give yourself _____ points.

A	+10
B	+6
C	+2
D	0

(If you marked A and are over 40, subtract 5 points. If you marked A and are under 10 years old, add 10 points.)

11. If you marked ____, give yourself ____ points.

A	+3
B	+1
C	+4
D	−1
E	−2

12. If you marked ____, give yourself ____ points.

A	+3
B	−5
C	−20

13. If you marked ____, give yourself ____ points.

A	+1
B	+2
C	+6
D	+4
E	0

(If you marked A, B, C, *and* D, give yourself 3 extra points. If you marked E but gave the person in question a verbal rain check, give yourself 2 points for awareness and verbalization. If you answered E but simply left the person hanging, subtract 3 points for mental and physical cruelty.)

14. If you marked ____, give yourself ____ points.

A	+8
B	0
C	+4

(If you marked C and you consider both of you touchers, give yourself 4 extra points for choosing a toucher for a partner. If you marked C and you consider both of you nontouchers, subtract 8 points.
Reality check: If you have marked A and your partner disagrees, subtract 5 points. If you marked B and your partner disagrees, give yourself 6 extra points. If you have marked C and your partner disagrees, subtract 4 points for being with a tactless person.)

15. If you marked ____, give yourself ____ points.

A	+10
B	0
C	+5
D	+4
E	+12

(Questions 16 and 17 concern background and self-perception and are not to be scored.)

Okay, everybody add up your scores and let's see what category you fall into.

0–25   You, friend, are a nontoucher. You may have been dropped as a baby. You undoubtedly feel uncomfortable in many social situations and you probably avoid crowds.

26–49   You are reserved in your touching and think of yourself as "formal." Other people almost always initiate physical contact with you—in handshakes, hugs, and so on—while you merely respond. People like you who are formal and somewhat physically reserved can get along beautifully in everyday life, especially if you are a "good talker" and are quick to respond verbally.

50–70   You are the outgoing type. You initiate contact with others instead of waiting for them to move first. Others probably regard you as friendly and social. If you scored 60 or above, you might be considered leadership material or someone with social ambitions. You are sensitive and thoughtful.

71–85   Howdy. To get a score in this range you have to have had either a childhood devoid of love and affection (and are now trying to make up for it) or a childhood filled with love and affection. It is important for you to be with people who respond to your physical warmth. Don't become self-conscious about your physicality; just give other people a little time to catch up to you. You can bring them along. You are a good teacher, so you know what we are talking about.

Over 85   Gang busters! You didn't need this test to tell you that you are Super-Toucher. If you scored above 105 you might consider taking up meditation or some other form of relaxation. You probably worry about being too emotional. Don't let other people's opinions bother you. You are (we feel sure) a happy person. To be completely happy, however, you need to find a partner toucher. Don't consider anyone who scores under 40. You will never be happy again. (Unless the person is so special, of course, that you are willing to go through life missing warmth and comfort for him or her.) If you scored over 115 you might try to find an outlet for your skin hunger. Have you considered taking up a regular contact sport? Buying a dog? Moving in with someone?

In designing the Touch Test we wanted to delve into several areas—your ability to talk about feelings, your relationships with parents and lovers, your self-perceptiveness, and so on. Briefly, we would like to describe what each of the preceding questions told us about you, and give you an idea how a sampling of 70 people answered the questions.

Questions 1 and 2 asked about your behavior with your parents—*how often* you touched them and *how* you touched them. Most people, 58% of the men and 63% of the women, hugged and kissed their parents on arrival and on parting. Another significant number hugged and kissed them frequently during their visits—16% of the men and 30% of the women. Twenty-two percent of the men reported hugging only their mothers but not their fathers, while a mere 4% of the women hugged only their mothers. By far, the largest number of respondents kept their parents at arm's length, except for greeting and parting shows of affection. Men and women reported about the same frequency of taking their parents' hands. Twice as many men as women said they sometimes put an arm around their parents' shoulders. Only a small minority of respondents reported touching their parents' faces. (The face is, it seems, an intimate part of the body—much more intimate than the hands or shoulders.)

On question 3 we asked how often you touched other people in public. Men and women reported almost the same, with slightly

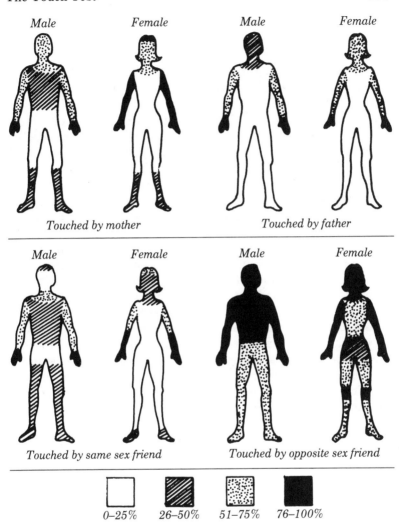

Jourard's study of how frequently and where we touch each other, inside and outside the family. Notice that we wear white "Long Johns," forbidden touching zones, with our mothers and fathers. After Jourard

more women than men saying they touched people "often." On one answer, though, there were significantly more men (21%) than women (4%). This was answer D, "only those of the opposite sex." Two men who gave this reply further commented that they worried about being considered "forward," "out of place," and possibly gay if they touched other men.

On question 4 we were trying to find out if you were a "touchy" person, someone who felt uncomfortable being touched on a "public" part of your body—the shoulder or the back, responses B and C. First of all, 58% of the men and 44% of the women reported they had *never* felt uncomfortable by being touched in one of the areas we listed. But, surprisingly, more men than women reported being uncomfortable on being touched on the shoulder or arm (men, 26%; women, 15%) and on the back (men, 26%; women, 11%). In the "private" areas—posterior and leg—women were more likely than men to report having been made to feel uncomfortable (women, 15% and 19%; men, 0% and 5%). Obviously you did not lose points for reporting that you had felt uncomfortable when someone touched you on a "private" part of your body, nor did you lose points for saying that you had not ever felt uncomfortable. Those of you who answered that you had felt uncomfortable when someone touched you on the arm or back may think our question unfair because the particular person who touched you was "creepy" or was making an egregious pass and *that* was the reason you felt uncomfortable. Perhaps so, but what interests us is that you have a strong body memory of just *where* that person touched you. One woman described the event—her boss had patted her on top of the head—as making her feel exactly like a dog.

About question 5, walking with an amorous companion: 37% of the men and 19% of the women reported not touching at all (the men and women in our sample were apparently not walking together). Almost the same numbers of men and women reported walking with arms around each other (58%) and hand in hand (63%). More men than women reported walking "shoulder to shoulder" and more women than men (women, 70%; men, 52%) reported walking arm in arm. We suspect that the arm-in-armers were of an older generation. The practice has sadly gone somewhat out of fashion.

Let's talk about your sleep habits. The same number of men and women, about a quarter of those who answered question 6, said they sometimes "rolled over and faced away from their partners." Another quarter answered that they slept side by side without touching. One man who considered himself a toucher revealed that he simply could not go to sleep if his partner was touching him or even was on his side of the bed. "Spoons" was a big favorite, getting the vote of 70% of the women and 63% of the men. Men seem to have less fondness for the position because in the usual organization (woman in front, man behind) the man sleeps with a face full of her hair and a paralyzed arm. More women than men (70% to 58%) reported throwing an arm over their partner's body. More men than women reported resting their heads on their partner's shoulder (63% of the men, 52% of the women). No one said that he or she preferred separate beds. Since the sales of these beds continue, we wonder if this answer was given truthfully.

Question 7 concerned touch substitutes. It seemed to us to be a harmless question. Little did we know that people would feel compelled to tell us their most intimate secrets, as if the mention of crumpled paper and hair touching was a Proustian excuse to recall other touch associations. First the results: Men and women seemed to answer each question in equal numbers except for C, which referred to picking lint off clothes. Twenty-two percent of the women said they picked lint; *none* of the men did. Men apparently took this question to mean picking lint off their partners' clothes, something they thought would insult any woman they were with. Women, on the other hand, see picking lint off a man's clothes as a way of showing they care.

Now for the comments: On lint picking we received this from a young Canadian girl: "I used to be fascinated by the lint in my mother's boyfriends' belly buttons and would often check [to see if it was there] so I could pick it."

A young man reported: "I don't pick lint, but ever since I was

a little boy I have picked the pills, the little fuzz balls, off blankets, put them between my lips, and rolled them into larger balls. I have already reduced several blankets to gauze."

On playing with the hair: "I had a roommate in college who, as a nervous habit, pulled hairs from the top of his head while he was studying. He would run the hairs through his teeth and then roll them into a wad and throw them under his bed, all without realizing it. At the end of his first year at school he discovered he was going bald and worried about it until I told him what he had been doing. He didn't believe me until I showed him the pile of hair balls under his bed."

And we received this comment in general: "I also pick my nose and roll the 'boogies' frequently, play with my navel, chew my nails, pick my teeth, and chew what I can reach of my moustache." You may not be happy to know that this man said he worked as a waiter.

Men and women gave almost the same answers about crying babies, question 8. A third thought they should be picked up and two-thirds thought they should be picked up sometimes but other times be left to cry it out. Obviously there were many variables on people's minds when they answered this question: their own experiences raising children, babies that might be colicky, babies of different ages and temperaments. What concerned us was that someone would answer that the baby should always be left to cry it out and sure enough one person, a man, gave this answer.

Some comments made by Burton L. White in his book *The First Three Years of Life* are interesting in connection with this question. Dr. White writes: "If [your baby's] cries are met with promptly, it seems to me reasonable that he would accumulate one kind of relatively desirable expectation about the degree of caring from the world around him. If on the other hand he is routinely not responded to (allowed to 'cry it out') I would expect that he would accumulate an importantly different set of expectations." Then later Dr. White says: "Infants brought up in institutions cry less and less as their first year of life proceeds. They seem to learn (at some primitive level) that crying usually produces nothing but fatigue. Home-reared infants whose cries are ordinarily responded to quickly do continue to cry more than institutionally reared infants, *but not as much as home-reared babies whose cries are responded to inconsistently.*"[2] (Our emphasis) In other words, the babies who were sometimes picked up and sometimes left to cry it out (the answer that two-thirds of our respondents gave) would be expected to cry more than the babies who were *always* picked up or were *always* left to cry it out.

Now on to question 9, the sensitivity question. Nearly twice as many women as men have asked to be held, and women were much more likely to have told their partners that they were being held the wrong way. Fifty-two percent of the women had told their partners not to touch them; 37% of the men had done likewise. One man may have been speaking for all men when he said that he worried about telling a woman she was touching him the wrong way because it would hurt her feelings. Over 80% of both men and women used touch when they couldn't think of what to say. That one quality about touch, its ability to communicate and comfort without words, is the whole point of this chapter. How often have we kept our emotions under control until someone touched us on the shoulder, and *only then* did we burst into tears?

Men, apparently, found it easier *not to* touch a person who didn't want to be touched than did women (men, 84%; women, 63%). These results suggest that men, because they tended to be non-touchers, found it easier to refrain from touching while women, because they tended to be touchers, found it harder to refrain from touching.

On the cuddling versus sex question (question 10) the results confirmed many recent studies that state that women often use sex as a way to get men to hold them. The same is not often true for men: five times as many women as men felt that cuddling was more important than sex. Almost twice as many men as women claimed that sex was more important than cuddling. The majority of men and women, however, ranked cuddling and sex as equals. We received several comments on this question, all of them from men. The sentiments were almost uniform: "It depends on the attributes of the lady in question."

With question 11 we were trying to find out what you knew about your "personal distance zone," the phrase invented by Dr. Edward T. Hall in his revolutionary study of people's use of the space around them. Dr. Hall outlined four categories: intimate (direct contact to between six and eighteen inches), personal (one and one-half to two and one-half feet), social (four to twelve feet), and public (twelve to fifteen feet).[3] In response to our questionnaire, 47% of the men said they stood less than two feet apart, sometimes touching, 32% said less than a foot apart, sometimes touching, and 21% said they stood further than two feet apart. The women's answers were 52% sometimes touching, less than two feet apart, 26% not touching, less than two feet apart, 15% sometimes touching less than a foot apart, and 11% more than two feet apart (some women marked several answers). What is interesting here is that twice the number of men as women claimed they stood less than a foot apart when talking to someone on the street. This is the distance that Hall calls intimate, and it is reserved for family and lovers. Perhaps these people who answered less than a foot apart had no idea just how close that is. Take a foot ruler and hold it between you and another person to get an idea of what intimate distance really means. Twenty-two percent of the respondents overall said they stood less than a foot apart. It is interesting to note that in breaking the figures down we found that 36% of the Jews answering our questionnaire said they stood less than a foot apart, therefore echoing, if only in self-perception, Efron and Hall's generalization that Jews stand closer together than WASP's and WASC's.

Men and women were nearly unanimous about having felt a "special thrill" at least once in their lives when someone touched them (question 12). For those who had not had this moment we awarded a 5-point penalty, but for those who weren't sure (how could you not be sure, we wondered) we took off a full 20 points.

For question 13, men seem to have been more interested

than women in massage, more of them having read books on the subject (by a small margin, 32% to 26%) and more of them having had professional massages (58% to 48%). Women, on the other hand, were more likely to have given a massage that was not a prelude to sex (women, 78%; men, 63%) yet slightly more women than men had also not reciprocated a back rub when it was expected of them (women, 19%; men, 16%). Our personal feeling is that an unreciprocated back rub should become grounds for divorce. Significantly more men than women had given a massage to a stranger (42% to 22%). As one man said, "It's a great way to meet girls."

How much do you touch your lover and how much does your lover touch you was the subject of question 14. Thirty-seven percent of the women felt they touched more often than their partners; 11% of the men felt *they* touched more often than their partners. Eleven percent of the men confessed to touching less than their partners and 19% of the women said the same. Most of the men were politic in their answers, 79% saying that they and their partners touched each other about the same, while less than half of the women (44%) felt that answer was true for them.

One might suggest that women do touch their men more often than the men touch their women. Let's quote Phyllis Chessler on the subject: "Psyche, an early prefiguration of the Catholic Madonna, embodies certain traits possessed by many women today. I am talking about female romanticism, tenderness, compassion and altruism. These traits are not devalued by either men or women. However, men benefit from such traits, almost exclusively, and reward them rather poorly."[4] It might be mentioned that men who are courting women touch them more frequently than they in turn are touched, but that once the two are living together or married it is the woman who touches more than the man. Men, unfortunately, often touch their women only when they want to make love to them.

As an experiment, for the next few days try to keep track of when and how you touch your partner and when and how your partner touches you. Then sit down and talk about the results. You mustn't go too far and start keeping track compulsively of who touches whom more often. There are days, weeks, even months when one person will need to touch more than the other. Touching can't be measured in ergs or numbers. All this record is meant to do is to make you more aware of what should be a vital resource in your relationship.

We added question 15 regarding crying to test our theory that people who cry easily are the same people who touch a lot. We tried to overvalue the men's scale for crying easily on the assumption that it would be much harder for men to admit that they cried. As it turned out, only one man said he cried "no matter who was watching."

In answer to question 16, exactly the same number of men and women considered themselves to be touchers—26%. More men put themselves in the category of nontouchers than did women (11% to 7%) which left the majority of people saying that they touched sometimes and sometimes did not touch, depending on the circumstances. Why don't you ask your friends whether they consider you a toucher, a nontoucher, or a little bit of both and listen to what they say. Their answers might surprise you.

In answer to the last question, 59% of the women and 47% of the men said that their parents were *not* touchers. Only 11% of the men and 15% of the women said that *both* parents were touchers. When asked if just their mothers were the touchers in the family, however, a surprising 42% of the men said yes, while only 7% of the women responded similarly. Did these sons just *think* of their mothers as being touchers? Or did the mothers actually touch their sons more. No men remembered their fathers as being the only toucher in the family, and only two women said that their fathers were the touchers. One of these two—a 25-year-old—explained: "He still likes for me to sit on his lap."

It would be interesting to ask the parents of these respondents how often they touched their children. We believe that children are touched more often than they remember, but less often than their parents think. Children have an almost endless need for touches, hugs, embraces, pats, squeezes, and strokes, in addition to the kinds of touch involved in getting a child dressed in the morning and getting his or her face wiped clean. The old saw about "Have you hugged your child today" is worth repeating and thinking about.

As questions 16 and 17 were included as guides to self-perception and not included in your scores, now is the time to consider your answers to these two questions in relation to your overall test scores.

In our informal survey we asked people to tell us their age, sex, marital status, nationality, and religion. Some of the results were so tantalizing that we could only wish the survey could have been larger and we could have asked additional questions. We wonder, for instance, if people who touch a lot have sexual intercourse more frequently than people who don't touch. Or, contrarily, perhaps people who are "touchers" have their touch-quotient satisfied without sex.

You might be interested to know that our top scorers in the men's and women's division were both Jewish, echoing Ashley Montagu's statement that "among Jews tactility is highly developed ... [they] tend to be tactually very demonstrative." The woman's score was 100 and the (heterosexual) man's a thumping 92. We have awarded these two our silver palm with a pointing finger, engraved with their scores. Our low scorer, a Protestant (Anglican) man who called himself a nontoucher, turned in a 22. By religion we found that the highest scorers were Jewish. Catholics were next. Those who touched least frequently identified themselves as some form of Protestant (the lowest scorers favoring the old Church of England).

In a separate category we must mention a 27-year-old gay male, with an Italian Catholic mother and a Russian Jewish father, who scored an astonishing 138. Needless to say, he considers himself a toucher. His largest single coup in collecting points was on the question, "Do you cry easily?" His answer: Yes and I don't care if anyone's watching. Plus 22.

7/ The Healing Hand

Part One/The Need for Touch

"The gods hear men's hands before their lips."

Algernon Swinburne

In the last chapter we asked you to consider whether you were a toucher or not. Perhaps it is time to talk about what touch means to us. Anna Freud writes, in *Normality and Pathology in Childhood*: "Being stroked, cuddled, and soothed by touch libidinizes the various

184

parts of the child's body, helps to build up a healthy body image and body ego, increases its cathexis with narcissistic libido, and simultaneously promotes the development of object love by cementing the bond between child and mother."[1] Making an even stronger claim for touching, Ashley Montagu says, in his book *Touching: The Human Significance of Skin*: "Hand-stroking is to the young of the human species virtually as important a form of experience as licking is to the young of other mammals."[2] Montagu then goes on to prove that mammals such as mice, rats, dogs (oddly, especially chihuahuas), and cats must be licked when they are newborn or they will fail to rally, process their food, and take hold of life. Even the rate of licking or stroking seems genetically predetermined: for baby rats, 6 to 7 times a second; for baby cats, 3 to 4 times a second; and for baby humans, according to Dr. William Greene, Jr.: at "approximately the mother's and/or baby's cardiac rate," which would be from 70 (for the mother) to 140 (for the baby) beats per minute, or between 1 and 2.3 times a second. For human babies the rate of the stroking or patting must be a calming reminder of the rate of the heartbeat in utero.[3]

Luckily for the human race, most babies inspire in us the urge to touch, stroke, pat, fondle, kiss, hug, groom, wipe, tend, lick, and snuggle them. But what if the baby *doesn't* want to be touched? Children can stiffen their bodies at an approaching hand, not give in to a hug, not allow themselves to be hoisted in the air. Their body language is clear; an insensitive adult would disobey at his or her own peril and to the accompaniment of outraged cries.

In "The Kids with the Faraway Eyes," an article about autistic children in *Rolling Stone*, Donald R. Katz writes: "Mothers often notice that their babies don't seem to want them; they go limp in their arms or hate to be touched."[4] The autistic child is the extreme of the child who occasionally shrugs off physical contact with others. The autistic child retreats entirely from the outside world, from the world of touching and being touched. He or she is tragically immune to any form of communication, totally "out of touch." Some attempts have been made (occasionally successful) to bring these autistic children back through the use of constructive, rewarding, insistently loving touch. For an idea of what autistic children go through in their contactless world, consider the results of sensory deprivation experiments in which volunteers are kept suspended in darkened, silent rooms so as to receive almost no skin sensations. The volunteers soon have psychotic-like episodes of disorientation, sometimes so severe that the experiments were discontinued so as not to risk permanent psychosis. For the autistic child, or for the laboratory subject in artificial isolation, the lack of contact with the rest of the physical world is a tragic condition.

We need to be touched and stroked from birth onward or we sicken and die; we need to be stroked and cuddled as children or our libidos fail to develop; we need to sense the outside world through our skins or we will go mad. Young parents are at the apotheosis of their careers as touchers; they touch their children and each other most freely. All too soon the inevitable barriers of separation, of the children's first pulling away and then leaving home, of the couple's sexual interest in each other changing, will leave them with less and less outlet for their need to touch. This is not always the case, of course. Some families continue being close and are always physically affectionate with each other. What does seem to be true, though, is that once the touch connection is broken, it is very hard ever to be as close again.

Sometimes, as parent becomes doting grandparent, there are renewed opportunities to touch. At other times, pets are brought into the home and lavished with the extra attention they might not have otherwise enjoyed. As Desmond Morris said in *The Naked Ape*: "Our naked skin may not send out very exciting signals, but other more stimulating surfaces are frequently available and are used as substitutes. Fluffy or furry clothing, rugs or furniture often release a strong grooming response. Pet animals are even more inviting, and few naked apes can resist the temptation to stroke a cat's fur or scratch a pet dog behind the ear."[5]

Family Health reported that stroking a pet not only relaxed the animal, slowed his heart and respiratory rate, but also relaxed the *person doing the stroking*. It feels as good to touch as it does to be touched. The healing hand heals both ways.

Our social training, however, has encouraged us *not* to touch each other. We step aside in the streets, move to separate corners in the elevator. If we accidentally brush against someone we quickly apologize so they won't think us rude. In 1965 Argyle and Dean published a paper outlining their "equilibrium theory" of interpersonal distance. Once people have established a comfortable social distance, they will actively seek to *maintain* that distance, leaning forward if the other person leans away or compensating by talking louder, making stronger eye contact, smiling, changing body orientation, or touching.[6]

The thing that complicates the equilibrium theory is that people from different cultures have different standards of "comfortable social distance." As one person seeks to increase the distance to what feels comfortable, the other person begins to feel rejected and begins compensating. Hall gives as an example the staid Englishman who wants to converse at a distance of two and a half feet and the Italian who wants to converse at a distance of one and a half feet. As the Italian moves closer, the Englishman turns sideways (a body orientation that seems to him less threatening). The Italian, not to be put off, moves to talk to the Englishman eye to eye; the Englishman turns again. The Italian reaches out to make body contact and the Englishman feels even more "rudely" approached. Around and around they go, neither one feeling comfortable, until the conversation is finished.

Montagu talks about the reserve of the typical Englishman: "The conditioning in non-tactility received by so many Englishmen of the upper classes seems to have produced a virtual negative sanction on tactility in English culture. This was so much the case that the sense of touch and the act of touching have both been culturally defined as vulgar."[7] He is no easier on the German character: "The emphasis on warrior virtues, the supremacy of the hard-headed martinet father, and the complete subordination of the mother in the German family made for a rigidified, unbending character which renders the average German, among other things, a not very tactile being."[8]

The French, on the other hand, seem to *enjoy* touching. Montagu reports that on a crowded Metro, "passengers will lean and press against others, if not with complete abandon, at least without feeling the necessity either to ignore or apologize to the other against whom they are leaning or pressing. Often the leaning and lurching will give rise to good-natured laughter and joking, and there will be no attempt to avoid looking at the other passengers."[9]

The Italians, the French, the Spanish, the Japanese, the Greeks, the Turks are all touchers. The English, Germans, most Swiss, Dutchmen, and Nordic peoples are *not*. These cultural variations are even carried into new societies; in Canada it is found that Canadians of English origin are nontouchers and French-Canadians are touchers. There are class differences as well, with those in the upper classes touching less often than those in the lower classes. The more immobile the class structure, the more these differences remain. In America, where "class structure" is less rigid than elsewhere because of social mobility, the difference between the tactility of the upper class and the tactility of the lower class may be slight. There remains, however, an idea that touching is "undignified," "rude," "vulgar," "pushy," "lecherous," "seductive," and "creepy," and nontouching, while "cold," "distant," and perhaps "stiff," is also thought of as "regal," "formal," and "proper."

Sensitivity to touch and to feeling "crowded," though based on highly individual values, is influenced most by your family, and, by extension, by the values of your culture. There may be, in addition, a biological or unknown personal factor involved. Studies have shown that inmates with a history of violent crimes, when tested on comfortable personal distance, felt that the interviewer was "up in their faces" and "crowding them" at distances normally considered unthreatening. Whether this feeling of needing extra room was a result of their scrapes with the law, or perhaps a cause of it, has remained so far unknown. Some studies have indicated that "anti-social" types sat farther away during interviews than those who felt socially comfortable in general. Other tests have indicated that it is possible to categorize babies at birth into three groups: outwardly directed, in between, and inwardly directed. These three categories are apparently recognizable throughout the child's growing years and correlate to physical ease in touching and being touched.

A 1977 study by Brittain in the *Human Ecology Forum*, entitled "Perceiving through the Body," revealed that a clear division occurred at 12 years of age between haptic types—those who reacted to the world in a body sense—and visual types. Brittain quotes Lowenfeld's study of 1,128 subjects, which gave the following statistics: 47% of the people were classified as "clearly visual," 23% were "clearly haptic" and 30% were mixed. "The haptic type," Brittain writes, "utilizes muscular sensation, kinesthetic experiences, touch impressions and all experiences of the self to establish his relationship to the outside world . . . the haptic person enjoys textures and feels objects pleasurably with his hands."[10] It is interesting to note that Lowenfeld's wide-ranging study reported almost the same percentage of "haptic types" (23%) as did our casual survey of self-reported touchers (26%).

Clearly there is something that makes some people touchers and other people nontouchers. And there is something that makes some people touchers at some times and nontouchers at others. The only real problem of touching–nontouching, and perhaps the reason for this chapter, is a personal one. If you have a need to be touched, and the person you love finds it hard to express himself or herself through touching, you might well feel literally unloved. It is as hard for a toucher to *stop* touching as it is for a nontoucher to *start*. A toucher might think that the nontoucher "doesn't care"; a nontoucher

Jack Stubbs, Fellowship of Christian Athletes

feels that the toucher is always "pestering" or "hanging on." A toucher may feel that the nontoucher makes skin contact only when he or she wants to make love; a nontoucher may feel that the touching partner is always ready for bed when in fact the toucher just wants to touch. Saying "I just want you to hold me" may sound like a sexual rejection to your partner rather than a statement of fact. The only answer can be that you must talk to each other, explain yourselves, and try to work it out. It helps to understand that the person you are with has needs different from your own, and that a hug from a nontoucher, though hard to come by, really means something when it is given.

Can a nontoucher change and become a toucher? If someone seems completely insensitive (as one man seemed to be whose wife complained that he gave back rubs as though he were Simonizing the car), can he or she ever *learn* to be sensitive? Is it possible to go against years, a lifetime, of training *not* to touch? The authors suspected that the answers to these questions would be no, but we asked a woman who uses her hands every day professionally in the healing trade. "It *is* possible," she said. "First of all it takes an unusual person, because they have to *want* to change. People around them have to be honest with them. They have to learn how to listen accurately with just their bodies. But people can do it. With practice they can learn to touch deeply, and sensitively."

Part Two/The Healing Professions

*Now when the sun was setting, all they that had any sick with divers
diseases brought them unto him; and he laid his hands on every one
of them, and healed them.*

Luke 4:40

*I think that's something nurses really have to stress. Touch makes the
patient feel more like a human being than anything else could. . . .
When somebody is really sick, maybe to the point of being powerless,
and I help the person to do certain things or do them myself—brush
his teeth, rinse out his mouth, shave him, wash his body off, put
lotion on his skin, put a clean gown on him, put Vaseline on his lips,
comb his hair, get him up or change his position—I feel really good.*

Peggy Anderson, Nurse

Asclepius was the Greek god of medicine, who, with his *theou cheir* or
"god hand," cured the sick and disabled and raised the dead. So
successful was he that, in the interests of population control, Zeus
eliminated him. Inevitably an Asclepian cult grew up in Epidaurus,
where the priests-physicians built a temple to him and began their
healing trade. Business flourished and the proceeds from it built the
famous theatre at Epidaurus, which can still be seen today, complete
with stone testimonials to the Asclepian powers. From the theatre at
Epidaurus to the ten million-dollar Oral Roberts University Prayer
Tower, healing with the hand has always been profitable.

Healing with the body—magic—was the first medicine known.
Powerful it was, too. One of the first miracle treatments involved the
transfer—by hand—of an illness out of a person and into a tree or
animal (preferably a goat), a practice that led to our term "scapegoat."
The magic wand was simply an extension of the already powerful
hand and was, according to Eric Maple, "identical with that of the
healing priests of antiquity, from whom it had in effect been bor-
rowed."[12] Pagan rituals employed arcane symbols that were traced

on the body by the healer's hand. Even today in Mediterranean countries Christian healers make the sign of the cross on a patient's forehead with a forefinger moistened with spittle.

Hands and the natural substances around the lowliest peasant (herbs, blood, water, mud, and for the upper classes, metals) were the entire medical supply closet of the early healers. Even when the use of surgical tools was known, most "good" doctors of the fourth century B.C. considered the use of them something entirely apart from the practice of *medicine*. The Hippocratic Oath in fact foreswore surgery. "I will not cut," they pledged, "even for the stone, but will leave such procedures to the practitioners of that craft." The practitioners of that craft—the laymen who cut people up—were *not* called *cheirourgos*, the Greek term which is the origin of our word "surgeon." To the Greeks a *cheirourgos* was a man who healed with his hands, particularly the first and the middle fingers (because they were closer to the heart) and later with the ring finger, which became known as the Physic or Healing Finger.

In Western medicine, the hand as healer would be almost entirely relegated to the mystical arts rather than the sciences. Medical science has always used the hand for diagnosis; occult science uses the hand for healing. The Old and New Testaments and Pliny all mention healing with the hand. Olaf of Norway, Philip I, kings Louis XIII through XVI of France, several English kings, and members of the Hapsburgs all practiced the Royal Touch, healing with the hands.[13] Scrofula (tuberculosis of the lymph glands of the neck) was known as the "King's Evil" because kings were called upon to heal it by the laying on of hands. Dr. Samuel Johnson was one of the last people to be brought before the throne for scrofula. He was then a child and Queen Anne reigned (the last monarch to perform the Royal Touch). The cure rate was apparently low, as Johnson bore the scars of scrofula for the rest of his life.

Cut-off hands and pieces of hands were thought to have magical healing powers. In the Middle Ages, in Transylvania, hands or fingers of dead men were considered talismans against disease and death.[14] According to Walter Sorell, "In older books we find accounts of Egyptian women wearing fingers from Christian or Jewish dead as amulets against diseases such as malaria."[15] And we can cite the ever-popular "Finger of birth-strangled babe" (recorded in Macbeth), the finger of a dead, unbaptized newborn, which was supposed to protect against any and all disease.

It was no coincidence that superstitions of all types flourished during the plague years in Europe, when even the best-trained doctors could do nothing. Although by the Middle Ages healers knew how to "set bones, extract teeth, remove bladder stones, remove cataracts of the eye with a silver needle and restore a mutilated face by skin graft from the arm,"[16] according to Barbara Tuchman, their idea for a plague cure was to fill the air with burning aromatics, to bleed patients, purge them with laxatives or enemas, apply plasters and compounds of spices, powdered pearls or emeralds. As Miss Tuchman notes: "The offensive, like the expensive, had extra value."[17]

Compared to these "cures," the waving of a magic wand or the finger of a birth-strangled babe in front of a plague sufferer was just as efficacious and more in keeping with the doctor's own pledge: "first, do no harm." As you can see, the medical sciences and the occult (healing with the hand) sciences ran about neck-and-neck in the Middle Ages. Hand healers were called "chiothetists," and were highly regarded, especially in the countryside where the city-trained medical doctors rarely ventured. In 1423, the English Guild of Physicians decided to put down their competition with a denunciation of all "Quacks and empirics and knavish men and women,"[18] in other words, the hand healers, witches, and druids. In 1540, English Parliament made it official: the only *true* healers were those who had trained at the College of Surgeons. The law began its quest against "impudent and ignorant buffoons prophets astrologers and healers."[19] One wonders how they thought to differentiate between the merely impudent and the truly ignorant, between the prophets and healers and the astrologers and buffoons. But they thought not to distinguish between them at all. Buffoon and prophet went out together, as, when you come to think of it, is often the case. No one had yet decided, of course, whether medicine was a matter of religion, philosophy, science, or magic. Everyone agreed that an analysis of the four humors had *something* to do with it. Leeches, bleedings, emetics, and torture were still considered elegant cures. And so it went.

Then in the seventeenth century that maverick, Paracelsus, a university-trained physician, said, "The universities do not teach all things, so a doctor must seek out old wives, gypsies, herb women, monks, and peasants and take lessons from them."[20] Carl Jung called Paracelsus "not only a pioner in the domains of chemical medicine, but also in those of an *empirical psychological healing science*"[21] (emphasis ours). In going to the "old wives, gypsies, herb women, monks, and peasants" Paracelsus discovered that some cures were effected not by putting something into or taking something out of the body, but by laying on the hands and talking to the patient. It was this blinding flash that gave the groundwork to the science of psychology: the idea that there were forces in the human body that could not be seen. The hand, remember, was a bridesmaid to this idea and became even more strongly wed to the psychological arts at the next stage, with the discoveries of Anton Mesmer.

Mesmer believed literally in Paracelsus's unseen body energy and set out to find it. He was another university-trained doctor, not some necromancer from the hinterland, and he conducted scientific experiments in search of "animal magnetism." A huge wood tub was filled with dilute sulfuric acid into which were plunged iron bars (thus constituting an electric cell). Patients sat in a circle around the tub, holding hands to increase the electromagnetic field. One by one the patients grabbed the iron bars to produce the cure.[22] These healing sessions were no doubt enhanced by the presence of Mesmer himself, dressed in a long purple gown and carrying a wand, which, for good measure, he touched to each person. For whatever reason, Mesmer's experiments "worked" and people were cured. All of Paris, especially the upper classes, flocked to him for treatment. (And needless to say, the local Parisian doctors immediately began proceedings, which proved successful, to have Mesmer declared a fraud.) But, as Paris Flammond wrote, "in this extraordinary compound of inductive brilliance, specific ignorance, essential confusion, slight charlatantry, and other ingredients, 'mesmerism'—the ability to introduce and implant suggestion of a mild intensity to near near total subjugation— was born."[23] The hand is once again present at and partially responsible for a gigantic leap in the practice of medicine, the scientific discovery of the power of suggestion.

Mesmer is falsely credited with having discovered hypnosis, the practice of which dates back to the Egyptians, who referred to it as "Temple Sleep." It was a pupil of Mesmer, Count de Puysegur, who published the first treatise on hypnotism, the inducing of an objective and intentional trance state in a patient.[24] And hypnotism, which allowed the unlocking of new fields of investigation, opened the door to that new branch of medicine, psychiatry, which finally understood the workings of suggestion.

"Suggestion" explained why all of those miracle cures, performed by hands and wands, had worked. But the hand, which *had* led science stumblingly to the discovery of the psyche, which *had*, after all, been the conduit for those miracle cures, which *had* induced the hypnotic trace, was immediately discarded, a classic case of the baby being thrown out with the bath water. Almost as soon as psychiatry began (*almost* as soon because Freud, in his earliest psychoanalytic sessions, did put his hand on the patient's forehead to start free associations coming, a practice he soon dropped) it was decreed: "Do Not Touch the Patient." We probably needn't mention that psychiatry established itself at a time and among a class that frowned upon any sort of bodily contact. Psychiatry's greatest champions were the English and the German-Austrians, who, if you will recall Montagu's assessments in Part I of this chapter, were dead set against touching. The hand in medicine was stupidly slapped down.

Before we continue with this discussion of the hand in Western medicine, which as you can see has just reached its nadir, let us look for a moment at the history of the hand in Eastern medicine. The Eastern "touch therapies" (acupuncture, acupressure, tai-yoga reflex massage, reflexology or zone therapy, jin shin jyntsu and shiatsu—the more recently developed Japanese finger massage) all began at a point commonly held to be five thousand years ago.

These systems of knowledge hold that there are body energies of which we are often unaware. The Chinese call these energies *ch'i*, the Hindus, *prana*. (Mesmer, *animal magnetism*; Reich, *orgone*.)

Here are the twelve qualities possessed by *ch'i*: it can heal; it penetrates everything; it accompanies solar rays; it is similar to but distinct from other forms of energy; it can be polarized and reflected; it emanates from the human body, *especially from the fingertips and eyes*; it can be conducted by metal, silk, and other substances; it can be stored within inanimate materials; it fluctuates with the weather; *it can be controlled by the mind*; it can cross distances and still have an effect; it can be used for good or evil.[25]

With these as the qualities of *ch'i* there is no wonder that Eastern medicine honored the hand, from which emanated the energy, and used it for healing, under the control of the mind. The idea in all of Eastern medicine is that *ch'i* flows freely in a healthy body along meridians, set pathways. Whether the healer practices acupressure or shiatsu—both of which use pressure from the hands to clear meridians for *ch'i* and use the hands' sensitivity to find where *ch'i* is blocked—the basic principles and lines of flow are the same. The invasion of Western medicine has never totally supplanted Oriental healing practice but now lives alongside it. Today in Japan, in the modern Tenrskyo Hospital there are 80 healers, practicing massage and laying on of hands, who act as a backup to the regular Western-influenced doctors and nurses.[26]

How different the Eastern mentality from the Western! Folk medicine and technological medicine easily coexist in the East. There is no adversarial struggle. There is no prejudice against the laying on of hands just because it is an old, and inexpensive, simple system. Eastern medicine didn't have to rediscover "touch healing"; it never discarded it.

Now that we have some cultural perspective, let us return to Western medicine, at a point in the early twentieth century when psychiatry was in and touching the patient was out. It was the time of distancing doctor from patient with tongue depressor, rubber gloves, stethoscope, and thermometer. It was the time of doctors and nurses touching the patient only to take a pulse.

At the turn of the century, in Davenport, Iowa, a man by the name of Daniel David Palmer began practicing a folk medicine that combined massage, the laying on of hands, and hypnosis. He called it "chiropractic." Today chiropractors are persistently popular in America, especially in the Midwest and in rural areas, where often they are the front-line medical practitioners. There are 420,000 medical doctors in the United States and 18,000 chiropractors.[27] (Heads up readers will have recognized the familiar Greek root *cheir*, "hand," the basis for the word "chiropractic.") When people with chronic problems—backaches, muscle spasms, arthritis, and so on— give up on "regular" doctors, they turn to chiropractors for sessions of spine realignment, touching, rubbing, a carefully prescribed diet, and instructions for rest and exercise. Sometimes chiropractors also offer whirlpool baths, hot and cold compresses, heat lamps, special shoes or shoe inserts to correct a misaligned walk, acupuncture, or enemas, when necessary.

A visit to a chiropractor is a physical *and* personal experi-ence, often in direct contrast to a visit to the physician's office. Frequently the people who go to chiropractors are old, with chronic problems requiring repeated visits, the kind of patient who gets the shortest shrift in conventional medical care. That an intimate "touch" therapy is available to them is a blessing and a salvation. Yet chiropractors are today regarded with as much fear and loathing by the medical establishment as were the "quacks and charlatans" of 1423 by the English Guild of Physicians. In 1963 the American Medical Association's Committee on Quackery charged that chiro-practic was "an unscientific cult whose practitioners lack the neces-sary training to diagnose and treat human disease."[28] And indeed one of the biggest problems with the use of chiropractors is the fact that people go to them for the wrong kinds of treatment—treatment for disease that should require laboratory tests and medical or surgical procedures the chiropractor is unable to provide.

Yet, used for the "right" kinds of ailments, chiropractors seem to be just as effective as medical doctors. A 1974 study at the Utah College of Medicine comparing treatment of back problems by medical doctors and chiropractors found that the two groups achieved about the same rate of improvement but that the chiropractors "generated *more* patient satisfaction than did the physicians, particularly in regard to the patient's response to the personality of the practitioner and his ability to explain the problem and its treatment."[29] (our emphasis).

By the time chiropractic medicine was being discovered there were proponents of touch healing even within the German psychiatric community. We are speaking, of course, of Wilhelm Reich, who gradually came to believe that psychosis was not only in the mind but in the body. Through touching of the body, manipulating it, breaking down physical barriers, the patient's mind could be freed also. Reich's notion of energy was quite similar to that of the Eastern touch therapies' notion of *ch'i*, a body energy that must flow freely if the person is to be healthy. Not all psychiatrists and doctors scorned Reich because of his ideas (he did have a loyal following of students and associates who carried on his work) but there was enough opposition to the man, especially to his later work, to have him branded no less a quack than the chiropractors, mesmerizers, and herbalist/conjurer/healers who preceded him.

Because medical science so closed itself off to the powers of the hand (which made effective the powers of the mind), people who needed this kind of treatment turned to "faith healers," spiritualists who used the available powers of the body to heal itself, often after the "healer" gives a charismatic touch, the laying on of hands.

One of the first requirements for a "faith healer" is a resonant, unforgettable name. Mary Baker Eddy, the founder of Christian Science, was herself a follower of the theories of Phineas Parkhurst Quimby, who practiced in Maine. Quimby believed that all illnesses were imaginary and could be overcome by the proper frame of mind. While he didn't necessarily touch his patients, he overwhelmed them with his personality and presence and his beliefs so that they were "touched" by him in another sense. Mary Baker Eddy parlayed these same beliefs and Quimby's forceful style into a new religion, one that forbade "artificial" healing and preached instead that love and faith would provide. Christian Science blossomed in the 1870's, a hundred years ago, and although its more radical teachings have been toned down—*some* medical intervention is now allowed in emergencies—it still preaches many of Mary Baker Eddy's and Quimby's beliefs that everything is "in the mind."

Edgar Cayce, working from the turn of the century to his death in 1945, diagnosed illness in a trance state achieved through self-hypnosis. Once a diagnosis had been made, Cayce treated the ailments with diet, chiropractic treatments, some medicines, and magnetic vibrations. Perhaps the best description of what Eddy, Quimby, Cayce, and others were up to was given a few years earlier in a book written by Samuel Hahnemann, a German. Hahnemann is the founder of homeopathic medicine, a field that has only in the last few years become well-known in America. In Hahnemann's *Organon of Medicine,* published in 1810, he wrote of Mesmer's cures through animal magnetism: "It is a marvelous, priceless gift of God to mankind by means of which *the strong will of a well-intentioned person upon a sick one by contact and even without . . . can bring the vital energy of the healthy mesmerizer . . . into another person dynamically."*[30] So with mystics and faith healers; healing is achieved by touch, and sometimes even without, simply because of the force of the healers' personalities. Some will take this statement in its figurative sense—that healers simply have forceful personalities—while others will take it quite literally—that the force is a God-given, magnetic, magical healing force—but here at last we have arrived at one definition of a touch healer.

(Granville) Oral Roberts, in his straightforwardly titled book *If You Need Healing Do These Things,* says: "I believe that the laying on of hands is one of the highest expressions of the Christian faith . . . that is one reason why I lay my hands upon the people when I minister to them . . . my hands serve as a point of contact for releasing my faith for the healing."[31] Roberts is probably the best-known and wealthiest contact healer.

Dr. John Lee Baughman of the Church of Truth has this to

say about the hand in faith healing: "Many people who have risen to some fame through the healing of hands have a rather primitive educational background. Yet, it doesn't really matter. . . . The point is that they begin to believe at an early age that something in their hands helped people. . . . The hands, like any other part of the body, do not perform of themselves. The hand is raised by one's mentality. . . . The hand is a sensitive instrument for [the healer's] consciousness, that is all. Now the question is whether the healer, by use of hands, leans to God . . . or simply believes in his hands."[32]

Not all faith healers use the hand. The late Kathryn Kuhlman, for instance, seemed first to heal people at a distance. Once they had received the cure, they came to the stage for an extra jolt of spirit, this time delivered by hand. Perhaps it would be instructive to relate to you what one of these "I believe in miracles" services is like. Here is Dr. William A. Nolen's description of Miss Kuhlman at work from his book *Healing*:

"It's hopeless for me to try to convey in words the charisma of the woman,"[33] Nolen writes. He describes how she made her entrance, called for an offertory, gave a short sermon. Then, he says, "she paused, eyes shut, one leg thrust forward. It was a tense moment, a dramatic moment, and the audience was silent.[34]

" 'The Holy Spirit is healing someone right now,' she said. 'It's a woman . . . [with] a cancer—a cancer of the lungs. And now . . . and now . . . she is being healed! You know who you are. . . . Stand up and come forward and claim your healing.'

"When no one came forward immediately, Kathryn suddenly pivoted and pointed toward the balcony. 'There's another healing.'

[Finally a bewildered looking woman is brought to the stage.]

" 'Do you see her?' Kathryn cried into the microphone. 'Lung cancer. And now she can breathe without pain. The Holy Spirit is surely working here today.'

"Then," Nolen writes, "she put her hands on either side of the woman's face . . . [and she] collapsed. The power of the Holy Spirit had knocked her right over."[35]

When Nolen checked on a large number of the Kuhlman

"cures," he discovered that "none of the patients ... had, in fact, been miraculously cured of anything, by either Kathryn Kuhlman or the Holy Spirit."[36] Persuing miracle healers even further, Nolen visited the Philippines to watch the famous "psychic surgeons," who reportedly removed tumors, gallstones, appendixes, and so on with their bare hands without using a knife and without leaving a scar. As might have been predicted, Nolen found no such miracles, but only the miraculous gullibility of desperate people of faith.[37]

There *are* people whose problems are solved by a visit to a faith healer. More likely than not, however, those problems resulted from a malfunction of the autonomic nervous system, malfunctions that can lead to headaches, ulcers, asthmas, skin diseases, and other nagging and severe complaints. Nolen writes, "a charismatic individual—a healer—can sometimes influence a patient and cure symptoms of a functional disease by suggestion, with or without a laying on of hands. Physicians do the same thing. These cures are not miraculous; they result from corrections made by the patient in his autonomic system."[38]

There are statistics that show that two-thirds of all people suffering from medical problems would get better *whether they sought medical treatment or not.* These people have what are called self-limiting diseases. When such strike us they will run their course; there is nothing much to be done except to treat nagging symptoms. Another study showed that 80 percent of all health problems involve psychosomatic effects, whether totally or as a contributing factor. That means that—*most of the time*—many or all of the symptoms we are experiencing are "in our minds" before they are in our bodies. That doens't mean we don't *feel* them, just that we feel them becuase *we put them there.*

Whether we like the idea or not, we feel better when we take medicine because *we believe in* medicine. We believe the doctor when he or she tells us, "You'll feel better in the morning." The use of placebos should not be seen as a dirty trick, but a wonderful cure. They are the safest medicines in a doctor's repertoire—no side effects, no possibility of overdose, no chance for addiction. These miracle pills, placebos, are even more effective if the doctor makes us feel more "treated" by touching us more, putting a comforting hand on our knee or shoulder, feeling that gland in our neck. What he or she is doing is no different from what the priest/healers did three thousand years ago, and it is just as effective, as long as we have faith in the doctor.

There is one problem, however. Many people no longer have family doctors, someone *named* "Doc" who delivered them, treated every ill, gave them shots, came to the house, and probably buried them as well. There are very few Dr. Welbys left, and it was these doctors who had the most potent medicine. In place of the comforting family physician, today we have acupuncturists and masseurs, we go to gyms and health food stores for cures. We have participated in primal scream therapy or Esalen, have taken up jogging or yoga, have done all these things to get back in touch with our bodies. We have, in the end, resorted often to Oriental teachings or have gone back and reread Wilhelm Reich with a new appreciation for the powers in the body. In response to all this, medicine has finally begun to change and to accept touch therapies.

Dolores Krieger, Professor of Nursing at New York University, teaches a course in "therapeutic touch." Krieger, a Ph.D. and Registered Nurse and author of *The Therapeutic Touch,* defines therapeutic touch as "a uniquely human act of concern of one individual for another, characterized by the touching of one by another in an act that incorporates an intent to help or heal the person so touched,"[39] a complicated way of saying that therapeutic touch is a healing touch.

Here is the method Krieger teaches: The healer holds his or her hands over the affected part of the body, which, most patients say, makes that part feel warm, even though the "healer" is not actually touching the skin. "The person playing the role of the healer becomes quiet, passively listening with the hands as she scans the body of the patient, gently attuning herself to the patient's condition. Then she places her hands on the area of the accumulated tension in the patient's body and redirects these energies."[40]

Throughout the healing, Krieger advises the healer to enter a state of deep concentration, meditation—"a total, effortless focusing of the mind."

Another person who practices touch healing has said, "Anyone who has lovingly touched another person has performed psychic healing. It's just one step beyond ordinary thought." And Dr. Nolen adds this suggestion: "All healers use hypnosis to some extent... and often with success. Making forceful verbal suggestions as one lays on hands or offers prayers works better than the laying on of hands or prayers used alone."[41]

From the god Asclepius, and the Greek physician/healers, from the *cheirourgos* and Royal healers, the chiothetists and druids, through Paracelsus and Mesmer, through Count de Puysegur, parallel with Eastern practices, slipping into America by way of chiropractic and faith healing, and now finally within the medical establishment, the hand has soothed and healed. So we can see that we've come full circle. What we long rejected as superstition or ignorance— the belief in the power of the healing touch—we now accept as insight and truth; that is to say, something scientifically proven. But did we really have to wait for science to come along and tell us that the hand is a healing instrument?

8/The Hands and Sex

Part One/Sex by Yourself

In sex, as in bridge, if you have a good enough hand you don't really need a partner.

American aphorism

Perhaps the greatest single misconception about sex is that, in adult relationships, it means nothing so much as, or more than, intercourse. This *idée fixe* has led inexorably to the enshrinement of the erect penis, the emphasis on male (penile) performance, and the myth of the vaginal orgasm. Luckily, in the last decade, we have had the advice, research, and counsel of Masters and Johnson, Hite,

Dodson, and many others to disabuse us of this notion, but herein Lee and Charlton will attempt to view the broad history of sexual relations from the roving viewpoint of the hand.

As one notable man about town has said, the hand's role in sex is rediscovered in old age, not even so much for giving oneself pleasure as for pleasuring others when all else fails. And, of course, the hand gives us our introduction to sex, first alone in our beds and then later with others. The hand was the first to brave those dark, damp, clothed recesses of the body, gave us our first thrill of exploration, brought us to heights of ardor, desire, and need unlikely to have been equaled since our days of parked cars, scratchy movie seats, and adolescence. Why, then, when we moved on to "adult sex," did we think we had to abandon the hand? Because, for many of us, the entire history of Western civilization was whispering, "Don't touch!"

Let us look first to our animal cousins who, though lacking hands, certainly enjoy and practice masturbation, whether by self-stimulation or with found objects. Ford and Beach would have us believe that "There is considerable evolutionary significance [in the fact] that female mammals of subprimate species indulge in self-stimulation much less frequently than do males,"[1] but most people who have owned female dogs given to wanton abandon with house guests' legs might argue with that claim. We might almost automatically ignore scientific observations before Masters and Johnson on the differences between male and female sexual conduct, because, as will be discussed shortly, many researchers had no idea what they were looking for (and some of them had no idea what they were looking *at*).

Perhaps we had better consider the monkey, a closer relative to man. In Mark Twain's famous address to the Stomach Club in Paris in 1879, a piece he called "Some Thoughts on the Science of Onanism," we are told:

"Give this ingenious animal [the monkey] an audience of the proper kind, and he will straight away put aside his other affairs and take a whet; and you will see by his contortions and his ecstatic expression that he takes an intelligent and human interest in the performance."[2]

Anyone who has taken a stroll through the monkey house, especially in the company of small, vocal, curious children, will be able to second Mark Twain's observations. We must not construe from what is quoted above that Twain was wholly convinced of the salubriousness of masturbation. As he stated further in his address:

"Of all kinds of sexual intercourse, this has the least to recommend it. As an amusement, it is too fleeting; as an occupation it is too wearing; as a public exhibition, there is no money in it. [Even writing in 1879, Twain must have been aware of the inaccuracy of this last statement.] It is unsuited to the drawing room, and in most cultured society it has long been banished from the social board."[3]

But how did it become banished? We suppose we must start with the Bible. The Concordance lists an amazing 1,227 references to the hand, mostly His hand, but not once do we read a proscription against touching yourself "there." Most people assume that the sin of Onan, the spilling of the seed, means masturbation when, in fact, it means coitus interruptus. (Even Twain in his essay makes this convenient mistake.) It would not be to the point to go into a long Talmudic discussion of the relevant passage (Genesis 38, verses 1 through 10), but we could make an argument that Onan was slain because he disobeyed his father's instructions (or even his Father's instructions), not because of the act of seed spilling.

In any case, by the sixteenth and seventeenth centuries, "touching yourself" had become an act so vile, so unspeakable, that only veiled references to it were accepted in polite company and in moral instruction. We will stop here to quote from an anonymous pamphlet, published in London in 1725, entitled "Onania, or the Heinous Sin of Self-Pollution and Its Frightful Consequences in Both Sexes."

"Self-Pollution is that unnatural Practice by which Persons of either sex may defile their own Bodies, without the Assistance of others, whilst yielding to filthy imaginations."[4]

The author pauses in the midst of his first chapter to ponder the idea that polluting oneself is worse than polluting another, in the same way that self-murder is worse than murdering another, then he rushes on to the crux of his argument:

"The crime itself is monstrous and unnatural . . . its consequences ruinous; It destroys conjugal Affection, perverts natural Inclination and tends to extinguish the Hopes of Posterity." [Yes, that's what he said, and that's what he meant.] The author repeats what everyone knew about masturbation—that it automatically hindered growth in both boys and girls—then goes on to report the results of his scientific investigations.

"In Men as well as Boys, the very first attempt has been occasioned a *Phymosis* in some and a *Paraphymosis* in others. I shall not explain these terms any further; let it suffice that there are accidents which are very painful and troublesome, and may continue to be tormenting for some time, if not bring on Ulcers and other worse Symptoms. . . . Whoever wants to know the significance of those words, any Surgeon will inform him.

"The frequent use of this pollution likewise causes *Stranguries, Priapisms* and other disorders of those parts but especially *Gonorrhaeas* more difficult to be cured than those contracted from Women. . . . This Distemper often proves fatal. . . . In some [masturbation] is the cause of Fainting Fits and Epileptics, in others of Consumptions; and many young men have been worn out by it. . . . In others again, whom it has not kill'd, it has produced nightly and excessive Seminal Emissions; a weakness in the Penis and Loss of Erection, as if they had been castrated."[5]

The author further states that it renders most men impotent, and if not impotent then infertile. If by some chance they should happen to get their wives with child, despite their heinous past, such children will be "weakly little ones, that either die soon or become tender, sickly people, always ailing and complaining, a Misery to themselves, a Dishonour to the humane Race, and a Scandal to their parents."

Women fare no better from such a sin:

"In Women, Self-Pollution, if frequently practis'd, relaxes and spoils the retentive Faculty, occasions the *Fluor albus,* an obnoxious as well as perplexing Illness attending that Sex. . . . It Frequently is the Cause of *Hysterick Fits,* and sometimes of *Consumptions,* but what it produces more than either is *Barrenness* . . . and all manner of *Gleets* and *Ouzings."* [6]

There was only one thing left for the author to warn against—that is, except for hairy palms, which affliction he seems to have missed: A young girl might "foolishly part with that Valuable Badge of the Chastity and Innocence."

Well! Such a pamphlet must certainly have had its desired effect on the populace. The author seems to have enjoyed an outpouring of grateful letters, many of them from clergymen. In addition to the warnings about what horrible afflictions might be visited upon anyone practicing the Sin, the author outlined some means for prevention and relief. First of all he advised parents to strictly forbid their children to touch either their eyes or their nose with the bare hand, but only with "their handkerchief, and that only upon very urgent Necessities." His feelings were that the "naked hand" touching bare, sensitive skin, might set off any number of ideas and profane desires. For men and women who had already fallen, he recommended a milk diet and cold bathing.

If that failed, there was the last resort. The author just happened to have invented two cures for self-pollution that could be purchased at the Sign of Seneca's Head, near Somerset House, the Strand. One, "The Strengthening Tincture," cost 10 s. the bottle and required two or three bottles for a cure. The other, the "Prolifick Powder," came in packets of 24 and required a continued course of treatment until a cure could be achieved. Judging by the author's previously demonstrated skills of scientific judgment and observation, we might guess that this was indeed a case of picking your poison.

There seems to have been a flowering of sexual freedom during the English Romantic period, which flowering included a *laissez-faire* attitude toward masturbation. But then, in response, came an even more violent prohibition. Some theorists, notably Rene A. Spitz, have found a parallel between the rise of Protestantism and the nearly hysterical attitudes toward masturbation, not only in time but also in place. In Austria, Germany, France, and England between 1850 and 1879, this all-out condemnation of masturbation reached its most inevitable conclusion with the advent of "surgical therapy" for masturbators. This may have been the origin of the custom of circumcising non-Jewish male babies, as circumcision was felt to inhibit masturbation. There also developed European clitoridectomy, which was felt to be a certain means of stopping little girls from touching themselves. Of course, this "therapy" worked extraordinarily well, since they had removed exactly what a little girl *could* touch. Sachs, in 1905, also recommended cautery of the spine, as well as "infibulation of prepuce and labia majora."

If you think this mania failed to catch on in the United States, you are wrong. Most "advanced" surgical procedures crossed the Atlantic, and so in 1890 there was founded in Chicago the Orifical Surgery Society, which advocated all manner of operations on prepuce, clitoris, and rectum; it flourished until 1925.

Not all "surgical" means were as extreme as those of Sachs and the Orifical Surgery Society. Some surgeons advocated breaking the childhood habit of touching oneself by mechanical restraints— splints attached to both arms so the child would be unable to finger himself or herself. This seems to have been practiced most frequently in England and may have been contributory to later English obsessions with bondage and restraints. We know that during Victorian times, when the bare hand was never allowed "out" in public and when there were the strongest social rules concerning touching oneself and others, people in private did as they pleased.

Masturbation, being an instinctive, natural act, seems to have continued no matter what laws and remedies were applied. We are reminded of the old joke about the father who walks in on his son masturbating in bed. The father delivers a long, impassioned lecture on the evils of masturbation, including the warning that it leads to blindness. Finally he extracts a promise from his chastised son that he will never do it again. As the father turns to leave, the son calls out, "Could I do it until I need glasses?"

With some reservations we will have to thank psychologists for enlightening the rest of society on the subject of masturbation. At a symposium in Germany in 1912, for the first time the world heard a cautious acceptance of masturbation—as long as it was not "excessive." Freud, of course, was at the center of this group and shared their views on masturbation. In his essay on Infantile Sexuality, Freud discusses masturbation as a developmental stage and makes a connection between masturbation and another form of sexuality involving the hand: thumb sucking.

"In the nursery, thumb sucking is often treated in the same way as any other sexual 'naughtiness' of the child. . . . Pleasure-sucking is often combined with a rubbing contact with certain sensitive parts of the body, such as the breast and external genitals. It is by this path that many children go from thumb sucking to masturbation."[7]

And even thumb sucking can then lead to other compulsive hand behaviors. Frances Millican and others, in a recent essay called "Oral Autoerotic, Autoaggressive Behavior and Oral Fixation," points out that "[Children] often transfer the oral pleasures to accessory patterns accompanying thumb sucking, particularly if thumb sucking has been forbidden by parents or when thumb sucking per se is given up. Sometimes they rub the skin areas near their mouth as a substitute, rub the nose with one finger while having one in the mouth. They also develop habits of rubbing or plucking at ears or hair, which later becomes a substitute."[8]

Playing with the hair, nail biting, smoking, compulsive eating and drinking—all these seem a part of the same satisfying behavior as thumb sucking and masturbation. We might call these "hand pleasures," pleasure derived from touching or stroking or feeding various parts of the body. It feels good, it is comforting, and it releases tension, a definition that might equally be true of the pleasures of intercourse.

The "Scientific" Campaign against Masturbation in the United States

Because American doctors in the nineteenth century were eager to keep up with the most recent medical "discoveries" in Europe, some of the most well-respected American doctors also uncovered bizarre results from habitual masturbation.[13] The physician Alfred Hitchcock, in a paper entitled "Insanity and Death from Masturbation," published in the *Boston Medical and Surgical Journal* 26 in 1842, warned that "self-abuse" could lead to death in as little as six years, by his own observation. A man considered to be the founder of American Pediatric medicine, Abraham Jacobi, blamed masturbation for causing polio and infantile rheumatism. A Chicago doctor, Allen W. Hagenbach, was particularly vehement on the subject of masturbators, saying that it caused insanity and homosexuality ("Masturbation as a Cause of Insanity," *Journal of Nervous and Mental Diseases* 6, 1879).

This latter idea was seconded in 1904 by, of all people, the man who sponsored Freud in America, psychologist G. Stanley Hall. As reported by Vern and Bonnie Bullough in their book *Sin, Sickness and Sanity,* Hall was explicit in ways to keep children from masturbating, warning parents "to watch carefully for the habit among their children, to be especially observant during springtime or when the climate was warm, to make sure that the children wore proper clothes, avoided rich foods and mental overwork." The Bulloughs also report that Hall believed that "a lack of cleanliness, nervousness, prolonged sitting or standing, monotonous walking, sitting cross-legged, spanking, late rising, petting and indulgence, corsets, straining of the memory, erotic reading, pictures, play, solitude, perfumes, overeating, fondling, rocking chairs, pockets, featherbeds, horseback riding, and bicycling all encouraged masturbation."

These fears, and what was obviously felt to be the need to help the young before they ruined themselves with featherbeds and rocking chairs, good food and mothers' kisses, resulted in a spate of "chastity" inventions, devices intended not so much to stop inter-

course but to stop the looking at, touching, or investigating of sex organs. Today one could imagine these devices in boutiques catering to sexual athletes and aesthetes. A series of devices intended to stop boys from masturbating or from even getting an erection(!) consisted of spikes or needles that would pierce the rising body. As the patent application for one of these devices stated, when "expansion in this organ begins, it will come in contact with the prickling points and the necessary pain or warning sensation will result." Other devices, some of them invented by women but for use on men (consider that for a moment), consisted of grippers or clamps that made any growth of the penis painful, as well as straps, plates, belts, and trap doors, all intended to be locked in order to keep hands away.

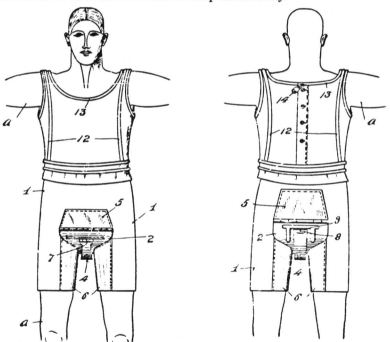

This anti-masturbatory device, patented in 1908 (patent number 875, 845), was invented by a woman from Minnesota. U.S. Patent Office

So we must thank Freud and his colleagues for defining the need for masturbation and for tracing the development of masturbation substitutes. On the other hand, we must hold against them their rigid definition of masturbation as "infantile," something to be thrown over for a better, more mature form of sexual activity. A large part of the blame must be placed squarely on Freud's shoulders, because he, with his incisive mind and his persuasive writing style, convinced the others that there were two types of female orgasm, the inferior, infantile clitoral orgasm, and the superior, mature vaginal orgasm. He clung to this belief despite his own observations to the contrary and thus condemned untold numbers of women to give up, or at least to enjoy in secret, the only way they could achieve orgasm. Let us quote here from Freud:

The chief erogenous zone in the female child is the clitoris, which is homologous to the male penis. All that I have been able to discover about masturbation in little girls refers to the clitoris, and not to the other external genitals which are so important for the future sexual functions. . . .

If a woman finally submits to the sexual act, the clitoris becomes stimulated and its role is to conduct the excitement to the adjacent genital parts; it acts here like a chip of pinewood, which is utilized to set fire to the harder wood. It often takes some time before this transference is accomplished, and during this transition the young wife remains anaesthetic. This anaesthesia may become permanent if the clitoris zone refuses to give up its excitability, a condition brought on by profuse sexual activities in infantile life. It is known that anaesthesia in women is often only apparent and local. They are anaesthetic at the vaginal entrance, but not at all unexcitable through the clitoris or even through other zones."[9]

We almost feel sorry for Freud, working so hard to make his observations fit his theories, fighting the easy answers (i.e., to change his theories to fit his observations), surrounded by contemporaries (Sachs, the church, popular belief) who were so far behind him they could offer no help whatsoever. And what imagery! The clitoris "acts here like a chip of pinewood, which is utilized to set fire to the harder wood." If only it were true, it would be profound.

Since in Freud's time the medical community's most advanced operation involving the clitoris was amputation, it is not hard to see how Freud came to be so grievously misled. We can only guess what enlightening things Freud would have to say now!

It would be a disservice, however, to leap from Freud to modern theorists, because it would mean overlooking Havelock Ellis, who, though suspicious of "excessive" masturbation again, was aware of its natural place in human development. "Masturbation," he says in *The Psychology of Sex,* "in the wider sense is an almost universal phenomenon among animals and man in all parts of the world. It is so widespread that we cannot, strictly, speak of it as 'abnormal.' "[10]

Ellis observes that masturbation is more widespread in female children than in boys, in adolescent boys more than in girls, and in adult women more than in men, an observation that has been seconded by more recent research.

As to Ellis's dislike of "excessive" masturbation—"Masturbation, when practiced in excess, especially if begun before the age of puberty, leads to inaptitude for coitus, as well as indifference to it, and sometimes to undue sexual irritability, involving premature emission, and practical impotence"[11]—we might comment that he was making an obvious error in logic. Excessive masturbation may have no more been the *cause* of the problems he observed than excessive eating, sleeping, or excessive television watching might be. Rather, any form of excessive behavior has deep roots that might also be responsible for sexual problems.

As we have seen, there was very little change in the attitude toward masturbation from 1725 to 1925. For the next 25 years Freud's view prevailed: masturbation was seen as something acceptable in children more than in adults, and only if practiced moderately. Then, in 1953, there was a bombshell: Kinsey's *Sexual Behavior in the Human Female* revealed that 70% of women, despite Freud, had remained faithful to their clitorises and had had adult masturbatory experiences.

It was also shortly discovered that, contrary to Freud, Ellis, and almost everyone else, it was the women who masturbated who reported the strongest and most frequent orgasms.

And when Kinsey did a statistical study comparing educational levels and present masturbation experiences, the results were thus:

Education	% Women	% Men
Grammar school	34	89
High school	59	95
College graduates	63	96

The differences between the men in the study were hardly significant, but look at the women. Twice as many college graduates reported masturbating as did women with grammar school educations. We could make endless speculations on the reasons for these figures but we will mention only one thing: the women college graduates had almost certainly read Freud during their educations, yet they were the most likely to ignore his assumptions.

It was this kind of feedback Freud lacked. Once Kinsey's report was issued, and others followed, psychologists could no longer assert that masturbation was rare, unnatural, evil, or a sign of incomplete sexual development. We might quote a recent commendable work, *Masturbation: From Infancy to Senescence,* edited by Irwin M. Marcus, M.D., and John J. Francis, M.D.:

Of special importance in connection with the theme of masturbation, and related to unique evolutionary shift to the permanent sexuality of the human female, is the evolution of the upright state, bipedality, and the consequent freeing of the human hand [their emphasis]. . . . *It is now the hands which are enabled to share with the mouth and tongue the expressions of physical affection. . . .*

. . . *Freeing the hand by the upright position made manual genital stimulation possible both in autoerotic practices and in the relations between sexual partners.*[12]

And here we are today: we recognize the naturalness of masturbation (to the point that we recognize that genital play will invariably appear in infants by the age of 18 months if they have had proper mothering); we accept clitoral response as the norm in women and hope that their male partners are able to locate and properly woo this sometimes illusive member; and we urge both men and women to find pleasure in their own bodies as is their wont.

Part Two/Sex With Others

Praeterea sentio vulvam Sacratissimae Majestatis ante coitum
diutius esse titillandam.
        Advice given to Empress Theresa of Austria by her physician[14]

Before little boys know quite what they are doing, they are using
their hands to attract the attention of little girls. Starting in third
grade (or even sooner) there is a lot of intrasexual punching, pushing, and pinching and also ponytail and pigtail pulling and dipping
going on. No sooner does puberty hit than the boys start snapping
the girls' bra straps in class, a source of great hilarity among seventh

and eighth graders. From here it is a short step to passing notes in class (early ninth grade) and before the year is out some of the girls are spending their lunch hours unwrapping and rewrapping their boyfriends' rings with surgical tape.

Next there is a day at the beach, with the girls asking the boys to help them put suntan lotion on their backs (or, something requiring even longer periods of hand-to-back contact, writing messages on the girls' backs with tape to block out the sun). Somewhere along the way there is the first date.

In a previous chapter we mentioned the Basal Hand Movement/per minute rate. Nothing increases the BHM/pm so much as a first date to the movies; that is probably why popcorn sells in such huge quantities. Once the popcorn and Pepsi are consumed, it is time for the real purpose of going to the movies, for the guy to get his chance to put his arm around the girl's shoulder. This can be accomplished through elaborate ploys: reaching out to yawn and then dropping the arm on her shoulder; pretending to be looking the other way and tapping her on the far shoulder (then leaving the hand there); talking to the guys in back of her and then, in turning around, letting an arm come "naturally" to the back of her seat. Whatever the *modus*, this is the point at which the boy will experience either his first rejection or his first romance.

No girl has even taken the initiative, at this age, to put *her* arm around *him*. That leaves her with few options: either she can cross her legs away from him, put her coat and purse on her lap, keep her hands on the side furthest from him, and lean forward when he puts his arm on the back of her seat (your basic "I'm not with him" technique), or she can make herself available to him and sink back onto his arm, which will, before the movie is over, be hot, sweaty, and sound asleep. Later, when they get in his car (city dwellers will note that we refer here to the real world, a world in which teenagers drive cars), she can signal her receptivity by where she sits—huddled against the door, noncommital in the middle of her seat, or snuggled close to the driver. We are assuming that this is a car without a floor shift and without bucket seats. Any boy rich enough to own a sports car is also rich enough to have his own room, apartment, or den/rec room for privacy and will dispense with the hours-long driving around in the car and the hand play that would otherwise follow a date at the movies.

Whether the boy and girl are in the front seat of the car, sitting on a beach blanket, or on the family couch, the next moves are inevitable. After some preliminary kissing he will touch her breast through her sweater or blouse. Then, after meeting no convincing resistance, he will move his hand to her back and work his way up her bare skin, untucking her shirt, if necessary, to do this. Next will come the treacherous bra-unhooking. Although they admire suave lovers who supposedly can do it with *one* hand, most men find it damn hard to do, even with *two*. There is no clumsier moment, they will tell you, than grappling with the darn thing (let's see? is it right over left? hooks inside or out? where *is* the hook?) only to have girl—who seemed willing—ask you "What are you doing back there?" when they can't effectively show her. The only worse moment is, of course, struggling to find the hook in back when it is in fact in front. Most girls will, at this stage, be helping as much as they can, either by drawing both shoulderblades together to make the bra hooks bunch up so he can find them and open them, or by gently taking his hand and leading it to the front hook, or—fast girls—by doing it themselves.

Once exploration on the upper body has been completed, the boy will turn his attention to the knees. His hand will perch briefly and then, with a circular motion of the thumb, will begin its upward progress. The first natural barrier is three to four inches above the knee. Here his hand will reach (a) the tops of her nylons (rather old-fashioned, but we like it), (b) the bottoms of her Bermuda shorts, if they are in style, (c) the hem of her cheerleader's pleated skirt or culottes, or (d) the soft, worn-by-rubbing patch on the inner thigh of her jeans. If none of these articles of clothing obtain, he will be able to tell when he has reached this spot by the fact that the hard, bony kneecap will have given way to the soft yielding flesh of the thigh. At this point he will meet resistance. She will apply the (a) hand block, (b) elbow across the knee barrier, or the dreaded (c) knee clamp.

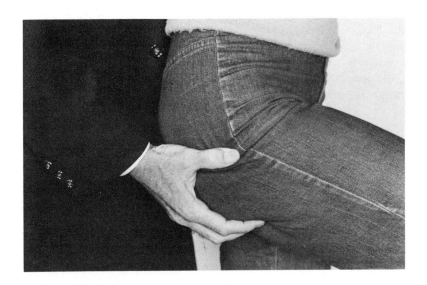

(Some boys believe that the only reason girls are required to take gym is to train their thigh muscles for the 100-pound-per-square inch knee clamp on the offending hand.) The boys' hands invariably are on the insides of the girls' knees; there being no point to running his hand up the *out*side of girls' legs.

If she finally allows him past the midthigh, his hand is then free to roam as far as the pantyline. One boy has told us that you can tell where to go and how far away the goal is simply by the heat and humidity. A really sensitive hand, he said, will home in with unfailing accuracy. It is, he said, a place suitable for growing orchids.

It is at this point that the boy tries surreptitiously to (a) fold back the car's airliner recliner seats (invented in 1959 for the American Motors Rambler), or (b) slide the girl down on the couch, or (c) lean her back into a horizontal position on the beach blanket. Occasionally a boy will suggest that they adjourn to the back seat of the car, which is awkward and a terrible mood-breaker. This suggestion can never be made on a first date.

Whatever happens next, one thing can be said to be true—
the hand is there first. No man will ever forget the first time he
touched a girl *there* through her cotton Lollipops. The first acquaintance with sex may happen at an earlier age today than it did twenty
years ago, but there is always a first time, and the hands are always
essentially involved.

To those of us who can think back ten, twenty, thirty, forty
years to the kind of experiences we've just been talking about, to
steamed-up windows and the "empty popcorn box trick" ("want
some popcorn? heh-heh-heh), to lovers' lanes and fast girls who
touched the zipper, to tickling a girl's palm or sticking a finger in a
boy's ear, to rumors that some girl in the *next town* (never your own
town) actually took it *all off* playing strip poker, the fact that the hand
and sex are inseparable is abundantly clear. What is so sweet about
those memories is that we were so innocent and so arousable, even
by a touch.

Compared to the lives of inexperience and ignorance we
actually led, the books we relied on for advice were exotic, to say the
least. Take that bible of sex education among junior high school
students, the *Kama Sutra*, which lists the 64 ways a woman marks
her readiness for sex. This does not include American practices like
checking out the car window to see if anyone is coming. No, instead it
lists things such as playing a musical instrument, drawing, making a
bed of flowers on the ground, cookery, and, number 64, making clay
figures. Many of these arts and sciences involve the hand, but in ways
your normal American school boy and girl may find hard to relate to.
No one, of course, read the *Kama Sutra* for sections like the one
above. What caught our attention were descriptions of impossible-
seeming sexual positions, with all of the interesting words rendered
in Hindi (yoni, linga, etc., leading to a lot of embarrassment for girls
named Joni and Linda), elaborate classifications of techniques (for
scratches, eight types), and the special circumstances for the various
techniques (on scratches, for instance, the *Kama Sutra* specifies they
be done "on the first visit; at the time of setting out on a journey; on
the return from a journey; at the time when an angry lover is
reconciled;" and last, when the woman is intoxicated—pretty heady

advice to be read by teenagers. The book also mentions the ways in which lovers can strike each other during the sex act, and the places on the body most responsive to blows, and warns that blows done with "the wedge, the scissors, the piercing instrument and the pincers" had caused serious injury and even death. (Even in the *Kama Sutra* passion had its limits.)

How much better today that school kids (and adults) can read books like *The Joy of Sex* and *More Joy of Sex,* the popular translations of Masters and Johnson's books, *The Hite Report,* and other sensible, enlightening books too numerous to mention. *The Joy of Sex* devotes four pages to "handwork," Dr. Comfort's term for masturbation either of oneself or of one's partner. "A woman who has the divine gift of lechery and loves her partner," it is said in *The Joy of Sex,* "will masturbate him well, and a woman who knows how to masturbate a man—subtly, unhurriedly and mercilessly—will almost always make a superlative partner."[15] As concerns men, the book says, "The main difficulty from the man's point of view is that the ideal pressure point [for a woman] varies from hour to hour so he should allow her to guide him to the right place. Most men think they know automatically, having succeeded once—they are often wrong."[16] In Shere Hite's book, one woman complained that her partner rubbed her clitoris "like he was trying to erase it,"[17] a remark that makes us laugh because it has been so often true of men's attempts to satisfy women.

As we have now reached a point beyond the high school front-seat grapplings, let's dispense with nostalgia for the days in which the hand was the only source of sexual satisfaction and talk about the role of the hand in the widest range of sexual activities. Even before you get ready for an evening together with a lover, the hand has played a role in your sex life. For women it has helped them avoid pregnancy, something that may be vital to their full enjoyment of sex. It has helped them groom themselves, apply makeup and perfume. It has bathed and scrubbed their bodies. For men the hand has bathed and shaved them, applied cologne, dressed them and groomed them. Together, their hands have stroked and touched— her fingenail run up the inside of his thigh, his hand on her breast, mutual holding and then undressing, all bring them to a more excited state for lovemaking.

Then the hands begin exploring the skin, roughly perhaps, squeezing the breasts and nipples, lightly (in a move *The Joy of Sex* calls *pattes d'araignée*, or spider's legs) in a tickling massage using only the fingertips on the body hairs.[18] The hands pull the two bodies together, bury themselves in hair, hold faces for gentle or intense kisses. The hands guide the lovers' hands, tongues, genitals to places that give them pleasure. The hands *give* pleasure, make each partner aroused. They guide the penis into the vagina. They maintain or prolong intercourse, bring one to climax. They pick parts and arrange them in more exciting, more satisfying positions, lift legs, hold buttocks, grasp breasts. For some people the hands spank, tie up, whip, throttle. For others, mostly women, the hand is the only way they can enjoy orgasm. Once intercourse is over, the hands maintain the contact, hug and squeeze, caress, thank.

To understand how essential are hands to most intercourse,

consider the difficulty of the "goldfish" postion mentioned in *The Joy of Sex*: "Two naked people tied and put on a mattress together to make love fish-fashion, i.e. no hands. [It was] originally a nineteenth-century Bordel joke. It *can* be done (if you are victims, try on your sides from behind)." Think how short the mating is of "handless species, and how boring.

Hands and hand-holds allow us to explore not only each other's body, but each other's fantasies and quirks also. Consider the erotic yet innocent quality of this sentence from the "Tale of Miriam" in the *Arabian Nights*: "he made his palm resound on the silken resilience of her backside."[19]

Because there are so many uses of the hand in sex we could not hope to give a comprehensive list, nor would we feel comfortable giving "rules" for the use of hands, but here is a list of our observations about the use of hands in sex:

1. One should never assume anything. If he or she responded to where you touched him or her last night, don't immediately try to do the same thing tonight. Masters and Johnson's new study found that the *average* time it took the males in the sample to touch the females' breasts was *30 seconds*.[20] This automatic treatment of the women was not always, or even usually successful. It seems to us that intelligent, sensitive, varied touching will undoubtedly be also the most stimulating, and the most complimentary. It shows that you are *there*, that you are aware of the other person and listening to his or her body.

2. Here are some suggested spots to touch while making love: touch the ears; touch the fingers (especially the insides of the fingers); tickle between fingers and toes; lick between fingers and toes; touch the back of the neck with the back of your thumb, and with your forefinger; hold the back of the neck with your whole hand; hold the waist with both hands; graze the thighs with your fingers; touch the insides of the thighs; touch the soles of the feet; touch the calves; touch the small of the back; touch the lips; touch the breasts and nipples of both men and women; touch her clitoris, the labia; separate the labia with your fingers; touch his penis, especially on the underside where it is most sensitive; on an uncircumcized man pull

back the foreskin; touch his scrotum; touch the crevice between the two buttocks; touch the armpit, the bend in the elbow, the hair, the eyes.

3. It is better to keep your hands flowing over your partner's body than it is to simply grab hold and make love. As your hands move, try to listen for body sounds, soft exhalations, groans, words, that will tell you what is pleasing.

4. Your hands should be on your partner's body before, during, and after you make love. If possible, fall asleep while still touching.

5. Controlling the man's ejaculation by touching him at the base of the penis, or at a spot halfway between the scrotum and the anus, can be enormously helpful in cases where the man worries about premature ejaculation. It allows the woman to be involved in helping the man, taking some of the pressure off of him, but it also necessitates good verbal or physical communication between the two of them, and some practice. Anything like this, arrived at mutually, can do nothing but improve the sexual bond between two people.

6. Know how much stimulation your lover can take and don't displease a lover by forcing a too-soon orgasm. Many couples like to come together, yet sometimes one partner first wants to try to get the other one to come *manually* once. This can diminish the force of the mutual orgasm, so ask before you start in.

7. Some people, however, are simply shy, or afraid of feelings, or afraid of being exposed. (When you are masturbated to orgasm the other partner is in control. Some men and some women are afraid they will look ugly, or simply "out of control" at the moment of orgasm, and so resist.) Without forcing your partner, try to convince your partner that you love him or her, will take care of him/her, will not be put off, and so on. This is better done, as are most sexual things, by showing your partner with your body rather than telling your lover with words.

8. Women, it is hard to find exactly the right method—one hand, two hands, forefinger-thumb ring, stroking, licking, mouthing, tickling, circular, top, bottom, combination—that is going to please

your man tonight. Have you asked him to show you how he does it for himself? Have you tried several different techniques? Do you enjoy doing it? If not, perhaps you are bored because you always do the same thing. Your hands can help you especially here. Read a sex-instruction book together in bed. Start on page 1 and see how far you get.

9. It occurs to us that men are often too rough or too perfunctory with women's clitorises, starting too hard, not allowing her movements, sounds, and comments to guide them to more excited touching. One woman in Shere Hite's book complained that "masturbation by men is usually to check if I'm wet." Others complained that if they asked for a particular kind of clitoral stimulation, the man sometimes did not listen to them (the "he thinks he knows what's best for me" routine) or "forgot" the next time they made love. It is apparently threatening for men to think that intercourse alone will not satisfy some women and that the lowly hand may be better than the sword.

10. The first person to study the use of the electric vibrator on women's sexual response was Robert Latou Dickinson (along with W. F. Robie and LeMon Clark);[21] he published a report in 1949. We would like to salute this man, who has added a Western equivalent to the ben-wa stimulators and other wonderful sexual devices created in the East. The vibrator may have forever let off the hook clumsy men, men with little staying power, or men whose sexual enjoyment proceeds at a different pace from that of their partners. It should not be seen as a replacement for the hand but as a valuable adjunct. Either the man or the woman can control it. The right vibrator can add greatly to either sex's enjoyment.

Before we leave this subject, we would like to mention one area of sex in which the hand is intimately, essentially involved—tickling.

The early teenage years are the high point of boys' goosing mania, which persists from late grammar school days through junior

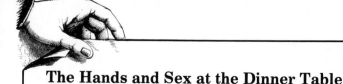

The Hands and Sex at the Dinner Table

Maurice Yaffé, a psychologist at Guy's Hospital in London, has found it possible to detect patients' sexual problems by the way they eat at the dinner table.[24] He is still in the midst of studying the diagnostic device, but has so far come up with four basic types of male eaters (women will be studied next:)

Slow, careful eaters seem to be the top sensualists in bed.

Slow eaters who show disinterest in food are reported to have difficulty in obtaining or maintaining an erection.

Fast eaters who enjoy food and are knowledgeable about it have a high incidence of premature ejaculation and are highly anxious. They find work pressures difficult to bear and, women report, are difficult to relax with in bed.

Fast eaters who are disinterested in food fall into four categories:

Those who are "presexual," who find it difficult to establish relationships, and who therefore have never had sex.

Sexual celibates who have a low sex drive.

Those who use food as a substitute for sex.

Those who find it difficult or impossible to achieve ejaculation and who are emotionally detached from their partners.

high and even beyond. For some boys the "goose" is the supreme form of combined threat and sexual contact.

Although boys goose each other, there is no goosing between girls. Girls tickle each other, if they touch at all.

When boys are with girls they tickle their palms. It is titillating because a positive response is supposed to mean that she will "do it." It is not the worst test in the world—the girl's reaction to *any* form of touch would indicate whether she was responsive to the approach—but compared to the Oriental sophistication of touch and response, the Western palm tickle is somewhat simplistic.

However, once we get beyond the palm, the subject of tickling is an interesting one in connection with adult sexual relations. Ellis states: "Ticklishness . . . is, as it were, a play of tumescence, on which laughter comes as a play of detumescence, to dispel undesired sexual emotions (as often among bashful sex-conscious girls). Ticklishness . . . tends to die out after adolescence, at the period during which sexual relationships normally begin."[22] He further notes that the tickle response may have originated as a kind of warning system because the most ticklish areas of the body—in order: the palms and soles of the feet, the armpits and stomach, the sides of the chest, the inner sides of the thigh, the knees, and the lips—are the parts that most need protection. Yet it is not as a warning signal but as a form of sexual pursuit that tickling interests us. "All forms of amorous contrectation, and especially the sexual embrace, have an intimate connection with the phenomena of ticklishness. . . . To tickle among some peoples has been to make love, and sometimes, as along the Fuegians, the same word is applied to the sexual embrace as to tickling. The German word for the clitoris, 'Kitzler' or tickler, indicates a similar connection of ideas."[23]

To tickle someone is to perform either an act of love or of aggression on him. An adult male who tries to tickle another adult male will be seen as a hostile aggressor, unless there is some specific agreement between them. The sensation of ticklishness is a remarkable one. When a friend tickles you, you laugh, but if an enemy tries to tickle you, you experience it as pain, or as no sensation at all. It is

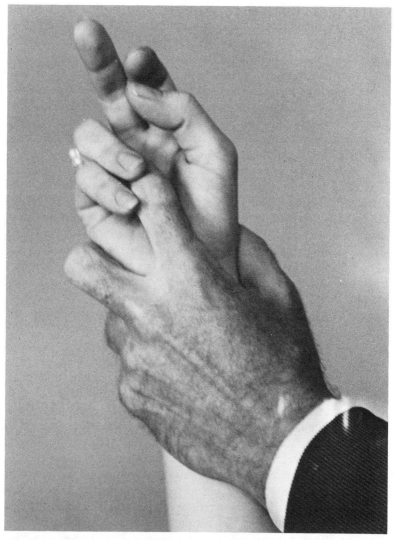

The great advantage of touch dancing was the chance to run your finger up the center of her palm to find out how willing she was.

certainly not with what we associate with a tickle: laughter, warmth, pleasure. (Try to remember what it was like when you were a child and a particularly odious, to you, adult tried to tickle you. Did you burst into tears? Or did you laugh?) In many ways this is comparable to intercourse and rape. What was pleasurable between friends is frightening and painful when forced on a woman or a man.

It shouldn't be surprising to learn that women begin to lose their tickle response to a man once they've started sleeping with him. As he becomes familiar he becomes like one's own hand—incapable of raising a laugh through tickling. (Try it. You can't tickle yourself. You might be able to get a ticklish feeling out of your lips, if you brush them lightly, but even this tickle response is more like an irritating buzz than a fall-on-the-floor-with-laughter tickle.) The same woman who has lost her tickle response to her husband, say, might be wildly ticklish with her husband's brother or his boss—any familiar, but not too familiar, man.

In both tickling and sex, with two people under the right circumstances there is the proper, wholehearted, unfaked response. But in tickling, unlike in sex, you can't please yourself, *by yourself.* Logically, then, in human evolution, we should reproduce not by enjoying sex but by tickling.

9/The Hand and Divination

... It is good to seek for the meanings of popular traditions ...good sense is often hidden beneath a cloak of folly.

Ad. Desbarrolles The Mysteries of the Hand, *1859*

From the minute humans began cerebrating, they began wondering how to predict what would come next. What, she wondered, would happen to her when she went around the next corner? How could he tell, in advance, what the hunting would be like if he moved his camp to the other side of the river? After a few rounds of operant conditioning—a fall through thin ice, an attack by a disturbed swarm of bees—people must have wanted, desperately, to be able to foresee future dangers.

Julian Jaynes, in his brilliant book, *The Origin of Consciousness in the Breakdown of the Bicameral Mind,* describes an early stage of consciousness when humans hallucinated hearing voices. Thousands of years later this evolved into the kind of process you see in Jaynes' book—any book—"subjective consciousness, that is, the development on the basis of linguistic metaphors of an operation space in which 'I' could narratize out alternative actions to their consequences. . . ."[1] In other words, people went from following their instincts to following their reason. *However,* during those few thousand years of confusion between finding one solution to the problem (instinct) and finding the other (reason), people had to make do with interim systems. What did they rely on? Gods, whose systems of belief were made evident through divination. (Think for a moment of the word *divine.* As an adjective it means "of or pertaining to God," while as a verb it means "to perceive through sympathy, or intuition; to detect, to conjure.")

But how were people to divine the Divine? Once again we will refer to Jaynes: "Attempts to divine the speech of the now silent gods work out into . . . four main types, which can be ordered in terms of their historical beginning and which can be interpreted as successive approaches toward consciousness[:] . . . omens, sortilege, augury, and spontaneous divination."[2]

Note: Those in a hurry to *get on* with palmistry, reading fingerprints and hand types, and graphology, should turn immediately to page 237.

The first method Jaynes outlines is the *omen,* which technique has now been popularized by a spate of recent movies. The omen is, of course, the most simplistic form of reasoning. *A* happened before *B* once, therefore we can expect *A* to happen before *B* again. (As you will later see, palmistry is one form of divining omens.) Jaynes pinpoints the second millennium B.C. as the heyday of omens and quotes several examples from the library of Ashurbanipal, of which our favorite is:

If a horse enters a man's house, and bites either an ass or a man, the owner of the house will die and his household will be scattered.

This is a specialized omen, indeed, but—who knows?—it may have once been true, of a rabid horse or a horse carrying tetanus. So it is with all omens. The fact that a connection may once have been made, especially if that connection is elucidated with gory details, makes us all stop for a moment and wonder—what if . . . ? Let us give you an example from *Medical Palmistry,* a book by Marten Steinbach that has developed almost a cult following:

A forty-year-old Los Angeles newspaper columnist whose hands I analyzed several years ago offers a good example. . . . [O]ne of the outstanding features of his palm was an island on the line of Apollo, occurring just below the heart line at about age forty-three. His life, heart, and fate lines all bore signs of difficulty or illness at the same period.

    I admonished him to give close attention to his health and his emotional life . . . during the next two or three years. . . .

    The advice, of course, fell upon more or less deaf ears. . . . Within two years, however, a bitter quarrel . . . cost him his lucrative contract. . . . During the same period of stress, he became emotionally involved with an Oriental exotic dancer—a liaison which caused the breakup of his marriage. When I last saw him, he had suffered a heart attack and was recuperating in a private sanitarium.[3]

Now there are some cynics out there who would suggest that this is the normal course of life for 40-year-old newspaper columnists. True, perhaps, but didn't the coincidence of the palm reading and this man's fate make us suspect, if for only an unreasoning moment, that there might have been something *predictive* in the palm?

    Omens have a mythic quality; we listen to them disarmed of

our usual skepticism; they are *satisfying* superstitions. Included in this category are teratological omens (if a pregnant woman sees a mouse, her baby will be born with a mouse-shaped birthmark; if she listens to music, her baby will be born with heightened musical appreciation), medical omens, physiognomical omens (hand morphology and palmistry, for instance), numerologies (biorhythms), and astrologies (horoscopes), among other sciences and psuedo-sciences, including the study of dreams. (Don't get us wrong. There are many scientific observations founded on omens, one occurrence followed by another, with later proof of causality. What appeals to many people, however, are the pseudosciences, the *Cults of Unreason* that Dr. Christopher Evans refers to in his book of that title.)

Before we go on to a description of the specific uses of the hand in divination, let us first finish Julian Jaynes' list of the four types of divination: omen, sortilege, augury, and spontaneous divination.

Sortilege is the casting of lots—throwing "sticks, stones, bones, or beans" on the ground.[4] In the East this resulted in the I Ching; in the West, in shooting dice.

Augury is a bit more complicated. It consists of being able to see metaphors for actual events in other mediums, and also of the literary and linguistic ability to describe these connections at length. The earliest form practiced—about one and a half millennia B.C.— was the pouring of oil on water, a technique that offered the "seer" as many opportunities for prediction as he might have had in describing the clouds in the sky. When oil on water went out of fashion—the latest example of it being, according to Jaynes, the reference to Joseph's silver goblet in Genesis 44:5, at about 600 B.C.—other auguries became common: ". . . the movements of smoke rising from a censer of incense held in the lap of the diviner, or the form of hot wax dropped into water, or the patterns of dots made at random, or the shapes and patterns of ashes, and then sacrificed animals."[5]

Reading the entrails of sacrificed animals—extispicy—became the number one form of augury, at least in terms of the number of texts devoted to the subject, and in its own misbegotten way it was probably the grandfather of anatomy and pathology. Today augury is practiced in the reading of crystal balls and tea leaves and in the writing of popular psychology and history.

Spontaneous divination, according to Jaynes, is a combination of the other three types. "The outcomes of undertakings or the intentions of a god are thus read out from whatever object the diviner happens to see or hear."[6] This technique, which some people might think of as simply "making things up," was probably useful in early church teachings as a way of making abstract concepts clear to local listeners. One simply pointed to nearby things: "Do you see those sheep? These children? These loaves and fishes? Well, so great is God that. . . ." In other words, it offered instructive parables which the people could easily understand. In this case divination, in the form of inspiration and rhetoric, is the closest we come in Jaynes' system to outright logic and narratized consciousness.

Such elegant forms of telling the future were not, as such, available to old Yorick, say, when he wanted to know how to meet his Griselda. Neither was there available to him the expense of extispicy—sacrificial animals didn't come cheap—nor oil on water, nor tea leaves, nor bones, nor beans. No, old Yorick had one thing and one thing only: he had his hand—if he had been a good boy, he had both of them—from which to tell his future. Palmistry was the poor man's entrails, parable, and I Ching rolled into one.

It amazes us, in fact, that palmistry, which requires no charts, no research into date, time, and latitude and longitude of birth,which is simplicity itself, has not gained far more advocates than has astrology. Perhaps it is the fear of on-the-spot performance that has scared people off. If that is the case, the next section is designed to put to rest those fears.

Part One/Palmistry

This section might well be entitled "How to Win Friends and In-fluence People through Hand Reading." All hand reading is based on simple prejudices, good judgment of character, and a few diagrammatic rules. Let us start with the prejudices.

The origins for the "Science of Palmistry" are invariably placed in India, China, Egypt, or Greece. "The earliest known written reference to palmistry occurs in the Vedic scriptures of India, dating from about 2000 B.C. Whether the system of hand reading in use at that time was developed by the ancient sages themselves or was a modified tradition having its origins in the even older cultures of Chaldea and Egypt is a question that will never be answered."[7] "It has survived over thousands of years, from the days of the ancient Hindus and Greeks."[8] The Chinese and Egyptians of centuries past used it to forecast the future."[9] Conventional wisdom has it that the gypsies learned palmistry from the Hindus and carried the knowledge of it to Europe.[10] All palmistry systems—and there are almost as many systems as there are palmists—share certain assumptions about the shape of the whole hand, and in each system the shape of the hand is the first thing considered.

In 1652 John Gaule wrote what he felt was a *parody* of palmists' hand classifications. From the quote that follows you will see that he has in fact written a good summary of the basic prejudices:

A great thick hand signes one not only strong but stout; a little slender hand one not only weak but timorous; a long hand and long fingers betoken a man not only apt for mechanical artifice but liberally ingenious; but those short on the contrary denote a foole and fit for nothing; a hard, brawny hand signes dull and rude; a soft hand witty but effeminate; an hairy hand luxurious; long joints signe generous. . . . Short fat fingers mark a man out for intemperate and silly; but long and lean for witty.[11]

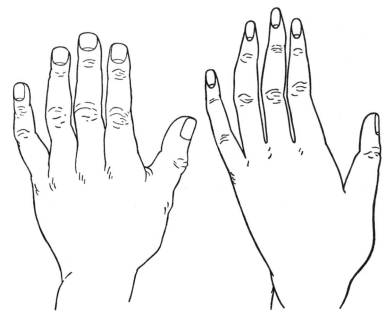

The Fat Hand. Cheiro   *The Thin Hand. Cheiro*

If this is the parody, listen to the seriously rendered modern classifications. We have the seven hand classifications of Count Louis
Hamon or "Cheiro" (1894), who simply copied the earlier classifications of D'Arpentigny (1843): The Elementary ("belongs to the
lowest grade of human intelligence . . . betokens a crass and sluggard
intelligence";[12] The Spatulate ("a woman with such fingers and a big
thumb will always be tidying up; a person with these hands will have
no taste for literature or art"[13]); The Conical or Artistic ("absolutely unfit for physical and mechanical pursuits"[14]); The Square or
Useful ("orderly, punctual and precise in manner, not, however, from
any innate grace of nature, but more from conformity"[15]); The
Knotty or Philosophic—the hand with "well-developed" joints—
("love, instinct, faith are all made subordinate to reason . . . we find a
large proportion of persons who become known as sceptics"[16] or, to
put it another way, "theirs the cloudland of thought, where the

dreaded grub-worm of materialism dare not follow"[17]); The Pointed or Psychic ("an otherworldly kind of person—contemplative, poetic, intuitive, often religious . . . fairly uncommon in Western countries")[18]; and the Mixed ("one finds in practice that almost all hands are 'mixed' "[19]). *That* simplifies matters.

In the interest of clarity we would like to divide all hands into two types—fat and thin—plus undecided—mixed. The fat hands are what have been described as Hippocrates' "pyknic types," or "Cheiro's" Elementary, Spatulate, and Square types. Thin hands are what Hippocrates would have described as the "Leptosomatic types," or "Cheiro's" Artistic, Philosophic, and Psychic hands. The third category—undecided—belongs to the otherwise-known-as-mixed.

Consider your own hand objectively, and categorize it under one of the three types. Later in this chapter we will provide a "reading" of your palm, based on your own careful classifications of your hands' morphology, lines, fingers and mounts. On a piece of paper write down 1 for this first question and A, B, or C for fat, thin, or other.

The next basic criterion for palms is "wet or dry, hot or cold." When you go to a professional palmist, a large part of his readings of your temperament will be based on these physical qualities. We like to think of these variables in terms of the chart below, which combines Galen's four temperaments (sanguine, choleric, phlegmatic, and melancholic) with the astrological four elements (water, earth, air, and fire). On your piece of paper, write down 2 and A, B, C, or D for which type most closely matches your own hand.

	Galen	*Astrological*	*type*
A. cold and wet	phlegmatic	water	emotionless
B. hot and wet	melancholic	earth	moody
C. cold and dry	sanguine	air	cheerful
D. hot and dry	choleric	fire	angry

If you have any trouble deciding whether your hand is cold or hot, take a look at its color. A cold hand is any hand that is not bright pink

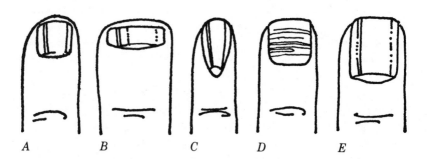

A   B   C   D   E

or red; it may be either white, pale pink, or blue. If it is blue, you should probably not be sitting there taking this test but should be under a doctor's care. You see? Your hand has already told you something about yourself.

Not only the shape of the hand and its moisture content and temperature, but its nails also tell us something of the character inherent in the hand. For question 3 on your paper, mark down which of the following you find in your hand:

A. Short nails, not reaching end of fingertip, of medium width (covering approximately two-thirds to four-fifths of the finger).

B. Short nails that cover more than four-fifths of the fingertip; nails that are more broad than long.

C. Oval or almond-shaped nails.

D. Nails with vertical or horizontal ribs.

E. Square nails, long and broad.

Now let's get down to some basic palm reading, which is essentially a look at four fingers, three lines, a thumb, and the Girdle of Venus. Believe us, the hardest part of palm reading is remembering which finger is which, which line means what. We have developed a simple pneumonic device to help you remember the fingers and the two major mounts: J. SAMMER MALU—J[upiter] S[aturn] A[pollo] MER[cury] MA[rs] LU[na]. This is a reading of the fingers, starting from top (the index finger) to the bottom (see illustration) plus the two mounts, Mars and Luna.

We have used the left hand here. For your own hand reading, you should be looking at your dominant hand. In palmistry the

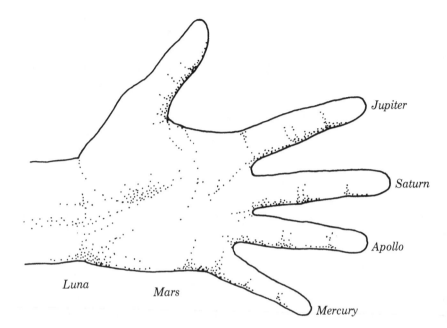

dominant hand reveals what you have made and will make of your life; the nondominant hand reveals what might have been. In the case of a surprising finding in the dominant hand, check the non-dominant hand for background information.

Once you've learned the names of the fingers, the associations are easy. Jupiter equals ambition; Saturn, sober restraint; Apollo (the Sun), artistry; Mercury (quicksilver), mental quickness. Or, if you are involved in astrology, think of the houses over which these planets rule:

       Jupiter: Sagittarius
       Saturn: Aquarius
       Apollo: Leo
       Mercury: Gemini and Virgo

The two mounts, Mars and Luna, rule, respectively war (Mars rules Aries) and imagination, someone being *"dans la lune"* (Luna rules Cancer). There is a third important mount on the hand, the mount of Venus, at the base of the thumb, which rules sex or, if you prefer, passion. Venus is associated with Libra.

In passing you might take note of the fact that Luna and Venus, the two feminine components of the hand, constitute what is referred to as the "heel."

Now, on to some reading. Let's look at the fingers Jupiter, Saturn, and Apollo. On your piece of paper, for question 4, mark down which of the following is true:

A. Jupiter (index) is longer than Apollo (ring)

B. Apollo is longer than Jupiter

C. They are about the same length.

Next, let's look at your "little" finger, Mercury. How does it measure up? This is question 5.

A. Tip falls below second knuckle (counting up from hand to nail) of ring finger.

B. Tip just reaches second knuckle of ring finger.

C. Tip extends beyond second knuckle of ring finger.

For the last "finger" of the hand, let's consider the thumb. Think of the thumb as the ego. Now, knowing that, admit which type of thumb you have, for question 6. Does your thumb reach (with your hand placed naturally, on a flat surface):

A. To the second joint of the index finger.

B. To the middle of the first phalanx (the part between the first and second knuckle) of the index finger.

C. Below the middle of the first phalanx of the index finger.

Now, place your hand naturally on a piece of paper and draw its outline. Finished? We're not going on with question 7 until you've done this. No cheating. Ready?

In your drawing, is your thumb:

A. Close to the palm of the hand.

B. Closer to a 45-degree angle.

C. Closer to a 90-degree angle.

For question 8 we have one last overall question before going on to the lines of the hand. Put your dominant hand—the one you've

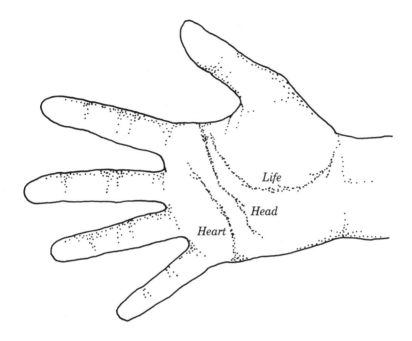

been "reading"—in you lap and shake it out. Let it relax. Now bring it up, elbow bent, hand facing forward, to shoulder height with the palm open. Turn your head and take a look at the hand. Is it:

A. Curled forward.

B. 80 percent erect.

C. Completely erect or even hyperextended.

The hardest part of reading the lines of the hand is remembering which line is which. Most everyone can remember which is the life line, although people have different systems for reading it, away from or toward the wrist. People often, however, confuse the head and the heart lines. We've found the easiest way to keep them straight is to think of the hand (left *or* right) always held sideways with the thumb up, as in the illustration.

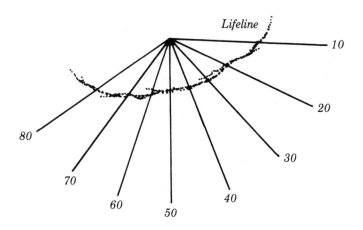

The Age Scale

If we think of the hand this way, it is easy to see that the head line is on top, on the "head" end of the hand, and the heart line comes from below, near the heart.

Now let's take a look at the life line. In all reputable palmistry systems, the length of the life line is measured from above the thumb toward the wrist. Note the Age Scale for the life line of the left hand (right handers please think mirror image). This reads properly for the hand held with the fingers pointing straight up.

You will first of all be glad to note that, almost without exception, life lines run long. This single fact is undoubtedly the key to palmistry's ongoing popularity. Beyond the potential in the hand for long life, however, the life line will also tell us at what point crucial events have and will occur. The Age Scale can be consulted also for the following question.

Question 9. At any point does a major line cross the life line:

A. Cutting upward.

B. Cutting across.

C. Forking off from.

Now to the head line. This line is considered a "character" line and tells us about your mental abilities and tendencies. It is not so much the length of the head line as its quality that informs us. First, for question 10, its beginnings. Does your head line:

A. Run contiguously with the life line for some distance.

B. Start from the same point as the life line.

C. Begin at a point separate from the life line.

Next, for question 11, let's consider its qualities:

A. Singular, clean, unwavering.

B. Chained.

C. Broken.

And finally, question 12, where is your head line headed?

A. Upward toward Jupiter (index finger).

B. Upward toward Saturn.

C. Upward toward Apollo.

D. Upward toward Mercury.

E. Straight.

F. Downward.

With your knowledge of what the different fingers stand for, you might already guess what your head line's direction indicates. If your head line does go straight across, it may in fact join the heart line, coming from the opposite direction. This is known as the Simian Crease and is typical of the hands of children born with Downes Syndrome, commonly known as Mongoloidism. It is called the Simian Crease because it duplicates the configuration on the hands of the apes and monkeys, whose hands lack the mobility of the human hand and therefore typically fold horizontally at the Simian Crease. *Do not be alarmed* if you find a Simian line in either hand. Although some palmists—even the modern ones like Broekman ("the infant is men-

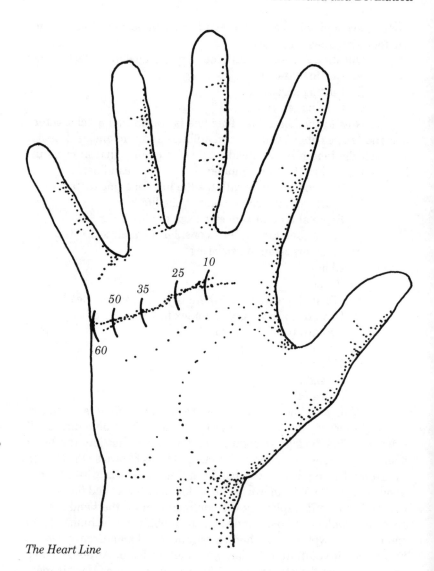

The Heart Line

tally doomed"[20])—consider this an aberrant sign and one that is undesirable in the hand, we like to think of the Simian line as a charming atavistic throwback to simpler times. Before humans evolved to their present complex state, the head and the heart were the same, thinking and feeling were synonymous. Of course, because we *do* live in complex times, a hand with a Simian line might predict an obstacle to be overcome—the entwining of thinking and feeling—but it might just as well indicate an elevated state of being, one for which many people strive. As for its unfortunate occurrence in the hands of those with Downes Syndrome, it is a necessary but not a sufficient sign of this problem, which usually also involves severe mental retardation. One need not look to the hand to discover this problem. For our purposes, the hand should be addressed when there is a need to look into the past and into the future and to consider the unknown and the unknowable in one's life.

The heart line also is a "character" line, this one of the feelings. The ages that indicate affairs of the heart are read from the center of the hand outward, as shown in the illustration.

As you can see, you have to go around the bend of the hand a bit to read this line for ages after 60. Take a look at your own heart line and then answer question 13. Is your heart line:

A. Forked at the beginning.
B. Doubled or tripled.
C. Interrupted.
D. Forked at the end.

In association with the heart line we have the lines of affection or marriage and lines of potential children. The lines of affection are found on the outside of the hand, parallel to and above the heart line. The number of potential children are found perpendicular to the lines of affection. The age at which these major "affections" occur can be read by considering the midpoint between the heart line and the crease of the little finger to be 25 with age increasing as you move toward the little finger.

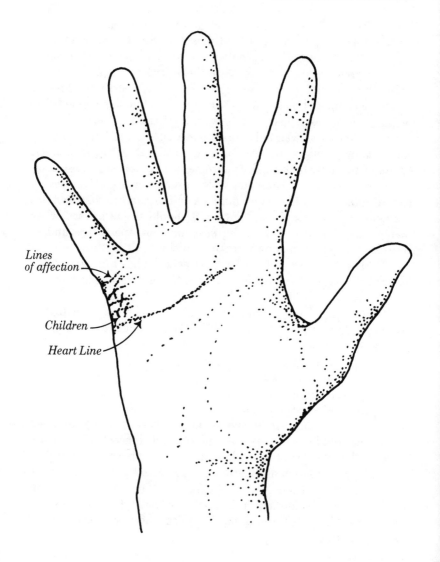

*Lines
of affection*

Children

Heart Line

Now let's go back to question 1 and see what we have found in your hand.[21]

The A hands, or "fat" hands, belong to people who are athletic, plain-speaking, and extremely honest. Type A hands have perseverance. They are not afraid of doing hard work, though there is a tendency toward giving in to laziness. A hands belong either to simple, earthy people or to romantic dreamers.

The B hands, or "thin" hands, belong to sensuous, cunning, and pleasure-loving people. Type B hands are artistic and belong to egoists. People with B hands may work hard, but it is only to put themselves in a position to enjoy more pleasure and more beauty. B hands may be generous to friends, but they are greedy, close-fisted hands to others. Fakers, eccentrics, and intellectuals have B hands. Type B's are enthusiasts, but only about the things *they* are interested in.

C hands have some of the A qualities and some of the B qualities. It is common for a hand to have some characteristics of each—fat palm with thin fingers, or fat fingers with thin, pointed tips. Some of the most interesting, vital people mix the best qualities of the two hands (or so a skillful palmist will tell you, neatly avoiding the fact that *most* hands are mixed).

Now to your temperament, question 2.[22] First let's take the A's, with cold and wet hands. You are passive, careful, sensitive and thoughtful. You like being in control, and if you feel you are not in control you become very upset. Usually you are at peace with yourself (some people would call you "out of touch" with the real world). You are calm and even-tempered, washing over most trials and occasions like the water sign you are.

B hands, hot and wet, belong to the melancholic. You are moody and anxious (that's why your hands are hot and wet, after all). You have a rigid personality and always see the pessimistic side to things. People think of you as sober, but that is because you are reserved and unsociable when you aren't fretting about something. Like the earth, you are quiet, practical, and rigid. You would like to be more outgoing, but your introverted nature pulls you back.

Type C hands belong to the sanguine. They are cold and dry. You are sociable, outgoing, talkative—the opposite of Type B. People think of you as an intellectual and a leader, and they like your carefree, lively, easygoing approach to things. You may be a bit *too* talkative in public, but because you are so responsive to the people around you, no one will care. You are air, light and vital.

Type D hands, hot and dry, belong to the touchy, restless, and aggressive folks. These are the opposites to the type A hands. While you are passionate, optimistic, and excitable, you are also changeable and impulsive. No one knows quite *what* to expect of you. Like fire, you go where there's fuel.

(Incidentally, on the subject of hot hands being red and cold hands being white or blue, certain Russian psychics claim to read these colors of subjects' hands while they are still blindfolded. Whether they can feel the relative heat or coolness or whether they can really "see" these colors has not been established.)

Now to the shape of your nails, question 3.

You Type A nails have been biting them, haven't you? That's because you're the critical type. Have your blood pressure checked.

The Type B nails denote a fighter, someone who is dogmatic and argumentative. You too probably bite your nails but not from nervousness, like the critic above. You bite your nails instead of biting someone's head off. Your Type B nails indicate a Type A personality for heart attacks.

The Type C nails, almond shaped, belong to compulsive workers who use up their nervous energy in short bursts. You may not be in the best physical health, but your nervous energy should carry you through.

You Type D nail owners probably didn't know that your shock, whatever it was, would turn up in your nails. These are called "Beau lines," for the French physician who identified them in 1846, and they indicate acute illness, like scarlet fever or typhus, as well as broken limbs or emotional shocks. Longitudinal ridges usually indicate a chronic physical condition, and white flecks occur when you are under stress or tension, or are anxious for any reason. Depression will also cause the little white specks. (Some of what we have just said has basis in fact, which is something palmists, who operate in a fairly fantastic field, latch onto with great glee. For a further discussion of medical diagnosis made from the nails, see the box at the end of this chapter.)

Happy Type E nail owners. You are open, honest, and, as far as we can see, healthy and well-adjusted. Other signs in your hand, of course, can change this picture.

Now we will move on to your fingers, question 4.

You people who answered A are Jupiter types. You are proud and have a desire to lead. You are sensual, and you love good food. Your capabilities are in the material world. This strong finger is often found in the hands of tyrants, school principals, and religious leaders in the Western world. Jupiterians are manipulators, if no other parts of the hand control them. Check your nondominant hand to see if your *potential* and your actual hand configurations are the same. If your Jupiter is not longer than your Apollo in the nondominant (usually left) hand, that means you have become a tyrant against your nature.

The long Apollo finger belongs to the artistic types. These are the B answers to question 4. You are charmers rather than manipulators, and you care about what people think of you. You may be fatalistic and sometimes gamble when you shouldn't. You should not work on your own, but learn to work in partnership with others, where you will be happier. Again check your nondominant hand to see if you were meant to be this way or just became this way.

If Apollo and Jupiter are about the same length, they are nicely balanced by the middle finger, Saturn, which is the longest finger on the hand. The Saturn character—serious and conservative— carefully weighs each situation and calls upon your leadership qualities or your artistic qualities as necessary.

Now to question 5. Ah, Mercury, you little devil. If your Mercury is shorter than the second joint on your ring finger, answer

A, you absorb things quickly but tend to be better in straightforward reasoning than in creative thinking.

If you are a B type Mercury, you are probably attracted to the sciences or to some business involving words.

The C Mercury types are tactful, great judges of human nature, adroit, crafty, and great talkers. They specialize in oratory, some are attracted to careers in the theater, *and* they are great business people besides.

And then there is your ego—your thumb—question 6.

Those of you whose thumbs reach the second joint of the index finger (answer A) have lo-o-o-ong thumbs. These denote tremendous willpower and logical ability. You are extravagant, and could one day be a great leader.

If your thumb reaches the middle of the first phalanx (the part of the finger between the first joint and the second joint), then you answered B. You are less energetic than Type A, but you still act with logic and determination.

If you have a Type C thumb, you have little use for logic and little energy to pursue your scatterbrained ideas. You are very easily led. Other signs in your hand may help counteract your short thumb. Check your other hand to see if you were born this way or if "something happened."

On the position of your thumb, question 7, the closer it is to the hand (answer A) the more you depend on other people. If you have a long thumb (6–A) but hold the thumb close (7–A), you have a lot of leadership ability which you are afraid to use. You are hiding your light under a bushel. The more your thumb stands out on its own (answer C), the more independent you are in your thinking. A short thumb (6–C) that stands at a 90-degree angle is compensating for little self-assurance by putting the person in a front position. Radicals and revolutionaries have widespread thumbs, but this sign in the hand too can be modified by other qualities.

On question 8, the straighter you hold your hand, the more self-realized you are. People who hold their hands almost curled are in poor health, either physically or emotionally, perhaps just today, perhaps chronically. A hyperextended hand, bent almost backward, belongs to a proud, healthy, effective, happy person.

On question 9, answer A, there are several possible interpretations of an upward line crossing the life line, depending on where the upward-sweeping line leads. Generally speaking, lines sweeping upward from the wrist denote success: if toward Jupiter (the index finger), it denotes academic or business success; if toward Apollo, an achievement in the arts; if toward Mercury, success in business or science. When that success occurs depends on where the upward sweeping line crosses the life line. See the Age Scale earlier for an idea of the time period.

If you answered B, check your hand again and make sure these are major lines and not just the fine lines that sometimes dominate the hands of sensitive or very nervous people. Event-lines will be deeper and longer than general disposition lines. If a major line cuts your life line but doesn't affect other lines, it indicates interference at that time in your life by your parents. If a line cuts across the life line, the head line, and the heart line, it indicates a serious loss of affections, perhaps a lost love. If the line crosses the life line smoothly and leads all the way to the middle finger, it could indicate a potentially dangerous accident. Check to see whether this has already occurred, and if not, take care to fasten your seat belts and look both ways in traffic.

Answer C, lines forking off of the life line, indicate obstructions, difficulties, and reverses in your life. The small lines that fork off at the end of your life line indicate your eventual physical weakening. A major branch leading off of the life line toward another part of the hand shows that at that point you will make (or have made) a major change in your life.

On question 10, if you answered A, that means that you are cautious, timid, that you quite literally didn't give yourself your head in life for some time. Caution is also indicated in a Type B head line, although it may be a healthy caution. For answer C, the wider the separation, the more you tend toward being reckless. A small separation means merely that you are independent.

As for your head line's qualities; question 11, an A line belongs to a practical, straightforward person. The chained head line, answer B, indicates a person who constantly changes his or her mind. And C, a broken head line, indicates serious trouble. If the breaks are actually islands, consider this a sign of serious injury to the head, either literally or by an emotional trauma.

And, most important, question 12, where is your head line headed? Answer A, toward your index finger (Jupiter), means you are headed for leadership. If it branches toward Saturn (B) you must be prepared for negative energy and a gloomy sense of fatalism. If the line heads toward Apollo it means that you want to be successful and popular. And if your line moves toward your little finger (D), it denotes talent in science or business. A straight line (E) shows your lack of imagination (on the negative side) but your practical nature (on the positive side). And a head line that heads downward (F) toward the heel of your hand, indicates a fertile imagination.

Most of you have probably been wondering about the love line, that is, your heart line. And so we come to question 13. A forked beginning to the line of the heart (answer A) indicates early conflicts within the family. You draw your ability to love from many sources, not just one cohesive one. A tripled or doubled heart line (answer B) indicates a double nature. You may have one life at home and another life completely separate and be able to keep both going without any interference between them. You truly have two faces which coexist without conflicting emotions. An interrupted heart line (C) can mean problems in love, or it can mean serious heart trouble. If you are worried that this might indicate the latter for you, have a checkup. (Palmists can never go wrong suggesting that their clients see a professional "if they are worried.") The forking at the end of the heart line indicates the normal weakening of the heart as you get older.

Well, how did you do?

What is interesting about palmistry is that it gives people a chance to consider the important questions of life: How long will I live? Am I a "good" person, a strong person? When will I marry? How many children will I have? Am I smart? Talented? Will I be successful? These are questions we would never ask another person unless we had the excuse of their "reading" our hands. But while they read the lines in our hands, they are also reading our personality. When we offer our hands for a reading, we can discuss personal topics without embarrassment or hesitancy. If you think that we did a good job in reading your character from your hand, you should be aware of a few things. First, if you are left-handed, you should know that the left hand has more lines than the right. Therefore left-handers' readings tend to show a more conflicted, complicated life. Palmists would make sense of this by saying that lefties are constantly faced with problems because of their minority status. It is not a devastating difference, but it is enough to add small tensions throughout their lives.

You might also look back on our "readings." As with astrological "readings," things have been put in easy-to-accept terms, what might be called glittering obfuscations. When you read your daily horoscope and it tells you to be careful in business dealings that day, it is good advice for anyone to follow, whether you are a Leo or not. Likewise when we say you should "take care to fasten your seat belts and look both ways in traffic," who, may we ask, shouldn't? And who hasn't had a devastating love affair at "around the age of 20"?

Third, you will see that most of our readings are positive, either of good things that have happened or of positive steps you can take to make things happen.

Also, remember, you "helped" us by making your own interpretations.

And finally, remember that you have perceived our readings
to be accurate using selective memory. What sticks in your mind are
the amazingly insightful things we have said about you, not the near
misses and the does-not-applies.

Now, armed with the skepticism we have just imparted, and
with this much knowledge of palm reading, you can go forth and read
other palms. What you don't know, make up. What better way to get
to know someone than to sit quietly with the person, holding his or
her hand, discussing his or her whithers and hences. This activity is,
needless to say, great at parties. Everyone has the necessary two
ingredients: a palm and curiosity.

Part Two/Fingerprints, Graphology, and Medical Diagnosis

In Eastern cultures the lines of the palm were used for divining the
past and the future, and so were the fingerprints. The Chinese used a
thumbprint as a seal for many hundreds of years, correctly believing
that such prints were varied enough to form a positive identification.
In Oriental occult practices the fingerprints were looked at to tell the
character. In the West even stone-age people had a look at those
strange lines on their fingers and made cave drawings of them,
possibly in the belief that fingerprints were magic.

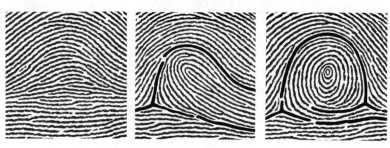

The three types of fingerprints are shown in the illustration. On the left is the arch, in the middle the loop, and on the right the whorl. Look closely at your own fingerprints to see which type you have.

The Chinese have a folk saying (similar to our "Monday's child is . . . ," which explicates the patterns on the fingertips:

One whorl, poor; two whorls, rich;
Three whorls, four whorls, open a pawn shop;
Five whorls, be a go-between;
Six whorls, be a thief;
Seven whorls, meet calamity;
Eight whorls, eat chaff;
Nine whorls and one loop, no work to do—
    eat till you are old.[*][23]

The Japanese had perhaps a more helpful system. Whorls signified dexterity and stubbornness. People with whorls on all ten fingers were restless, doubting, sensitive, clever, eager for action, and inclined to crime. Loops indicated lack of perseverance, arches a merciless, crude character, someone who was ambitious, cold-blooded, stubborn, disobedient, defiant, and rebellious. Mixtures of loops and whorls denoted neutral people who were kind, truthful, yet sometimes disobedient and impatient.[24]

You might be interested to know that loops (lack of perseverance, according to the early Japanese) are the most common configuration in America, with a large number of people having loops on all fingers.

In criminal fingerprinting systems, the hands are categorized by a numerical index based on whorls (16 points for a whorl on one thumb, 32 for a whorl on both thumbs, etc.). Such a system is necessary because the FBI holds 180 million sets of fingerprints, most of them, obviously, from noncriminals.[25]

---

[*]*We want you to know that one of the authors almost made it, clocking in with eight whorls, one loop and a delta.*

The Hand and Medical Diagnosis

There *are* diseases that can be spotted in the hands, though not the ones that palmists say can be found there.[35] One medical doctor, a specialist in endocrinology, said he could spend two hours talking on symptoms and signs of disease found in the hand.

Obviously, crippling diseases like arthritis are immediately recognizable in the hands. Heberden's nodes are a specific form of osteoarthritis of the hands that often affect women after menopause, resulting in unsightly but relatively harmless enlargements of the end joints of the fingers. Rheumatoid arthritis, in which the body attacks itself, is a more common cause of swollen knuckles.

Dupuytren's contracture, contrarily, is more common in men. It starts with a small nodule opposite the base of the ring finger or little finger, and progresses to the formation of tight bands in the palm that pull the fingers into a claw hand. It is often associated with alcoholism and is also thought to be hereditary.

Marfan's Syndrome, sometimes known as Lincoln's Disease, gives the hands a characteristically elongated appearance. The disease also affects other long bones and internal organs, which continue to grow until they misfunction. A curious disease known as "penile strabismus" or a bending of the penis, is presaged by an inward curving of the hand. Cystic fibrosis might be suspected in a baby born with hammerhead nails.

Leathery (sclerodermatous), cold hands might indicate Reynaud's Syndrome, a vascular problem. Blue nails would mean that you've become cyanotic; in other words that you are not getting enough oxygen and are either in immediate danger or have a chronic illness. And hands that sweat easily might point toward Basedow's Disease, which causes a thyroid problem.

DeQuervain's disease results in pain at the base of the thumb, radiating to the nail and up to the forearm. This condition, more frequently seen in women, is also known as stenosing tenosynovitis and is aggravated by constant use of the thumb in work such as typing and household chores. The problem is caused by thickening of the sheaths of the thumb tendon.

Carpal tunnel syndrome sometimes occurs during pregnancy, and is often seen in women over 40. The median nerve to the hand is compressed as it passes through the wrist, resulting in tingling, pain or numbness in the thumb and index finger, and sometimes in the long fingers. These symptoms often occur at night, when the patient has gone to bed.

"Trigger finger" is so-named because a snap is heard as the finger bends or extends, the result of a small nodule of tendon that is moving through a constriction. "Buttonhole deformity," a result of a blow or injury to the middle finger, when fully developed results in the middle joint being flexed while the other two are extended. Immediate medical care can solve both trigger finger and buttonhole deformity. The so-called "baseball" finger is characteristically caused by the miscatching of a baseball, which strikes the tip of the finger and ruptures or tears the tendon. Immobilization will usually repair the injury.

The clubbing of the fingertips is a sign of hyperthyroidism or heart disease.

Trembling of the hands can be a sign of nervous disorder, palsy, or too much drink, hyperthyroidism, Parkinson's Disease, Wilson's Disease (a liver disorder that produces a slight hand tremor that becomes an up and down beating-the-wings movement when the hands are held at shoulder height), senility, neurasthenia, hypoglycemia, ataxia (frontal lobe lesions), narcotic addiction, multiple sclerosis, chorea, hepatic coma, or poisoning from heavy metals.

The skin on the hand can give an indication of health and disease, as can its temperature and color. Warm hands can mean high blood pressure, gout, diabetes, arteriosclerosis, or rheumatoid arthritis. Cold hands can mean anemia, problems with circulation, shock, or neurasthenia.

If for any reason you are concerned about something you see in your hands, go to a doctor for professional advice.

We don't divine the past and future of a person just by looking at his or her hands. We also look at the tracings the hands make—a person's handwriting. Handwriting analysis was developed in France in the nineteenth century and was elevated to a university level of study by the Germans. In Germany, handwriting analysis was taught as part of the medical curriculum or in the psychology division, with as much as three years of study possible.[26] No other country has been so fascinated with the study of graphology, except perhaps America, where the New School for Social Research, founded by Germans, offers courses in graphology.

Graphologists think of handwriting as concretized gesture. We are surely influenced by the copybook method of writing we were taught in grade school; but the further we get from Miss Knickerbocker's class, the more our handwriting takes on a personal look, and the more it tells about us. As graphologist Klara Roman said: "It retains the essential characteristics through the years. It's continuously in the process of change, reflecting growth and aging, the impact of crucial events . . . [yet] it retains its consistency through the years."[27]

One thing that is sometimes apparent from a subject's handwriting is the country in which he or she was raised. In the Swedish copybook handwriting model, for instance, the *i* is dotted with a circle. There is a theory that the size of the writing correlates to the size of the country in which you learned your writing. Australians write large, Britons smaller, and the Swiss smaller still. Once handwriting style is set, a later move to another country and copybook system usually fails to influence it.[28]

Dorothy Rice's system for classifying nationality had to do with character types:

Spanish and Italian is characterized by flowing capitals indicating gaiety and love of beauty; French by meticulous little forms showing logic, fine sensibilities, by prominence of the letter "M"; German by its

intricate angular letter forms [which dominate the capital letters that
characterize German nouns]; Russian by its overornamented capitals,
long connecting strokes, and sprawling rhythm, pointing to talkative-
ness and outgoing personality. . . . Russian is similar to English and
American [handwriting].[29]

One authority claims that intelligence can be gauged from handwriting. In a 1966 study of Mensa members, about 11 percent
showed a highly irregular handwriting, of which 1 percent showed
disconnected writing and 8 percent showed a highly original script.
These 11 percent were thought to be the most talented and creative
people, but people whose personal lives were characterized by
chaos.[30]

Other authorities feel that handwriting analysis can give
valuable clues to a person's health. Eisenhower's handwriting dis-
integrated noticeably during his presidency, especially after his
stroke. Robert Wasserman looks for signs of psychic ability in the
handwriting of patients—"disconnected letters, light pressure of the
pen, high upper loops, unusual writing, and the final strokes of the
last letter rising ususually high."[31]

Then there is the American graphologist Paul de Sainte
Columbe, who claims that he can "cure" homosexuality, laziness,
and stuttering, stop a person from smoking in eight weeks, stop an
alcoholic from drinking in nine months—all by handwriting therapy.
He also helps the timid, the emotionally unstable, and those who lack
confidence.[32]

One last thing before we go on to explain the ways in which
you can analyze handwriting. It is important to watch the speed with
which the writing is done. Roman, in her *Encyclopedia,* says that
tempo in thinking and writing are intimately connected. The rush of
ideas carries the writer along. Girls are writing at full speed by the
time they are 14, but boys don't reach their full speed until they are
18,[33] a factor that could make a difference in grades on essay exams
in high school. Great speed is usually associated with intellectual
ability.

Have your subject sit in a comfortable chair and give him or her unlined paper on which to write. An ink pen will give a truer indication of the person's writing style than will a ball-point pen. If the writer is used to a ball-point, however, it is better not to switch to a fountain pen. You should ask him or her to write several short sentences, with all of the letters of the alphabet included, but a special emphasis on *g, y, q, z, f, l* and *h.*

After your subject has written, first get a general impression. Look at where the writer started on the page—at the very top, a few inches down, or in the middle. The higher on the page, the more assertive the subject. The very cautious will start in the middle and then regret it (feel they are wasting paper) when they run out of room at the bottom, where they will start to write smaller. These people are bad planners, with little awareness of the immediate future.

Look at the flow of the writing. Is it well regulated? Or does it seem stilted and forced? Is it self-conscious? Or is it filled with jerks, starts, and stops, indicating haste and repressed hostility.

Next let's look at the "zones" of the writing. Obviously some letters go up and some go down. It is the emphasis of the up and down, however, that counts. In Freudian terms the upper zone is the superego, the middle zone is the ego, and the lower zone is the id. The upper is the realm of the intellect and spiritual consciousness, the middle range is of the individual consciousness, and the lower represents instinct and materialism. All movements (of a "straight" right-hander) that enter the lower zone are going back toward the writer, while all movements in the upper zone are going away from the writer. Pronounced lower loops—see the *y* above—are connected to material well-being—food, sex, money, traditions, and possessions. The ascenders of upper loops (*t, l, h,* etc.) indicate attitudes toward ideals, morals, and religion.[34]

It is the middle zone, though, that is most important. It mediates between the material and the spiritual world. Here we find the writer's attitudes toward family, work, and the immediate environment. If the writing has minimal ascenders and descenders and

The little boy with the

tends to concentrate in the middle range, it shows intense concentration on the here and now.

Now let's take a look at the slant of the writing. Most people, left- or right-handers, slope their writing to the right. Graphologists have little good to say about southpaws who slant their writing "backwards." The left, to graphologists, represents the past, reversion to the mother figure, and to the feminine in general. Anything slanting toward the right (ah, the old prejudices) is toward the father, the male, and the future. (Remember how the Australians called left-handers "Molly dookers," or woman-handed?) One authority mentioned a tendency in children when they reach the age of puberty to switch briefly to leftward (backward) slant, perhaps as an indication of the intense conflict and the growth of sexual forces.

So there you have three ways to read a person's future, past, and personality by his or her hands: palmistry, fingerprint reading, and graphology. What do the authors think of all this? Can't you really *tell?* Quite honestly, we think these methods are, respectively, nonsense, of interest to forensic pathologists only, and sometimes interesting and predictive. We have tried, however, to give you a fair sampling of the thinking of others on these subjects. We have enjoyed testing ourselves and our friends. If these techniques provide another way of looking at people, and especially if they get the people thinking about and talking about their own feelings and their past, there can be no harm in any of it.

10/ Obsessions, Compulsions, Decorations

Not all kisses equal thumb sucking, no, no, by no means all. One cannot describe the enjoyment that goes through the entire body when one sucks one's thumb: one is far from this world; one is absolutely satisfied and supremely happy. It is a wonderful feeling. One only wishes quiet; quiet that nothing can interrupt. It is simply, indescribably wonderful; one feels no pain, no sorrow, and oh! one is transported into another world.

A grown-up girl patient, a compulsive thumbsucker,
recorded by Dr. Galant, 1919

We have already mentioned some of the obsessions, compulsions, and decorations associated with the hand: the wearing of amulets in the form of various obscene or holy hand gestures, the cutting off of "birth-strangled babes' " fingers or the fingers of hanged men for good luck, the cutting off of fingers and thumbs as a form of punishment, and masturbation, just to name a few.

For some people the hand has a special significance, beyond that most of us accord it. To some Irish, for instance, the O'Neills in particular, *Lamh dearg Eirin*, "The Red Hand of Erin," is a reminder of a clansman O'Neill who, on being told that the first hand to touch shore would claim the land there, and seeing another boat edging ahead, cut off his own hand and threw it to the shore, thus winning the race. The "bloody hand" appears also on several badges and coats of arms, signifying bloody deeds and battles.[1]

Some people merely collect "death hands," casts made of the hands of the great and beautiful when they die. Others sculpt, draw, or paint nothing but hands. Ray Shaw, a Manhattan sculptress, is a self-admitted maniphiliac. She has sculpted the hands of Franklin D. Roosevelt, Jack Dempsey, Helen Hayes, Lauren Bacall, Jimmy Doolittle, and Albert Einstein, among others. When she asked Einstein what instrument she should include in her sculpture of his hands to symbolize his work, he thought for a moment and then said, "A pencil, my child, is my only weapon." Thus Einstein's hand sculpture carries a pencil in its right hand.

The modern French artist César Baldaccini has made several sculptures of the thumb alone. His most monumental work is a three-foot-tall bronze called César's Thumb, obviously a self-portrait.

There are people who collect hand *prints,* in the belief that these tell us something about the person's heredity or artistic bent. Sorell, for instance, dedicates almost twenty pages of the book, *The Story of the Human Hand,* to hand prints of the great (Maurice Maeterlinck, Edgard Varèse, Jean Cocteau) and the ungreat (friends with interesting palms), in a section he calls "The Mainstream" in which he sets out to prove how Cocteau's thumb, for instance, points to someone who "must and cannot help but succeed."

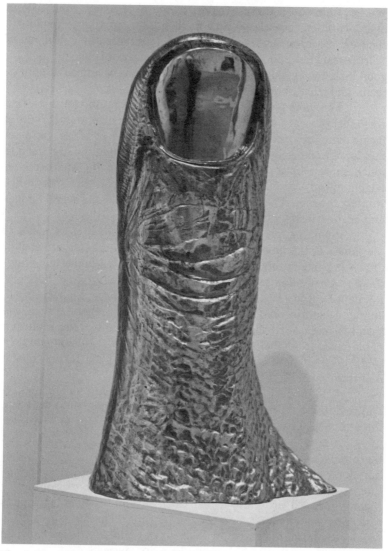

César's Thumb. Andrew Bradke

There are people obsessed with palmistry just as there are people obsessed with astrology. And there are people who always look at another person's hands first because that is the part of the body that most attracts them.

There are people who go still further into obsessions in regard to the hands. Compulsive hand washers, for instance, "may have a history of punitive early toilet training," but this is not an unequivocable background, according to Beech in his *Obsessional States*.[2] Grooming behavior, according to Zeigler, is a way of unloading a situation, and hand washing is an extreme form of grooming.[3] Some people worry incessantly that their hands are dirty but restrain themselves from washing them as often as they would like. Others let their urges rule their lives and wash their hands as many as fifty times a day. One man of our acquaintance, a noted New York critic, washed his hands so often he had a permanent red band of irritation around his wrists where the washing stopped.

One way of breaking a compulsive hand washer is with the paradoxical intention, in which the patient is taught to think: "I love germs. I like my hands to be as dirty as possible. Who wants to be clean?" This method could lead to paradoxical reversals of the hand washing compulsion, though. Perhaps a better method is to demonstrate patiently to the compulsive that his or her hands are *not* dirty and that not washing the hands does not inexorably lead to disease and disaster.

This kind of compulsion is what psychologists call a displacement activity. The classic study in this area concerned the stickleback fish. When two male sticklebacks meet over a boundary area between their territories, instead of fighting, as might be expected, both sticklebacks immediately and compulsively begin nest-building activity. Displacement activity, according to Zeigler, occurs when there is motivational conflict, frustration, thwarting of drives, or perhaps exposure to novel situations. All of these conditions obtain in the lives of people living in large cities and it is a wonder there isn't more frustration displaced into activities like washing the hands or biting the nails.[4]

Of all hand compulsions the oldest, and still favorite, is thumb sucking. Even before we are born, we are sucking at our thumbs and they are our first refuge in the cold, dry, outside world. In his essay "Infantile Sexuality" Freud says: "The pleasure-sucking is connected with a full absorption of attention and leads to sleep or even to a motor reaction in the form of an orgasm."[5]

And, later in the same essay, he says: "The child does not make use of a strange object for sucking but prefers his own skin, because it is more convenient, because it makes him independent of the outer world which he cannot control, and because, in his way, he creates for himself as it were a second, even if an inferior, erogenous zone. . . . I believe [we are justified] in claiming thumb sucking as a sexual activity."[6]

Who would have it otherwise?

As children we suck our thumbs: the forefinger and middle finger, all three fingers, all four fingers, we suck the back of our hand, we suck our forearm. We do it in times of stress, at bedtime, when we are hungry. It is a never-to-be-lost, all-purpose, anatomically correct pacifier. Boys suck their thumbs, fingers, or hands more than do girls (perhaps because, as they are more sensitive to pain, they need this solace during teething). Boys persist in sucking their thumbs long after most little girls have stopped. Later girls are more likely to seductively or reflectively suck their thumbs, men to smoke and drink. As Dr. A. A. Brill said in 1922, "neurotic smoking . . . represents a regression to infantile autoeroticism . . . its infantile root is thumb sucking."[7] Gum, lollipops, erasers on pencils, bows of eyeglasses, and food sometimes make satisfying substitutes for the beloved thumb.

In times of worry or anxiety many of us revert to a modified form of thumb sucking. We bite our thumbnail or tap it against our front teeth, neither of which seems quite as *verboten* as putting our thumb in our mouth would be. Thumbs are dirty, "bad," they are sucked only by "babies." And so we put them aside except during lovemaking, when we might put our lover's thumb in our mouth, to tease it with pleasure, or might put our own thumb to our mouth afterwards in an orgy of self-satisfaction.

Dr. Joseph C. Solomon sees thumb sucking in children, as well as rhythmic rocking and nail biting, as "self-containment" devices, "a method of defending the formative ego against the feeling of being abandoned. . . . It is as though someone is always there."[8]

Well, someone *is* there. It is our old friend, the hand.

Nail biting is known as *onychophagy*. There have been several famous people who habitually bit their nails, including Robespierre and Napoleon[9], the latter only in moments of extreme irritation, as during his stay on St. Helena. One of the few "sure cures" for nail biting is to turn the compulsion the other way, toward nail growing, perhaps with an expensive manicure to boot.

The Chinese developed a cult of the nail, with ladies of the court enclosing their long nails in silver or gold sheaths to guard them. Chinese Mandarins gilded their nails to indicate rank, showing that they were not only rich but also that they were idle rich. In some parts of the world—the Philippines is one—a man's thumbnail is grown long to show that he doesn't perform manual labor. In Greece it is the little fingernail that is grown long for the same purpose. This practice may be a holdover from the seventeenth-century court in Europe; here the little fingernail was also grown long but not to show that its bearer performed no manual labor. (They were at court, after all.) Long nails were necessary because no one was allowed to knock at the door of royalty or high dignitaries; rather, petitioners were instructed to scratch, *softly*.[10]

Nail painting was originally practiced to guard the fingers and the hands from evil spirits. The women of Ancient Egypt used henna to dye their nails, and it also dyed their palms as they used it. Other women varnished their nails to cover up imperfections (of which there were many, as healthy nails were a reflection of good nutrition).

Cromwell denounced enameling nails as an evil custom, but the Restoration reestablished the right of ladies to paint their nails.

Queen Victoria, however, disliked the custom and made no effort to hide her disapproval. The custom waned until her death, but soon painted nails were back again. Each time the custom disappeared and reappeared, it gained more practitioners. Painted nails, once the sign of a "bad" woman, are now considered fairly tame.

Even more acceptable than painting nails is the wearing of rings and bracelets. Wedding rings symbolize the marriage contract and bond. They are common throughout the world, extending to Assam, Zambesi, Central Africa, and so on. The rings are not always worn on the third (ring) finger of the left hand, as we wear them in America and Europe, but might be worn on the forefinger of either hand or, as in Colombia, South America, on the ring finger of the *right* hand. One theory holds that the ring finger was so chosen because it moves on its own the least of any of the fingers and therefore the wedding ring has less chance of being lost or scratched on that finger. Others say that the ring finger has a special nerve, vein, or artery connecting it directly to the heart, but this belief has no basis in fact.

Desmond Morris reports a nineteenth-century proposal that all husbands (today we would include wives, too, as they are now let out of the house) have their ring finger tattooed to discourage errant ways and bigamy; when divorced, a man would have the tattooed ring X'ed out, only to be tattooed a second time if he remarried.[11]

Sad to say, the wearing of gloves, especially white gloves, has passed its heyday. Gloves have been worn almost as long as people have had hands. According to Tabori, even cave dwellers had a primitive form of them. Early gloves often covered only the palm and back of the hand (leaving the fingers free for work), thus the origin of the name, from *glof*, Anglo-Saxon for "palm." Only during the thirteenth century did gloves take on an ornamental rather than a practical appearance. During this time also they began to be worn indoors. They also began to be long, sometimes elbow length. By the sixteenth century gloves, along with most other things, reached a peak of decoration and elaboration. They were collected, given as presents, and considered as art objects. Kings were buried with their gloves on. A glove was removed and flung down or used to slap an

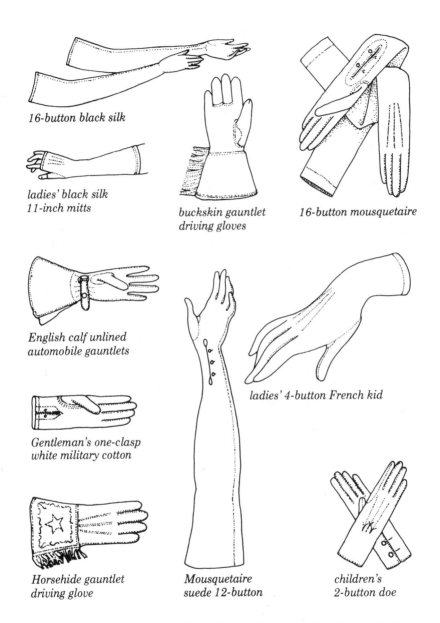

16-button black silk

ladies' black silk
11-inch mitts

buckskin gauntlet
driving gloves

16-button mousquetaire

English calf unlined
automobile gauntlets

Gentleman's one-clasp
white military cotton

ladies' 4-button French kid

Horsehide gauntlet
driving glove

Mousquetaire
suede 12-button

children's
2-button doe

A selection of gloves advertised in England and America from 1890 to 1910.

opponent's face as a form of challenge. And gloves, which were easily removable, were offered as a formal symbol of an agreement to make a payment.[12]

Now we consider them almost relics, along with spats, wing-tip collars, and buggy whips. But perhaps gloves have fallen out of favor simply because no one makes a perfectly fitted glove anymore.

We have talked about the hand's importance in making tools and in making art; how the choice of left- or right-handedness has influenced our brain organization; how we learn hand gestures at our mother's knee and from our motherlands; how the hands get us jobs, take us to parties, and help us seduce a mate. We have talked about the emblems of hands in power and how manipulators have learned to use their hands in the pursuit of power. We have shown that hand words are insidiously present in many objects and acts of daily life. We worship with our hands and make love with them. We try to find our future or our past in them. Hands help us into the world, and, if we are lucky, someone's hand will be there to help us out of it. The touch of someone you love is different from the touch of anyone else on earth. To take a loved one's hand is to take his or her soul. The trembling, the return pressure, the intensity and conviction there—what surer way to know what someone is feeling?

And still we haven't said enough. Our hands are our enigma, the symbol of the human race. They are our vassals and our masters, both translators and shapers of the outside world. They are the agents of our minds, the symbols of our development, the seat of our humanity. Yet they are clowns too, sometimes even ugly, clumsy, dopey, inappropriate. Like an old hound dog that's become part of the family through devotion, occasional service, and longevity, our hands have found a warm spot for themselves in the sun.

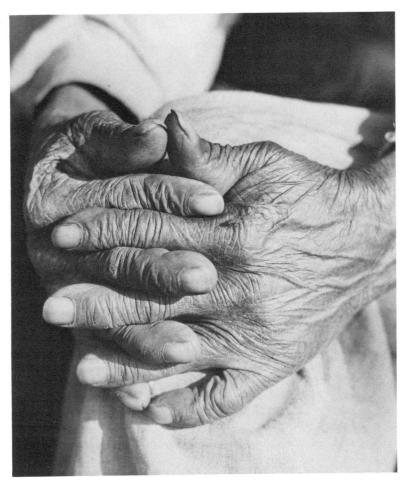

The hands that felled trees also cut umbilical cords; the hands that wrung the necks of chickens and butchered hogs also nudged African Violets into bloom; the arms that loaded sheaves, bales, and sacks rocked babies into sleep. They patted biscuits into flaky ovals of innocence—and shrouded the dead. They plowed all day and came home to nestle like plums under the limbs of their men. Toni Morrison, The Bluest Eye. *Jack Delano, The Library of Congress*

Notes

Introduction

1. Tabori unfortunately does not further identify the author of this quote and its source. It is, however, so much a statement of our feelings, we could not resist using it.
2. Frank Caplan, *The First Twelve Months of Life,* p. 9.
3. Luigi Giacometti, "Thumbs Up," *Human Nature,* November 1978.
4. Cresollius quote as translated in Macdonald Critchley, *Silent Language,* p. 3. Kant as quoted in Walter Sorell, *The Story of the Human Hand,* p. xvii.
5. Giacometti.
6. We are grateful to Tabori for collecting the many proverbs from which our favorites were chosen.
7. Revesz quote from Sorell.

Chapter 1

1. Helical plant information from Jack Fincher, *Sinister People: The Looking Glass World of the Left-Handed,* p. 94. Flounder information from Michael Barsley, *The Other Hand,* p. 149. Mice studies from Fincher, pp. 98–100.

2. Jaynes' test from Julian Jaynes, *The Origins of Consciousness in the Breakdown of the Bicameral Mind,* p. 120.

3. Bruning and Kaeppel's test from Tabori, p. 132.

4. Fincher, p. 116.

5. Based on "Chapter One," Barsley.

6. Fincher, p. 148.

7. "But Why Did They Sit on the King's Right in the First Place?", G. William Domhoff, *Psychoanalytic Review,* 56 (1969–70), reprinted in *The Nature of Human Consciousness,* edited by Robert E. Ornstein.

8. Gertrude Hildreth, *The Development and Training of Hand Dominance,* "Journal of Genetic Psychology," p. 49.

9. Paul I. Yakovlev and Pasco Rakic, "Patterns of Decussation of Bulbar Pyramids and Distribution of Pyramidal Tracts on Two Sides of the Spinal Cord," Transactions of the American Neurological Association, 1966, as quoted in Fincher.

10. A. Gesell and L. B. Ames, "The Development of Handedness," *Journal of Genetic Psychology.*

11. Carl Sagan, *The Dragons of Eden,* p. 180.

12. Desmond Morris, *The Naked Ape,* pp. 106–7.

13. Gertrude Hildreth, pp. 73 and 76.

14. Barsley, p. 37.

15. Sorell, p. 104.

16. Fincher, p. 58.

17. Ibid., p. 62.

18. Sorell, pp. 105–6.

19. Colin Blakemore, *Mechanics of the Mind,* pp. 143–45.

20. Sagan, p. 166.

21. Michael S. Gazzaniga, "The Split Brain of Man," in *The Nature of Human Consciousness* ed. by Robert E. Ornstein, pp. 87–100. The article first appeared in *Scientific American*, 217, 2, pp. 24–29, August 1967.
22. Sagan, pp. 97–98.
23. "New Findings about Left-Handed People," *U.S. News and World Report*, June 20, 1977, pp. 33–34.
24. Barsley, p. 178.
25. Fincher, pp. 175–87.
26. Ibid., p. 176.
27. *U.S. News and World Report*, p. 34.
28. Ibid.
29. Fincher, p. 186.
30. Fincher, p. 173.
31. Tabori, p. 145.
32. Fincher, p. 26.
33. These terms are collected by Fincher, Tabori, and Sorell.
34. Fincher, p. 37.
35. Stekel is quoted in Sorell, p. 116.
36. Fincher, p. 46.
37. Ibid., p. 143.
38. Barsley, p. 178.
39. Hildreth, p. 47.
40. Ibid., p. 42.
41. Beech and Fransella, *Research and Experiments in Stuttering*, p. 6.
42. Ibid., p. 8.
43. Hildreth, p. 43.
44. Barsley, p. 162.
45. Tabori, p. 146.

Chapter 2

1. Washington *Post*, April 8, 1979, p. F7.
2. Critchley, p. 135.

3. *Life,* January 9, 1950, article by Mario Pei, p. 54.
4. Sorell, p. 135.
5. David Efron, *Gesture and Environment,* p. 39.
6. Ibid., p. 31.
7. Critchley, pp. 141–42. (In this and in what follows Critchley is summarizing the invaluable work done by Efron.)
8. Ibid., pp. 142–43. (Again following Efron.)
9. Ibid., pp. 143–44. (Following Efron)
10. Summarized from Efron, *Gesture and Environment.*
11. Critchley, p. 141.
12. Sorell, p. 138.
13. Sorell, p. 41.
14. W. A. Rose, "The Language of Gesture," *Folklore* magazine, p. 314.
15. Critchley, p. 144.
16. Eugene Linden, *Apes, Man, and Language,* Chapter 2.
17. Ibid., Chapter 3.
18. William Philo Clark, *The Indian Sign Language,* Chapter 2.
19. Critchley, p. 71.
20. Ibid., p. 72.
21. Laurence Wylie, *Beaux Gestes,* p. xiii.
22. R. Brasch, *How Did It Begin?,* p. 78.
23. Desmond Morris, *Manwatching: A Field Guide to Human Behaviour,* p. 191 caption.
24. Garrick Mallery, "Sign Language among the North American Indians," *1st Annual Report of the Bureau of Ethnology,* p. 302.
25. Wylie, p. 26.
26. Morris, *Manwatching,* p. 189.
27. Wylie, p. 49.
28. Morris, *Manwatching,* p. 186.
29. *Time,* June 13, 1969, p. 86.
30. Critchley, p. 115.
31. Robert Saitz and Edward Cervenka, *Colombian and North American Gestures: A Contrasting Inventory,* p. 119.
32. Addison Burbank, *Guatemala Profile,* p. 24.

33. Wylie, p. 63.
34. Morris, *Manwatching,* p. 197.
35. Wylie, pp. 32–33.
36. Thomas Burke, *Streets of London,* Chapter 9.
37. William Shakespeare, *Romeo and Juliet,* Act 1, scene 1, lines 40–50.
38. Morris, *Manwatching,* p. 193.
39. Critchley, p. 118.
40. Morris, *Manwatching,* p. 198.
41. Anecdotal material, conversation with John Giroux.
42. Morris, *Manwatching,* p. 201.
43. Wylie, pp. 72–73.
44. Ibid., p. 43.
45. Ibid., p. 77.
46. Morris, *Manwatching,* p. 198 caption.
47. Anecdotal information from Olivia Guerrero, Debbie Steinbach, and Rick Van Waggonen.
48. Saitz, p. 21; Burbank, p. 24.
49. Saitz, p. 78.
50. Wylie, pp. 6 and 30.
51. Morris, *Manwatching,* p. 39.
52. Mallery, p. 296.
53. Critchley, pp. 119–20.
54. Morris, *Manwatching,* p. 38.
55. Wylie, pp. 55 and 59.

Chapter 3

1. Anne F. Fenlason, *Essentials in Interviewing,* p. 137.
2. Sorell, p. 122.

    Werner Wolff first proposed this theory. Recently a research team composed of Dr. Harold Sackeim, Dr. Ruben Gur, and Marcel Saucy, working at the University of Pennyslvania, confirmed Wolff's claim. The left side *does* show more emotion—at least it does to subjective viewers. "Turning the Other Cheek, a Psychological View," *The New York Times,* November 14, 1978. Tabori, however, disagrees by saying that in right-handed people, the right eye, right side of the mouth, and so on are also dominant. "All this makes clear that, with the normal right-handed man, the right side of the face is the more expressive . . ." *The Book of the Hand,* p. 138.

3. Critchley, p. 144.
4. Ibid., p. 135.
5. Ashley Montagu, *Touching: The Human Significance of the Skin,* p. 208.
6. Sandor Feldman, *Mannerisms of Speech and Gesture in Everyday Life,* Chapter Six.
7. Quoted in Julius Fast, *Body Language,* p. 95.

Chapter 4

1. Albert E. Scheflen, *Body Language and Social Order,* p. 37.
2. D. Mornet, *French Thought in the 18th Century,* p. 52.
3. Francis Hayes, "Gestures: A Working Bibliography," *Southern Folklore Quarterly,* p. 280.
4. Much of the information in this box comes from Robert Haberstein, *Funeral Customs the World Over.*
5. Alfred Adler, *Problems of Neurosis,* quoted in Sorell, p. 134.
6. Geza Revesz.
7. Hayes, p. 322
8. Elizabeth Marbury, *Manners: A Handbook of Social Customs,* unpaged.
9. Ibid.

Chapter 6

1. Montagu, p. 34.
2. White, *The First Three Years of Life,* p. 29.
3. Edward T. Hall, *The Hidden Dimension,* pp. 111–125.
4. Phyllis Chesler, *Women and Madness,* pp. 266–67.

Chapter 7

1. Anna Freud, *Normality and Pathology in Childhood,* p. 199.
2. Montagu, p. 37.
3. Ibid., p. 135.
4. *Rolling Stone,* Nov. 15, 1978.
5. Morris, *The Naked Ape,* p. 206.
6. W. Lambert Brittain, "Perceiving Through the Body," *Human Ecological Forum,* p. 8.
7. Montagu, p. 263.
8. Ibid., p. 264.
9. Ibid., p. 268.
10. Brittain, p. 9.
11. Sorell, pp. 16–17.
12. Eric Maple, *The Ancient Art of Occult Healing,* p. 20.
13. Sir James Frazer, The Golden Bough, p. 221.
14. Revesz, p. 126.
15. Sorell, pp. 18–19.
16. Tuchman, p. 106.
17. Ibid.
18. Maple, p. 22.
19. Ibid.
20. Mary Coddington, *In Search of the Healing Energy,* p. 61.
21. Ibid., p. 59.

22. Ibid., p. 68.
23. Paris Flammond, *The Mystic Healers,* pp. 24–26.
24. Ibid., p. 26.
25. Coddington, p. 15.
26. Neil Chesanow, "Is It Time to Take Psychic Healing Seriously?" *Family Health,* p. 22.
27. Joseph B. Treaster, "Chiropractic Comes of Age," *Family Health*, pp. 26–29.
28. Ibid., p. 54.
29. Ibid.
30. Coddington, pp. 99–100.
31. Flammond, p. 69.
32. Ibid., p. 137–38.
33. William Nolen, *Healing,* p. 61.
34. Ibid., p. 62.
35. Ibid., pp. 63–64.
36. Ibid., p. 64.
37. Ibid., p. 90.
38. Ibid., p. 282.
39. Chesanow, p. 22.
40. Ibid., p. 26.
41. Ibid., p. 26.

Chapter 8

1. Charles N. Sarlin, M.D., "Masturbation, Culture and Psychosexual Development," in *Masturbation: From Infancy to Senescence,* p. 358.
2. Privately published.
3. Ibid.
4. *Onania,* unpaged.
5. Ibid.
6. Ibid.

7. Sigmund Freud, *The Basic Writings of Sigmund Freud,* ed. by Dr. A. A. Brill, pp. 585–87.

8. Millican, in *Masturbation: From Infancy to Senescence,* p. 146.

9. Freud, p. 613.

10. Havelock Ellis, *The Psychology of Sex,* p. 97.

11. Ibid., p. 98.

12. *Masturbation: From Infancy to Senescence,* pp. 355–56.

13. Based on readings in Vern and Bonnie Bullough, "The Secret Sin," *Sin, Sickness and Sanity,* especially Chapter Five.

14. "It is my feeling, therefore, that the vulva of her Most Holy Majesty be titillated for a longer time before coitus" (translation by John Drakeford). If some one throws this quote at you, you might respond with Juvenal's *Parce, Quinte, digitis! Quod perdidis vir est.* ("Spare thy fingers, oh Quinte. What you are losing is your virility.")

15. Dr. Alex Comfort, *The Joy of Sex,* pp. 116–18.

16. Ibid., p. 118.

17. Shere Hite, *The Hite Report,* p. 345.

18. Comfort, p. 193.

19. Tabori, p. 94.

20. Masters and Johnson in an interview on the Phil Donahue Show, April 1979.

21. Bullough, pp. 222–23.

22. Ellis, p. 43.

23. Ibid., p. 44.

24. *Manchester Guardian,* 4 December, 1977.

Chapter 9

1. Julian Jaynes, *The Origin of Consciousness in the Breakdown of the Bicameral Mind,* p. 236.

2. Ibid.

3. Marten Steinbach, *Medical Palmistry,* pp. 111–12.

4. Jaynes, p. 239.

5. Ibid., pp. 242–43.

6. Ibid., p. 244.

7. Steinbach, p. 3.

8. Henry Frith, *Palmistry Secrets Revealed,* p. 4.

9. Edith Niles, *Palmistry; Your Fate in Your Hands,* p. 7.

10. Ibid., pp. 8–9.

11. As quoted in Fred Gettings, *The Book of Palmistry,* pp. 21–22.

12. Ibid., pp. 25–26.

13. Frith *Palmistry Secrets Revealed,* pp. 9–10.

14. D'Arpentigny, quoted in Gettings, p. 29.

15. Gettings, p. 31.

16. Ibid., p. 31.

17. Cheiro, quoted in Gettings, p. 32.

18. Steinbach, p. 29.

19. Gettings, p. 34.

20. Marcel Broekman, *The Complete Encyclopedia of Practical Palmistry,* p. 25.

21. Our analysis of findings in the hands is based on readings in Gettings, Broekman, Steinbach, Niles, and interviews with two palmists, plus our own reaction to the look of the hand.

22. With apologies to Eysenck.

23. Sorell, p. 190.

24. Ibid.

25. Stuart Kind, Michael Overman, *Science Against Crime,* p. 67–68.

26. Huntington Hartford, *You Are What You Write,* Chapter 3.

27. Ibid., Chapter 2.

28. Manfred Lowengard, *How to Analyze Your Handwriting,* Chapter 1.

29. Hartford, p. 47.

30. Noel Currer-Briggs, Brian Kennett and Jane Patterson, *Handwriting Analysis in Business,* Chapter 4.

31. Robert Toogood. "How to Tell Psychic Ability Through Handwriting." *National Enquirer,* Jan. 1978, p. 13.

32. Currer-Briggs, Noel, Brian Kennett, and Jane Peterson. Chapter 6.

33. Hartford, Chapter 1.
34. Lowengard, Chapter 2.
35. Based on readings in Brokeman, Korman and Hurwood's *Hands: The Power of Hand Awareness;* John M. Ellis, *The Doctor Who Looked at Hands;* and "Your Health in Your Hands," *Self,* July 1979. Additional information from Dr. Ken Miller.

Chapter 10

1. Tabori, p. 47.
2. H. R. Beech, *Obsessional States,* p. 84.
3. Ibid., p. 165.
4. Ibid., pp. 165–66.
5. Freud, p. 587.
6. Ibid., p. 588.
7. Brill, "Psychopathology in Everyday Life," *Fundamental Concept of Psychoanalysis,* p. 193.
8. As quoted in Montagu, pp. 133–34.
9. Tabori, p. 102.
10. Ibid.
11. Morris, pp. 228–29.
12. Tabori, pp. 105–109.

Bibliography

Anonymous. *Onania, or the Heinous Sin of Self-Pollution and its Frightful Consequences in Both Sexes,* London, 1725.

Barsley, Michael. *The Other Hand,* Hawthorne Books, Inc., N.Y., 1967.

Baker, Frank. "Anthropology Notes on the Human Hand," *American Anthropology,* Vol. 1, No. 1, 1888.

Beech, H. R. and Fay Fransella. *Research and Experiment in Stuttering,* Pergamon Press, London, 1968.

———, editor. Obsessional States, Methuen & Co., London, 1974.

Birdwhistle, Ray. *Introduction to Kinesics,* University of Louisville Press, 1952.

Blakemore, Colin. *Mechanics of the Mind,* Cambridge University Press, Cambridge/London, 1977.

Brasch, R. *How Did It Begin? Customs & Superstitions and Their Romantic Origins,* Longmans, Green and Co., Ltd., Melbourne, Australia, 1965.

Brill, A. A. *Fundamental Concept of Psychoanalysis,* Harcourt, Brace, and Co., New York, 1921.

Brittain, W. Lambert. "Perceiving through the Body," *Human Ecology Forum,* 7:8–10, Winter, 1977.

Broekman, Marcel. *The Complete Encyclopedia of Palmistry,* Triune Books, London, 1974.

Bronowski, Jacob. *The Ascent of Man,* Little, Brown & Company, Boston/Toronto, 1973.

Bullough, Vern and Bonnie Bullough. *Sin, Sickness and Sanity: A History of Sexual Attitudes,* New American Library, New York, 1977.

Burt, Sir Cyril. *The Backward Child,* University of London Press, 1937.

Burke, Thomas. *Streets of London,* 4th edition, London, 1949.

Caplan, Frank. *The First Twelve Months of Life,* Bantam Books, New York, 1978.

Chesanow, Neil. "Is It Time to Take Psychic Healing Seriously?", *Family Health,* January 1979, Vol. 11, No1.

Chesler, Phyllis. *Women and Madness,* Doubleday & Company, New York, 1972.

Clark, William Philo. *Indian Sign Language,* Philadelphia, 1885.

Coddington, Mary. *In Search of Healing Energy,* Warner Books, New York, 1978.

Comfort, Dr. Alex. *The Joy of Sex,* Simon & Schuster, New York, 1976.

Critchley, Macdonald. *Silent Language,* Butterworths, London, 1975.

Cratty, Bryant and Robert Hutton. *Experiments in Movement Behavior and Motor Learning,* Lea & Febiger, Philadelphia, 1969.

Currer-Briggs, Noel, Brian Kennett, and Jane Peterson. *Handwriting Analysis in Business,* Associated Business Programmes, London, 1969.

Efron, David. *Gesture and Environment,* Kings Crown Press, New York, 1941.

Ekman, Paul and Wallace V. Friesen. "Hand Movements," *Journal of Communications,* Vol. 22, 1972.

Ellis, John M. *The Doctor Who Looked at Hands,* Arco, New York, 1966.

Ellis, Havelock. *The Psychology of Sex,* Emerson, 1964.

Elworthy, Frederick T. *The Evil Eye,* London, 1895.

Evans, Dr. Christopher. *Cults of Unreason,* Farrar, Straus, and Giroux, New York, 1973.

Fast, Julius. *The Body Language of Sex, Power, and Aggression,* M. Evans, New York, 1977.

———. *Body Language,* M. Evans, New York, 1971.

Feldman, Sandor S. *Mannerisms of Speech and Gesture in Everyday Life,* International Universities Press, New York, 1959.

Fenlason, Anne F. *Essentials in Interviewing,* Harper and Row, New York, 1962.

Fincher, Jack. *Sinister People: The Looking-Glass World of the Left-Hander,* G. P. Putnam's Sons, New York, 1977.

Flammond, Paris. *The Mystic Healers,* Stein & Day, Briarcliff Manor, New York, 1974.

Frank, Lawrence. "Tactile Communication," Genetic Psychological Monograph 56, 1957.

Frazer, Sir James. *The Golden Bough,* Macmillan, New York, 1922.

Freud, Anna. *The Writings of Anna Freud, Vol. VI. Normality and Pathology in Childhood: Assessments of Development,* International Universities Press, New York, 1965.

Freud, Sigmund. *The Basic Writings of Sigmund Freud.* Edited by A. A. Brill, Random House, New York, 1938.

Frith, Henry. *Palmistry Secrets Revealed,* Melvin Powers, Wilshire Book Company, North Hollywood, California, 1975.

Gesell, A. and Ames L. B. "The Development of Handedness," *Journal of Genetic Psychology,* 1947.

Gettings, Fred. *The Book of Palmistry,* Triune Books, London, 1974.

Giacometti, Luigi. "Thumbs Up," *Human Nature,* Vol. 1, No. 11,

November 1978.

Goffman, Erving. *Behavior in Public Places,* Free Press, Glencoe, Illinois, 1963.

Haberstein, Robert and William Lamers. *Funeral Customs the World Over,* Milwaukee, 1973.

Hall, Edward T. *The Hidden Dimension,* Doubleday & Company, New York, 1966.

——. *Beyond Culture,* Anchor Press, Doubleday Company, 1976.

Hartford, Huntington. *You Are What You Write,* Macmillan, New York, 1973.

Hayes, Francis. "Gestures: A Working Bibliography," *Southern Folklore Quarterly,* Vol. 21, 1957.

Hendrick, I. *Facts and Theories of Psychoanalysis,* Knopf, New York, 1941.

Hite, Shere. *The Hite Report,* Macmillan, New York, 1976.

Hildreth, Gertrude. "The Development and Training of Hand Dominance," *Journal of Genetic Psychology,* Vol. 75, 1949.

Hughes, Albert. *Self-Analysis Through Your Handwriting,* Thorsen Publishers Ltd., London, 1966.

Jaynes, Julian. *The Origins of Consciousness in the Breakdown of the Bicameral Mind,* Houghton Mifflin Company, Boston, 1976.

Jourard, Sidney. "An Exploratory Study of Body Accessibility," *British Journal of Social and Clinical Psychology,* Vol. 5, 1966.

Kind, Stuart, and Michael Overman. *Science Against Crime,* Doubleday & Company, Garden City, New York, 1972.

Kittridge, George. *Words and Their Ways in English Speech,* New York, 1911.

Krieger, Dolores. *The Therapeutic Touch: How to Use Your Hands to Help or Heal,* Prentice-Hall, Englewood Cliffs, 1979.

Linden, Eugene. *Apes, Man and Language,* Atlantic Monthly Press, New York, 1977.

Lowengard, Manfred. *How to Analyze Your Handwriting,* Marshall Cavendish, London, 1975.

MacDougall, Robert. "The Significance of the Human Hand in the Evolution of the Mind," *The American Journal of Psychology,* 1905.

Mallery, Garrick. "Sign Language Among the North American Indians," *First Annual Report to the Bureau of Ethnology,* Government Printing Office, Washington, D.C., 1881.

Maple, Eric. *The Ancient Art of Occult Healing,* The Samuel Weiser Inc., New York, 1974.

Marañon, Gregorio. "The Psychology of Gesture," *The Journal of Nervous and Mental Disease,* December 1950.

Marcus, Irwin M. and John J. Francis, editors. *Masturbation: From Infancy to Senescence,* International Universities Press, New York, 1975.

Montagu, Ashley. *Touching: The Human Significance of the Skin,* Columbia University Press, New York and London, 1971.

Morgan, Anna. *An Hour With Delsarte; A Study of Expression,* Lee and Shepard, Boston, 1889.

Mornet, D. *French Thought in the Eighteenth Century,* New York,

Morris, Desmond. *The Naked Ape: A Zoologist's Study of the Human Animal,* McGraw-Hill, New York, 1967.

———. *Manwatching: A Field Guide to Human Behavior,* Harry Abrams, Inc., New York, 1977.

———. *Intimate Behavior,* Random House, New York, 1971.

Niles, Edith. *Palmistry: Your Fate in Your Hands,* H C Publishers, New York, 1969.

Nolen, William A. *Healing: A Doctor in Search of A Miracle,* Random House, New York, 1974.

Orme, J. E. "Lefthandedness, Ability and Emotional Instability," *British Journal of Clinical Psychology,* 1970.

Ornstein, Robert E., editor. *The Nature of Human Consciousness,* W. H. Freeman and Company, San Francisco, 1973.

Revesz, Geza. *The Human Hand,* Routledge and Kegan, London, 1958.

292   Bibliography

Rose, H. A. "The Language of Gesture," *Folklore*, 1919.

Sagan,Carl. *The Dragons of Eden: Speculations on the Evolution of Human Intelligence*, Random House, New York, 1977.

Saitz, Robert and Edward Cervenka. *Colombian and North American Gestures: A Contrasting Inventory*, Centro Colombo Americano Publishers, Bogotá, Colombia, 1962.

Schefflen, Albert E., M.D. *Body Language and Social Order: Communication as Behavioral Control*, Prentice-Hall, Englewood Cliffs, New Jersey, 1972.

Scheinfeld, Amram. *Twins and Supertwins*. J. P. Lippincott, Philadelphia, 1967.

Solomon, Shirl. *How to Really Know Yourself Through Your Handwriting*, Taplinger Publishing, New York, 1973.

Sorell, Walter. *The Story of the Human Hand*, Bobbs-Merrill, New York, 1967.

Steinbach, Marten. *Medical Palmistry*, University Books, Secaucus, New Jersey, 1975.

Tabori, Paul. *The Book of the Hand: A Compendium of Fact and Legend Since the Dawn of History*. Chilton Co., Philadelphia, 1962.

Travis, Edward Lee. *Speech Pathology*, Appleton Century, New York, 1931.

Treaster, Joseph B. "Chiropractic Comes of Age," *Family Health*, December 1978, Vol. 10, No. 12.

Toogood, Robert, "How to Tell Psychic Ability Through Handwriting," *National Enquirer*, January, 1978.

Tuchman, Barbara. *A Distant Mirror*, Knopf, New York, 1978.

Twain, Mark. "Some Thoughts on the Science of Onanism," Address to the Stomach Club, Paris, 1879. Privately published.

White, Burton L. *The First Three Years of Life*, Prentice-Hall, Englewood Cliffs, New Jersey, 1975.

Wolff, Charlotte, *The Hand in Psychological Diagnosis,* Philosoph-
          ical Library Inc., New York, 1952.
————. *The Human Hand,* Methuen, London, 1937.
Wylie, Laurence and Rick Stafford. *Beaux Gestes: A Guide to French
          Body Talk,* The Undergraduate Press, Cambridge, Massa-
          chusetts, E. P. Dutton, New York, 1977.
Ziff, William. "Your Gestures Give You Away," *Reader's Digest,*
          August 1951.

Index